T0337420

IN THE FOOTSTEPS OF GEORGE BORROW

In the Footsteps of George Borrow

A Journey through Spain and Portugal

GUY ARNOLD

Signal Books
Oxford

First published in 2007 by
Signal Books Limited
36 Minster Road
Oxford OX4 1LY
www.signalbooks.co.uk

A catalogue record for this book is available from the British Library

ISBN 978-1-904955-37-5 Cloth

Cover Design: Baseline Arts
Cover Images: Alexandru Teodorescu/istockphoto; Adam Korzekwa/istockphoto;
Miguel Angelo Silva/istockphoto

Photos and illustrations: Guy Arnold
except: i Peter Williams/istockphoto; viii Ken Sorrie/istockphoto; 7 Leeman/
istockphoto; 66 Rafael Laguillo/istockphoto; 75 Brandon Laufenberg/
istockphoto; 85 Duncan Walker/istockphoto; 121 Hannu Liivaar/istockphoto;
147 Juan Olvido/istockphoto; p. 159 José Luis Gutiérrez; p.187 Jarno Gonzalez
Zarraonandia/istockphoto; p.198 Pasha Patriki/istockphoto; pp.220 & 236
David Pedre/istockphoto; p.236 Graham Heywood/istockphoto; p.244 Arturo
Limon/istockphoto; p.259 magui80/istockphoto; p.277 Ricardo Sánchez/
istockphoto; p.295 Mariano Heluani/istockphoto; p.321 Guillaume Dubé/
istockphoto

Printed in India

Contents

MAP

Bay of
Biscay

FRANCE

ANDORRA

SPAIN

PORTUGAL

Atlantic Ocean

Vivero
Ribadeo
Luarco
Naval
Gijón
Ribadesella
Llanes
Santander
Ferrol
La Coruña
Oviedo
San Vicente
Corcubión
Muros
picos de Europa
de la Barquera
Cape
Finisterre
Noya
Lugo
Puerto de
León
Padrón
Santiago de
Piedrafita
Burgos
Compostela
Ponferrada
Astorga
Vigo
Palencia
Zaragoza
Barcelona
Valladolid
Medina
del Campo
Salamanca
Segovia
Sierra de Guadarrama
Peñaranda de
Bracamonte
Ávila
MADRID
Escorial
Mallorca
Navalmoral
Talavera
Aranjuez
Tagus R.
Jaraceijo
Toledo
Valencia
Trujillo
Guadiana R.
Ibiza
Sintra
Elvas
Mérida
Manzanares
Formentera
LISBON
Entremoz
Badajoz
Setúbal
Évora
Valdepeñas
Montemor-o-Novo
Vendas Novas
Guadalquivir R.
Bailén
Cartagena
Córdoba
Andújar
Seville
Carmona
Mediterranean
Sanlúcar de Barrameda
Granada
Sea
Jerez de la Frontera
Almería
N
Cádiz
La
Línea
0   100
Algeciras
GIBRALTAR
km

Introduction

THIS is not just a book about George Borrow: it is also about Spain and England and their conflicting histories and about the changing world of travel. It is almost impossible to write a travel book that takes the reader into remote unknown places because just about everywhere has been explored and even the most inaccessible places are now invaded by "adventure" travel groups: provided you can afford to pay you can trek through the Himalayas to a ready-made camp, or canoe down a Borneo river to be entertained overnight in a longhouse by bored Dayaks. I decided, therefore, to write an old-fashioned style travel book about the Iberian Peninsula—Portugal and Spain.

My inspiration for this journey was George Borrow's masterpiece *The Bible in Spain*. I had read *Lavengro* and *The Romany Rye*, his two autobiographical books, when at school, but came to *The Bible in Spain* much later. George Borrow, the scholar-gypsy and English eccentric, went to Spain on behalf of the British and Foreign Bible Society in 1835 and remained there for five years, attempting to sell Protestant Testaments to the Catholic Spanish; the sub-title to his book is "The Journeys, Adventures, and imprisonment of an Englishman in an attempt to circulate the scriptures in the Peninsula." *The Bible in Spain* was published in 1842 and became an instant bestseller; it has been constantly reprinted ever since.

During his five years in the peninsula Borrow travelled to many parts of Spain at a time when the country was wracked by the Carlist civil war while bandits and brigands always made travelling a dangerous hazard. Borrow was sometimes reproved by the Bible Society for his presumption: he was a loner, he much preferred low to high company, he became an acknowledged expert on gypsies and was to write another book about his experiences in the peninsula, *The Gypsies of Spain*, as he also translated parts of the Bible into their language. Above all, *The Bible in Spain* is a travel book and it

1

is the account of his adventures and the people he encountered while travelling in Spain which ensured the book's enduring popularity.

The Bible in Spain appeared in 1842 to critical acclaim although the *Dublin Review* was sufficiently churlish as to complain that "Borrow was a missionary sent out by a gang of conspirators against Christianity." The immense popularity of the work rested upon its unique departure from normal missionary accounts: it was a book of adventure, travel, danger and high romance, full of wonderfully strange characters, some of whom appear from a mysterious and only hinted-at past, and many who might read other missionary works from a sense of duty could read this with pleasure. Possibly, before the appearance in 1850 of *Lavengro* which outraged because of its so-called vulgar tastes—it attacked "gentility nonsense", was called an "epic of ale" and offended by going against the kid-glove literature of the day—parents might have allowed *The Bible in Spain* as Sunday reading matter for their children though not, perhaps, if they had read it themselves. Richard Ford, who was Murray's reader and recommended *The Bible in Spain*, described it as *Gil Blas* with a touch of Bunyan. Both Ford and Herbert Jenkins, one of Borrow's biographers, describing his reactions, assume automatically that Borrow was a missionary. As Jenkins says:

> *Thieves, murderers, gypsies, bandits, prisons, wars—all knit together by the missionary work of a man who was persona grata with every lawless ruffian he encountered, and yet a sower of the seed. The Religious Public did not pause to ponder over the strangeness of the situation. They had fallen among thieves, and with breathless eagerness were prepared to enjoy to the full the novel experience.*[1]

But if the religious public did not pause to ponder over the strangeness of the situation, who else did? In answer to Harriet Martineau's suggestion that Borrow was a sham in the religious sense, Borrow's apologists have leapt to his defence to dismiss her claim. Whatever the truth, Borrow, Jesuit-like, would have found such arguments and perhaps still more the defences of his faith a cause for wry amusement and no little satisfaction.

⌘

I decided to follow Borrow's trail. More than a century and a half was far enough in the past to ensure that enormous changes would have taken place but not so distant that comparisons become meaningless or resolve themselves into dry history lessons. I have tried to achieve a balanced mix: a description of the Spain I travelled through compared with Borrow's Spain. Portugal formed only a small part of Borrow's initial travels as it did with mine, but both countries offer rich tapestries of history to comment upon.

Borrow came to Lisbon by boat in 1835 and after visiting Sintra and Mafra to the north of the capital made his way to Madrid. His normal mode of travel was by horse and the distance he could cover in a day became the general guide for my own daily journeys. After a period in Madrid Borrow returned briefly to London and then came back to Spain, this time landing at Cádiz. Borrow's longest and most exciting journey was from Madrid north to La Coruña, south to Vigo, back north to Padrón and then out to the westernmost point of Spain, Cape Finisterre; then he travelled along the north coast from La Coruña to Santander before returning to Madrid. Except for minor deviations for purely practical reasons I followed Borrow's itinerary as closely as I could. My aim, if possible, was to visit all the places Borrow named in his book: he was in Spain for five years, I was there for three months so that I was on the move all the time. Comparisons were not always easy. Sometimes Borrow describes a day in which he covers forty or more miles on horseback, at others he covers a more modest twenty or so. I employed three modes of travel: bus, train and walking which was my equivalent of riding horseback. My normal day's travel was between two towns or villages at which Borrow had stopped; if the distance was a reasonable one I walked, if too long I took a bus or, more rarely, a train.

During the months before I went to Spain I endeavoured to learn the rudiments of the language so that I had at least some elementary Spanish on my arrival in the peninsula and this improved with constant use, though I would not claim to be a linguist, unlike Borrow whose command of languages was phenomenal. As he says, on his arrival in Lisbon:

> *The next day I hired a servant, a Portuguese, it being my invariable custom, on arriving in a country, to avail myself of the services of a native, chiefly with the view of perfecting myself in the language; and, being already acquainted with most of the principal languages and dialects of the east and the west, I am soon able to make myself quite intelligible to the inhabitants. In about a fortnight I found myself conversing in Portuguese with considerable fluency.[2]*

Borrow kept a journal, which he used as the basis for long letters to the Bible Society in England. Later, he used the material from his letters when he wrote *The Bible in Spain* and some of the descriptions are taken almost verbatim from his letters.[3] At different times Borrow used Toledo and Segovia as bases from which he visited the surrounding villages to distribute his tracts. I did not have time to visit the villages round Toledo though at the very end of my journey I did manage to visit some of the villages near Segovia. Otherwise I visited, more or less in the correct order, almost all the other places mentioned in *The Bible in Spain*.

❧

There are many enigmas about Borrow, not least perhaps, why he should have accepted a mission to distribute Protestant Testaments in Catholic Spain, for while his defenders assumed he was a dedicated Christian his detractors suggested he was a sham. Perhaps the right explanation, if hardly romantic, is the simplest: he needed a job—and having obtained his post he carried out his duties in an unique and startling fashion upon which much of his later fame came to rest.

❧

This journey, *In the Footsteps of George Borrow*, was made by me in the mid-1990s and has lain dormant for some years, hence the references to pesetas rather than euros, while the perceptive reader may come across allusions which could strike him or her as dated. This in no way detracts from the narrative. The landscape of Spain and the many places visited on this journey will have altered little in the intervening years and any changes that may have occurred make no difference to this account of a journey through Spain.

1

Lisbon: "A Huge Ruinous City"

Arrival in Lisbon—effects of the earthquake— the Inquisition—the aqueduct—the Citadel—the poet Julio Martins

LISBON, like Rome and Tulcea on the Danube Delta, as well as other more obscure claimants to the distinction, insists that it is founded upon seven hills. The city certainly enjoys one of the most magnificent settings anywhere in Europe, sitting as it does on a half circle of hills facing the great pool of the Tagus. It looks spectacular from the air with the sunlight reflected off the wide waters of the river while its long waterfront includes many traces of the earlier Lisbon of a century and a half ago.

Borrow complained that disembarkation at Lisbon was a matter of considerable vexation, with exceedingly uncivil customs officers examining every article of his baggage "with the most provoking minuteness." By contrast I was able to dispense with all but the most elementary formalities, due to the fast-entry policies of the European Union, and make my way into town and a hotel with the minimum of delay so that in little more than an hour after my arrival I embarked upon my first exploration of the city.

Borrow tells us that his "first impression on landing in the Peninsula was by no means a favourable one," and he describes Lisbon as "a huge ruinous city, still exhibiting, in almost every

6

direction, the vestiges of that terrific visitation of God, the earthquake, which shattered it some eighty years ago."[1] In 1755 one of the greatest earthquakes ever recorded struck the city on All Saints Day (1 November) when the people were crowded in the churches; the waters of the Tagus were uplifted and roared through the city, followed by fire, and 30,000 people were killed and 9,000 buildings destroyed. Later, Borrow found much to admire and after visiting the main square and remarking upon the houses being "as high as castles" admits that "With all its ruin and desolation, Lisbon is unquestionably the most remarkable city in the Peninsula and, perhaps, in the south of Europe."[2]

I made my way down the broad Avenida da Liberdade and then along the crowded Rua Augusto and through an imposing baroque marble archway onto the Praça do Comércio from whose eastern corner the ferries ply back and forth all day long to the Alemtejo.

In Borrow's time this splendid square was known as the Plaza of the Inquisition. The square was almost the first place Borrow mentions after his arrival in Portugal; although open to the river on its fourth side it has an extraordinarily exact symmetry. The triumphal arch through which I had entered the square forms the centre of the

longest side facing the waterfront while the façade of all three sides is identical: a covered arcade runs behind elegant arches and above each of these rise tall, perfectly proportioned windows whose wrought-iron balconies look set to do duty as the dress circle of a vast theatre although every window was firmly closed. The next storey up and a further set of windows, only half the size of those below, suggest in their symmetrical turn even greater height to the whole building than the reality while a white balustraded parapet guards a red-tiled roof. The effect of the whole is to project an image of eighteenth-century elegance and order. The square is 200 metres long and the main façade lies 150 metres back from the waterfront. Behind the square lay an altogether different kind of bustling street with room only for restaurants whose proprietors stood in their doorways to call out greetings in all the tongues of Europe and urge the passers-by to enter for refreshment.

Borrow was interested in aqueducts and he described that of Lisbon in eulogistic terms:

> *I boldly say that there is no monument of man's labour and skill, pertaining to either ancient or modern Rome, for whatever purpose designed, which can rival the waterworks of Lisbon; I mean the stupendous aqueduct whose principal arches cross the valley to the north-east of Lisbon...*[3]

I inquired the way of a small man who came hastening towards me with every appearance of determined purpose, yet on discovering that I was a stranger his haste evaporated and he proceeded to give me elaborate instructions. My Spanish was no match for his Portuguese and, after my second plea that he should proceed more slowly, he inquired politely whether I was Spanish and then expressed charmed surprise when I told him I was English. Like Borrow on another occasion, I suspected "that there was some covert satire" in his speech although I was "Jesuit enough to appear to receive it as a compliment." My guide now led me through several streets to make sure I was on the correct path and only when it was impossible for me to miss my way did he leave me after we had shaken hands with expressions of mutual friendship and appreciation.

The aqueduct is indeed striking: it crosses a deep wide valley to the north of the city while under it an endless stream of traffic rushes on its way to Lisbon's first bridge over the Tagus, the Bridge of April 25. In Borrow's day the valley would have been a quiet country place across which the great aqueduct "walked" on its immense yet elegant arches in even more inspiring grandeur than it achieves today over a modern highway. Then I set off in search of other of Borrow's Lisbon landmarks including the Church of Belem, which was founded on the spot from which Vasco da Gama embarked in 1497 to circumnavigate Africa.

The Citadel, "which is the boldest and most prominent object to the eye, whilst surveying the city from the Tagus,"[4] is crowned by the Castle of St George which rises from this loftiest of Lisbon's seven hills to dominate the old medieval city. The first castle was built by the Visigoths in the fifth century, later to be refortified and expanded, first by the Moors and then by the Portuguese. It was a popular attraction for Lisbonites on their afternoon off as well as for the ubiquitous tourists who jostled one another on the walkways or apologised in many languages when they met in the angles of narrow stone stairways as they explored every turret and tower. The moat, now sheltered by luxuriant green trees, had its swans, while peacocks strutted and displayed the great fans of their tails in a garden beneath high grey stone walls, swans and peacocks between them softening the stark grimness of former days.

I needed a walking stick for my coming journey and was directed to a fashionable shop near the Praça do Comércio where amidst a collection of smart black canes with silver tops—"walking sticks for the occasion"—I found one remaining cane, stout yet elegant, that suited me exactly and would be my companion for the next three months. Then, hot from too much tourism, I made my way to the Avenida da Liberdade where I sat at a table under a tree to take refreshment and watch the world go by. And there I met Julio Martins.

My café was little more than a large kiosk under the trees although it had three rows of tables, perhaps twenty-four altogether, stretching in military precision away from it. Only a quarter of these were then occupied for it was still early afternoon and I soon discovered the disadvantage to sitting there for in the time it took me to drain half a beer several beggars who clearly regarded the occupants of the tables as fair game had approached and demanded alms; they did so with courtesy and without passion and a quick shake of the head was enough to send them on their way.

I sat facing up the Avenida towards the Marquês de Pombal statue on its column; the traffic roared up and down the avenue to my left and pedestrians passed to the right while directly to my front other café-kiosks with their attendant tables stretched away under the trees. I watched increasingly fascinated by his apparently haphazard method of locomotion as Julio Martins approached. He was a squat, heavy-built man in a shabby-genteel old suit with a satchel suspended from his left shoulder. His square, pugnacious face gave him an air of nobility that allowed him to rise above the indignity of his present occupation or, at any rate, gave to it a certain respectability that defied any easy dismissal. He would not be lightly brushed aside. He breathed with effort, a wheezing harsh sound that revealed more of his real state than all his elaborate front was able to conceal, and he needed the support of the walking stick which he grasped firmly with his right hand. He took his time, stopping every few yards to survey whoever might be sitting at the nearest table to his slow progression so that he could appraise their worthiness. Once he approached a table where he stood for several minutes talking to a trio of two men and a woman but, alas, without advantage to himself. They were too far away for me to hear what was said. Then he continued his progress with me firmly in his sights, as I had known myself to be from his first appearance beneath the trees. He came at an angle, straightforward yet sidling, as though he had not seen me and must pass my table by and leave me unrecognised. But then, almost as an afterthought, he turned just as he levelled with my table. He stood for a full minute wheezing while he got his breath back as, no doubt, he also considered what tactics to employ. On closer inspection I saw that he was older than I had at first thought, at least seventy or even more.

"Ah, English", he said and took a step towards my table. I said nothing. He came up to the table and placed his left hand on the back of the vacant chair opposite me. "You speak English," he insisted with a certainty that defied denial.

"A leetle," I said, "just a leetle."

"Good, good, I always know the English. You permit?" and without waiting for my reply he pulled the chair out and sat down.

I have an affinity with a certain kind of rogue and Julio was one; he was possessed of that indefinable air which says, "you must take me as I am, I cannot help it and I cannot change." He knew that I saw him as a rogue and the candour of his eyes invited me to agree with a fact that neither of us could alter. Julio did the talking. Or rather, he orchestrated our conversation, careful to maintain a flow which was designed to disarm and forestall any unwelcome termination of our talk before he had reached his objective. It was clear that he did not like to be hurried and followed a plan of campaign which, no doubt, he had sharpened and modified over the years. He began by praising my limited Spanish but did not make the mistake of bestowing upon it more of an encomium than it deserved; then he extolled the English and their long connection with Portugal—he twice mentioned John of Gaunt although he pronounced him as gent with a soft gee, before inquiring, courteously, why I had come to Portugal. With the first phase of preliminaries completed we were, I sensed, moving towards more serious business. I could have answered merely that I was on holiday but by then I was intrigued to know, as he had correctly calculated, what line he would pursue so I told him that I was following a trail in order to write a book. At the word write a gleam came into his eye. "I knew", he said, "oh yes I knew," and with this assertion he settled back comfortably to give us both a breathing space. Now his statement went contrary to his earlier mode of approach during which he had most carefully avoided looking at me, even once, until he was right beside my table. Nonetheless, I acknowledged his claim with an inclination of the head. "What a pleasure to meet another writer," and he sighed and clasped his hands across his ample stomach and smiled his approval at me. He nodded in comprehension at the discovery that we shared the same occupation; now, clearly, he had no intention of hurrying.

After a pause, during which he paid a few more compliments to the perceptive characteristics of the English, he reached for his satchel from which he extracted a white pamphlet. "I am a poet," he said, "and as one artist to another I present this to you." I took the little booklet which he offered me to examine; it was a mere forty pages, indifferently printed on poor quality paper: (*Nostalgia Poetica*) Poetical Nostalgia, Volume I was its title; below this was a photograph, the centrepiece of the cover, showing a much younger, fierce-looking author who stared belligerently out at an unappreciative world and underneath his portrait was the date 2-1-86 and the legend "From Julio Martins". This was the English version, which he had plucked from his satchel, but as I had watched him select this from a small collection while rejecting others I speculated that perhaps he also had translations into other European tongues—German, Italian, French?

The Preface detailed the poetical pleasures to follow:

> *Opening this book the reader will*
> *find a pleasant reading not only*
> *for the contents but also for the*
> *clearness of the inside poems.*

It was signed Julio Martins and inscribed some way below was the legend "Translation: Jose Oliveira". I made a pretence of glancing through it though in reality I was watching Julio whose face betrayed him. He was calculating what to ask; I think he was also hungry.

"I give it to you for a mere 1000 escudos" he said; and he shrugged eloquently, adding "a trifle, it is hardly worth mentioning."

As I hesitated, saying nothing, he reached across to take the little book: "Look, I inscribe it for you. May I inquire your name?" I told him. He took out a pen and with a flourish wrote above the Preface: "For Guy Arnold with best wishes of the author", followed by the date and his signature written with splendid strokes in an ornate hand. Below the Preface he added the place, Avenida da Liberdade, Lisboa, Portugal, and then the time, 16.20 hours. This addition in his wonderful script clearly doubled the value of the booklet, which I had as yet still to agree to buy but how could I now refuse? I extracted a note for 1000 escudos and gave it to him. We shook hands and he heaved himself to his feet, his business accomplished and, as he said with grave courtesy, a meeting of like minds that "had worked to our mutual satisfaction." Then his eyes lighted upon my brand new walking stick. It was similar in style but greatly superior to his own which was scratched and worn, its ferule missing, ready to be discarded. He needed a replacement and the sudden gleam in his eye told me he had seen mine in that role. For a brief moment the carefully cultivated nobility of his poetical features was replaced by a more earthy expression of covetousness. He reached for my cane which he grasped with such firmness of purpose that I thought he intended to make off with it at once, but he restrained himself although he could not resist a descent from the character of noble poet to that of sharp bargainer of the streets: "We change sticks, mine is..."—and he paused in his search for the appropriate word— "vintage." But I had had enough of Julio by then and I reached out firmly for my cane which he surrendered to me. With a final salutation he passed from my sight and I sensed rather than saw him pausing to survey other potential customers for the *Nostalgia Poetica* of Julio Martins. I searched his little book to find an appropriate verse to mark the occasion of our meeting:

> *Friendship comes first and*
> *That is the naked true*
> *But saying that I love your money*
> *That's a false thing that you do.*

2

George Borrow,
Eccentric

*Lavengro and The Romany Rye—Isopel (Belle) Berners—
the man in black—the postillion—Jasper Petulengro and
the gypsies—Belle's departure—an army childhood—
languages—wanderings—his "veiled period"—gentility—a
man of mystery—the Bible Society—St Petersburg—Spain*

FEW passages in English literature are more compellingly strange
than the final chapters of *Lavengro* and the first chapters in *The
Romany Rye*, Borrow's autobiographical-fantasy books in which
he describes his wooing—or non-wooing—of Isopel Berners in
a dingle somewhere in the middle of England.[1] Borrow, then aged
twenty-two, had just embarked upon his gypsy life of roving and was
recovering from a fit of the "horrors", for he was a manic depressive,
when the solitude of his dingle was invaded by the arrival of a man,
two women and their two horses and carts. The man is the Flaming
Tinman, renowned for his strength and ferocity as a fighter, one of
the women is his vulgar wife, the other is Belle or Isopel Berners.
Borrow stood six foot two or three and he describes Belle as an inch
taller than himself:

> *(…) an exceedingly tall woman, or rather girl, for she could scarcely have
> been above eighteen; she was dressed in a tight bodice, and a blue stuff
> gown; hat, bonnet or cap she had none, and her hair, which was flaxen,
> hung down on her shoulders unconfined; her complexion was fair, and*

her features handsome, with a determined but open expression.

She strikes Borrow a blow on the face that nearly fells him; then he is obliged to fight the Flaming Tinman and wins by a combination of luck, the fact that Isopel takes his side to ensure fair play and his final use of a Long Melford (a right-handed punch) instead of the lefts he employs through their fight. When the Flaming Tinman recovers, for Borrow has knocked him insensible, he leaves the dingle in a sulky fury with his wife but refuses to take Isopel who remains behind. And then follows Borrow's strange courtship of this Wagnerian giantess. They live for some time together in the dingle in their separate tents, he practising his new trade of tinker, she periodically disappearing about her own mysterious affairs.

Borrow sets about his wooing by questioning her. Indeed, with Borrow it might be more appropriate to say "puts her to the question," she reproves him for his forwardness and makes tea, and he discovers that she was brought up in the workhouse. He in return confides his fear, not of the Flaming Tinman but of the evil one, which is another way of describing his fits of the horrors. On Belle's suggestion that ale will assist his recovery, Borrow visits a public house that lies two miles from their dingle where his bruised hand attracts the landlord's attention; the defeat of the Flaming Tinman is already the local sensation. There he listens to a conversation in which a man in black attacks the Church of England while another man, a radical, lauds America at England's expense; this combination of outrages is enough to draw Borrow into the conversation. On his return to the dingle he assures Belle that the ale has driven away the horrors and strengthened him. They drink tea together and Belle warns Borrow that she does not like scoffers and mockers; they discuss America and then, following a silence between them, Borrow proposes to teach her Armenian. "I suppose you mean no harm," says Belle but they are interrupted by the arrival in their dingle of the man in black from the inn.

Real or imagined, the man in black is one of Borrow's most intriguing and sinister characters, a disguised Roman Catholic priest bent upon converting the English—or rather particular and preferably rich and influential English—back to Rome. They have a long discussion in the dingle, Borrow demonstrating the range of his learning and reading, the man in black both puzzled and wary, Belle a bemused spectator.

Borrow and Belle continue to live in the dingle, known as Mumper's or Gypsies' Dingle, and Borrow says: "If I am asked how we passed the time when we were together in the dingle, I would answer that we passed the time very tolerably, all things considered; we conversed together, and when tired of conversing I would sometimes give Belle a lesson in Armenian."

The man in black visits them again and admits that he hopes to bring the country back under the banner of Rome; a long chapter describing the conversation between the man in black and Borrow is designed to show up the duplicity and untrustworthiness of the priest and the cleverness of Borrow. In the intervals between the visits of the man in black, Belle's periodic disappearances about her own affairs and his forging of rough horseshoes for his little pony, Borrow conducts his wooing. He calls Belle the Queen of the Dingle; they have tea; he talks to her of China, explaining that is where her tea comes from, and teachers her more Armenian.

Then a new person invades their dingle: following a thunderstorm and the fall in a nearby field of a fireball they entertain a postillion whose coach has lost its wheel. Belle reassures the man, who is understandably suspicious of these strange characters in the dingle, while Borrow calms his horses, which had become unmanageable. The suspicious postillion is soon won over by their kindness and remains as their guest for the night, now convinced that they are runaway lovers who have come from Gretna Green, and will not abandon the idea until Belle tells him that "I am nothing to the young man, and he, of course, nothing to me." The postillion tells his story and turns out to have been the servant of an aristocratic family into whose services the man in black had insinuated himself with the object—in which he very nearly succeeded—of converting the ladies of the family to Rome.

After the postillion has departed (Borrow mends his wheel) and following a further visit from the man in black, the field beside the dingle is taken over by the gypsy band of Borrow's friend Jasper Petulengro. His sister, Mrs Chikno, asks Borrow whether Belle is his wife and finding that she is not declines to join them for tea: "When ryes and rawnies live together in dingles, without being certificated, I call such behaviour being tolerably deep in the roving line, everything savouring of which I am determined not to sanctify." However, Mr and Mrs Petulengro do visit the dingle for tea and Mrs Petulengro insists upon braiding Belle's hair in gypsy fashion. The gypsies remain for some time to visit a local fair and they assume that Borrow and Belle are living together as man and wife.

Eventually, after more Armenian, which sometimes drives Belle to tears, Borrow proposes that they marry and go to America. She thanks him for the suggestion, which comes matter-of-factly after many strange conversations, but asks for time to consider. He tells her to make up her mind at once and suggests that they should try a fall together: "Brynhilda, the valkyrie, swore that no one should marry her who could not fling her down." The next day Borrow is to accompany Petulengro to the fair and when he rises early is surprised to find Belle already dressed. She is in a strange mood and has not slept and when he takes her hand he finds it ice cold. Yet Borrow appears not to see anything significant in her condition. Before leaving with Petulengro he bids her farewell:

> *God bless you, Belle, I shall be home tonight, by which time I expect*
> *you will have made up your mind; if not, another lesson in Armenian,*
> *however late the hour be. I then wrung Belle's hand, and ascended to the*
> *plain above.*

Belle has gone when Borrow returns and he never sees her again. In *The Romany Rye* he makes Belle write him a long letter, which is delivered to the dingle by an old woman, in which she explains why she has left him. Borrow scholars have suggested that no such letter would have been written and that it is a device to explain the end of the courtship.[2] In it Belle thanks him for his offer of marriage, explains that she might have accepted him if he had made it sooner (rather, one assumes, than subjecting her to so many philological discourses and lessons in Armenian); points out that at root she believes he is mad; and reminds him of the fact that she had been brought up in a workhouse. She encloses a lock of her hair. If, as seems likely, the letter is an invention, it tells the reader a great deal about this strange man; most important, it reveals the reasons why he did not want to be married and tied down. Borrow clearly wishes to indicate that, as a general proposition, he would like to be married, but in fact is determined to continue his single roving life and not commit himself to matrimony.

❧

George Henry Borrow was born at East Dereham, Norfolk, on 5 July 1803, the second son of Thomas and Anne Borrow. His father, who had started life as a private in the Coldstream Guards, ended a long military career as adjutant of the West Norfolk Militia. He retired in 1816 to live in Norwich and sent George to the Grammar School there but George, who had already spent his early life following his father's regiment all over England, never settled down to school discipline or learning; what he liked to do was wander on his own to meet with gypsies and other "doubtful" characters. But he had early demonstrated an astonishing flair for languages and by the time his father died in 1824 when Borrow was twenty-one had taught himself or at least obtained a working knowledge of Danish (he developed a great interest in the Norse sagas), Hebrew, Welsh, Gaelic, Armenian, Latin, Greek, Irish, French, Italian and Spanish. On the death of his father he set of for London where he tried to make a living as a journalist. Then, in 1825, he embarked on a period of wanderings about which very little is known. These continued to 1832. During these years he certainly travelled a good deal in Eastern Europe as well as with the gypsies in England whom he had first come to know on Mousehold Heath just outside Norwich. In the byways of Norfolk, when they were both boys, Borrow first met the gypsy whom he calls Jasper Petulengro in *Lavengro*.

Lavengro: The Scholar, The Gypsy, The Priest must be one of the most extraordinary autobiographies in the English language. Indeed, in a preface to the first edition (1851) Borrow begins by claiming:

"I have endeavoured to describe a dream, partly of study, partly of adventure, in which will be found copious notices of books, and many descriptions of life and manners, some in a very unusual form." *Lavengro* means the philologist and its sequel, *The Romany Rye*, the Gypsy Gentleman. Borrow's use of the word dream in the preface provides a clue to what has puzzled many Borrow readers ever since: how much of what he tells is true? And how much is fiction, for he was certainly a great romanticiser? The two books bring us to 1825 when Borrow was twenty-two and embarked upon his "veiled period" about which we know very little except that he travelled much and must have lived rough, often perhaps as a vagabond.[3] There are many contradictions in Borrow: he wanted to be a scholar yet sought the independence of the road and tells in *Lavengro* how he purchased the necessary tools including a pony and trap to allow him to become a tinker: "A tinker is his own master, a scholar is not."

Much of Borrow's life was a revolt against gentility—he spoke of "this gentility nonsense"—and in Spain, for example, he avoids contact with the upper echelons of society, moving instead among the gypsies and lower orders, and though he might claim that the poor and ignorant ought to be the natural targets for his efforts in spreading the Gospel they were clearly also the people among whom he chose to move. And this raises another interesting question about Borrow. At the beginning of *Lavengro* he describes his father's background and then adds: "I mention these particulars that the reader may see at once that I am not altogether of low and plebeian origin." What seems clear is that the gentility against which Borrow rages nonetheless bothered him. He could claim to be a gentleman in what he describes as an aristocratic age, although his father was little more than an impoverished and undistinguished army officer constantly moving round England with his family and lacking any connections that might lead to advancement. But though Borrow despised the trappings of gentility and much preferred the rough life of a wanderer and adventurer, which had its climax in his five glorious years in Spain, he never lets anyone forget that he is a gentleman.

Borrow's knowledge of the gypsies both in England and in Europe, especially Spain, was unique and of all the mysteries he cultivated that of the gypsies was most dear to him. Jasper Petulengro, based upon the gypsy Ambrose Smith, whose appearances in the pages of *Lavengro* and *The Romany Rye* always enliven the narrative, is one of the most attractive figures in English literature.[4] His phrase "the wind on the heath, brother" must have acted as a spur to many would-be "gypsy" wanderers. Borrow, however, did not entirely embrace the gypsy life and turns down his mentor's offer of a Romany bride. When he had settled at Oulton on the Norfolk Broads, long after his years in Spain, and applied to the Lord Lieutenant of Suffolk to be made a magistrate (despite his objection to gentility nonsense) his request was turned down, and it seems likely that one reason for the refusal was the fact that gypsies were often the offenders who were brought before magistrates and Borrow was not seen as likely to be impartial. He never refused leave to the gypsies to camp on his land and would sometimes join them.[5]

As Herbert Jenkins, his biographer, claims of the years 1825 to 1832 when he disappears from view, while Borrow determined to keep sacred to himself the "veiled period", "In all probability it was a time of great hardship and mortification, and he wished it to be thought that the whole period was devoted to 'a grand philological expedition,' or expeditions. There is no doubt that some portion of the mysterious epoch was so spent, but not all. Many of the adventures ascribed to characters in *Lavengro* and *The Romany Rye* were, most probably, Borrow's own experiences during that period of mystery and misfortune."[6] He was never persuaded to talk about these years. Much later, writing in *The Bible in Spain* he claims, for example, to have lived in different parts of the world "much amongst the Hebrew race, and I am well acquainted with their words and phraseology,"[7] and elsewhere in the same book he says: "I have seen gypsies of various lands, Russian, Hungarian and Turkish; and I have also seen the legitimate children of most countries of the world."[8] In both *The Bible in Spain* and *The Gypsies of Spain* there are many references, often consciously mysterious, to places Borrow must have visited at an earlier stage in his life and this could only have been during the "veiled period".

Borrow, then, was a man of mystery, a pose he liked to cultivate and enhanced by always dressing in black. He was fiercely independent so that it is not surprising that he hardly ever had what a later generation would have described as a steady job and, perhaps, was only able to work for the Bible Society as long as he did because they sent him as their agent to faraway countries where he could play a lone hand. His sense of independence meant, among other things, his belief that he could tell people what he thought of them and their beliefs, which he was only too ready to do, so that at the best of times he must have made a most difficult and uneasy companion. Solitary and a brooder whose fits of the horrors or depressions must have added to his own sense of isolation and uniqueness, he is a most unlikely figure to have been selected for its work by the British and Foreign Bible Society. He liked ale and brandy, his views on the former being sufficient to persuade Walter Rye, a one-time Lord Mayor of Norwich, to decline attending the Borrow celebrations of 1913 with the remark: "I cannot understand how Mr. Jarrold who is so great an apostle of temperance can have anything to do with glorifying the memory of such an admirer of strong ale."[9] Borrow never holds back on his prejudices while his independence was aggressive and offended people. Indeed, pride stood in the way of his success and in 1831, before he was first employed by the Bible Society, his brother John wrote to him: "I am convinced that your want of success in life is more owing to your being unlike other people than to any other cause."[10] As Jenkins says, after listing as obstacles to his advancement such things as his choice of friends, his hatred of gentility and humbug, his attacks of the "horrors" and his grave bearing, "The world in return could make nothing of a man who was a mass of moods and sensibilities, strange tastes and pursuits."[11] He was, indeed, the archetypal "loner". As his Danish friend Hasfeldt was to write to him from St Petersburg: "Doubtless you are not troubled with many friends to visit you, for you are not of the sort who are easily understood, nor do you care to have everyone understand you."[12]

Now this strange, proud, moody man who loved to show how clever he was at other people's expense, who never believed in half measures and whose pride made him assume that others would understand his virtues and capacities without any need on his part to advertise them, was at best a difficult choice for the Bible Society. It was the Rev. Francis Cunningham of Lowestoft who saw how useful Borrow's talent for languages would prove to the Bible Society. It is probable that Borrow had been introduced to him by the widow Mary Clarke whom later he married. Cunningham recommended him to the Bible Society, which was favourably impressed by his letter of introduction. They asked Borrow to come to their Earl Street headquarters in London for an interview; as it happened the Society was then looking for a suitable candidate to send to Russia to produce a Manchu Testament. Borrow both impressed and astonished the committee. He was asked to learn Manchu and subsequently offered employment once he had shown his proficiency in that language. After a few weeks study Borrow wrote to the Bible Society's literary superintendant, Rev. Joseph Jowett, that he was already able to translate Manchu without great difficulty. Later he had talks with the Society's secretary, Rev. Andrew Brandram, about the gypsies and their lack of religion. After seven weeks study of Manchu Borrow could write "I am advancing at full gallop," although he does confess that want of a grammar was a drawback. However, nineteen weeks from the date he started studying Manchu Borrow wrote once more to Jowett to say "I have mastered Manchu, and I should feel obliged by your informing the Committee of the fact." Borrow was invited to London for an interview in which he acquitted himself well; he returned to Norwich to await the results and on receiving an encouraging letter from Jowett (though not a confirmation that he had the job) he wrote back to say "What you have written has given me great pleasure as it holds out hope that I may be employed usefully to the Deity, to man and myself."[13] Jowett replied with a charming admonition in which, among other things, he said: "I am sure you will not be offended if I suggest that there is occasionally a tone of confidence in speaking of yourself, which has alarmed some of the excellent members of our Committee." He then suggests that some were upset by the reference to the Deity in Borrow's letter: "It is where you speak of the prospect of becoming 'useful to the Deity, to man, and to yourself.' Doubtless you meant the prospect of glorifying God."

Borrow got the job and did wonders in St Petersburg, not only as far as the production of a Manchu Testament was concerned but also in business terms, for he saw to every aspect of the printing and production and obtained the necessary materials far more cheaply than anyone who knew Russia at that time could have believed possible. He turned out, in the phrase of his biographer, "a prince of bargainers". So well had Borrow performed in Russia that, as he wrote to his mother, he had every hope that the Bible Society would continue to employ him. Revealingly, he said "I have of late led an active life, and dread the thought of having nothing to do except studying as formerly, and I am by no means certain that I could sit down to study now."[14]

The Bible Society did decide to use him again, sending him initially to Portugal rather than Spain in order to discover the opportunities for "promoting the circulation of the Holy Scriptures in Portugal," but though there was ample evidence of the need for proselytising in that country it was to Spain that Borrow soon directed his attention and was to work for the next five years. Spain, at this time, was in the middle of a brutal civil war between the adherents of the child queen Isabella II, whose father Ferdinand VII had overturned Salic Law to ensure that she should succeed him, and the followers of her uncle, Don Carlos (the late king's brother), who claimed the throne according to the same Salic Law. The resulting war was bitter and cruel and raged through Spain during the time of Borrow's work there on behalf of the Bible Society. It was, therefore, an inauspicious time for such work. Spain, in any case, was the most Catholic country of Europe and as Borrow discovered, he would be thwarted wherever and whenever possible by the Roman Catholic priests and hierarchy. Such obstacles, however, made his task all the more congenial to him. It is in keeping with Borrow's obdurate and perverse character that on his arrival in Spain at Badajoz, across the border from Portugal, he spoke of his "humble hope of being able to cleanse some of the foul stains of popery from the minds of its children, with whom I had little acquaintance."[15]

And so, after a slow and extraordinary start in life for so talented and ambitious a man, Borrow was ready to embark for the Iberian Peninsula and five more years of work for the Bible Society which, in retrospect, he regarded as the happiest period of his life.

3

To the Portuguese Paradise

Sintra—the Pena Palace—Colhares—the discomforts of walking—Mafra—the library

BORROW'S first excursion outside Lisbon to acquaint himself with the state of religious affairs in Portugal was to Cintra:

> *If there be any place in the world entitled to the appellation of an enchanted region, it is surely Cintra; Tivoli is a beautiful and picturesque place, but it quickly fades from the mind of those who have seen the Portuguese Paradise.*[1]

Like Lord Byron, who eulogised Cintra in *Childe Harolde*, Borrow tends to hyperbole whenever he approves.

Sintra (the modern spelling) is certainly a spectacular place: the town itself, the palace and villas, and the great crags surmounted by the ruins of the ancient Moorish castle which was once the stronghold of the Lusitanian Moors, the whole region densely forested. Borrow, who could be laconic to the point of minimalism in his descriptions of places, waxes eloquent over Sinta: "Oh! There are strange and wonderful objects at Cintra, and strange and wonderful recollections attached to them."

The extraordinary Pena Palace, on its crag with its many-sized turrets and a square clock tower with four miniature pinnacled corners, the whole a mixture of grey stone, red-chocolate brown and bilious yellow, is a mid-nineteenth-century folly which was built after

Borrow's visit—or it must surely have elicited some comment from him. When I had toiled up the hill to view this rival to the more ancient Moorish ruins on a neighbouring ridge of crags I entered the courtyard to find myself surrounded by a group of noisy tourists. But from the battlements of this architectural absurdity I was able to view across a rich canopy of green forest, and beyond the dark silhouette of a great statue that reared above the distant trees, the grey rolling Atlantic, for the day was overcast with black clouds. The extensive remains of the huge sprawling Moorish castle which rose black against the sky from the adjoining crags were far more to my taste.

At Colhares, a village two leagues from Sintra, Borrow visited the village school where he inquired of the teacher who was in the middle of taking class whether he placed the Scriptures in the hands of the children only to be told that long before they could understand them they were removed by their parents to work in the fields and that the parents in general "were by no means solicitous that their children should learn anything, as they considered the time occupied in learning as so much squandered away." Borrow spent four days at Sintra, traversing the country in all directions and, as he wrote to Rev. Jowett in London, "riding into the fields, where I saw the peasants at work, and entering into discourse with them, and notwithstanding many of my questions must have appeared to them very singular, I never experienced any incivility, though they frequently answered me with smiles and laughter."[2]

I decided to make my first serious walk from Sintra to Mafra. Borrow says it was about three leagues from Sintra: "The principal part of the way lay over steep hills, somewhat dangerous for horses; however, I reached the place in safety." The distance by modern road was twenty-two kilometres and this was sufficient for me to discover some of the discomforts of walking: part of the road was dreary, lined with marble factories. At one point, far from shelter, I found myself trudging forlorn and miserable in a hailstorm so that I arrived in Mafra with chattering teeth and well-soaked—though a hot meal and brandy put me right. Then, helped by a friendly policeman, I found a room in Mafra's most expensive inn which, with his aid, I had mistaken for its cheapest.

Mafra has been called the Escorial of Portugal and the extent of the palace is prodigious; it is celebrated for its library. When Borrow visited Mafra, especially to see the library, there were no longer any monks in residence as there had been at the beginning of the century. "They had been driven forth", he tells us, "some to beg their bread, some to serve under the banners of Don Carlos, in Spain, and many, as I was informed, to prowl about as banditti." The palace of Mafra is in the form of a vast square whose four sides of grand halls and galleries enclose a huge basilica in the centre; it is possible to look down into this from a gallery above. I arrived at the palace in the late afternoon, just in time to be included in the last group to be shown round on a tour before the palace closed and a dozen of us set off in the care of a little round fat friendly guide. A French couple with a son of about ten and myself were the only foreigners, the others were Portuguese, and for reasons best known to himself our guide singled me out for his special care and concern. On discovering my nationality, the French boy attached himself to me to improve his English and we were able to divert ourselves during the more uninteresting parts of the tour. I asked the guide more than once about the library which was the feature I was particularly concerned to see and he assured me we would come to it in due course, which we did almost at the end of our inspection. We filed into one end of the library, which is truly magnificent. It contains 30,000 vellum bound books stacked high up the walls while a gallery runs round all four sides of the oblong chamber which is perhaps eighty metres in length. But there was no sign that the library was ever used. Instead, as though in a zoo, the huge volumes are stared at by carefully shepherded visitors. Our guide had led us at a certain speed, not quite hurrying us but not allowing us to loiter either, partly because the castle is so enormous, and partly, I suspect, because it was the end of his day. Later that evening, when the setting sun shone on glistening yellow stone surfaces after a fresh downpour of rain, the grandeur of the palace was enhanced as though it had just received a new coat of paint.

4

No Longer a Stranger

*Modern easiness of travel—television—the day's routine—
finding accommodation—plastic cards—bargaining—
roadside bars—the solitary walker—Borrow's purpose—
strangers no longer strange*

SOMETIMES, when talking about my travels in other parts of the world and wrapped up in the adventure of it, I have been asked to explain quite ordinary details: how much could I walk in a day, what did I do when my feet hurt, how often did I wash my socks, did I always carry plenty of money? In Spain, following the route George Borrow took, I was also forced to reflect upon the vast changes that have occurred in the easiness of travel: where in his time a coach and four would take twenty-four hours over dangerous dirt roads to cover a quite modest distance a modern inter-city bus on its macadamised highway will accomplish the same journey in two hours. The train had not yet appeared in the Spain that Borrow travelled and the great railway boom that swept Victorian England in the 1840s only occurred after his return home.

My own travel was to be a mixture: whenever the distance to be covered in a day, as well as the nature of the road, suggested it, I walked; otherwise I took one of the inter-city buses and occasionally a train. I rarely stayed in any place for longer than a single night though there were exceptions—Madrid, Seville, Córdoba, La Coruña. An ideal walk was about thirty kilometres though towards the end of my travels this distance had increased substantially to between thirty-five and forty a day and on several occasions I walked as much as forty-two kilometres. There was no pleasure to be had from walking major highways because of the ceaseless volume of traffic though sometimes it was unavoidable; nor was there any enjoyment walking out of big cities through stretches of built-up areas. During my three months in Spain I walked a total of 1,207 kilometres (750 miles), travelled 3,160 kilometres (1,963 miles) by bus and 1,141 kilometres (705 miles) by train. At the end of my trip I found that on average I had walked every other day. Although I had heard tales about the slowness and late arrival of Spanish trains those that I used came on time and reached their destinations on time. The big long-distance buses were comfortable and clean, and rarely late. They would turn into the appropriate bay at the bus station on the hour, pick up the waiting passengers and depart again on schedule and the elevation of the seats provided an excellent view of the countryside.

When walking I liked to get away from my inn as early as possible in the morning so as to enjoy at least two or three hours of relative coolness before the sun moved into its zenith and usually I would purchase rolls, cheese or fruit for my walk the previous evening since the Spanish, sensibly, pursue a leisurely routine at the beginning of their day and more than once, if I left a fair-sized town early enough I did so without having found even a café open for a cup of coffee.

The first undersea telegraph cable to link England and France was laid in 1850 and the first transatlantic cable in 1858. When, as a traveller, Borrow arrived in a Spanish town or village he was regarded with double interest: as a source of news about the place from whence he had come; and in himself since travellers were a rarity. Perhaps nothing has so revolutionised travel since his day than the electronic media. Travellers are unlikely to possess any information from outside the local community that is not already available since anything newsworthy and much that is not will have preceded the traveller by way of television. Almost every roadside bar or café up to and including the most prestigious restaurants had their television sets on and if, as sometimes, I found myself the first to enter a dining room for my evening meal a thoughtful waiter would come at once to turn on the television for me, even if I then had to wait half an hour before any food was forthcoming. Once, in the early days of my travels when I had taken the corner table in an elegant little restaurant of excellent cuisine and was enjoying a bowl of gaspacho, I gradually realised, as I thought, that everyone else in the dining room was staring at me. Startled at this unlooked for attention, I began to study the other diners more closely only to realise that I was sitting beneath the television set and that they were all staring above my head which allowed me, in my turn, to study their upturned faces.

Borrow and his servant travelled by horse and had to hire mules and guides, the latter often proving unreliable, drunken or scoundrels. Moreover, he would be obliged to rise very early to oversee the preparation of his animals or find a guide with the expectation of travelling upon an unknown road or track to his next destination. My departures were far simpler, a matter of packing my rucksack, settling the bill and then setting off. My day followed a routine that only varied according to the mode of travel—walking or bus; otherwise, the mornings were spent in travel. On arrival at my day's destination my first concern was to find a place to stay. Thereafter, most days followed a similar pattern: a midday meal and drink, a shower and change into my town clothes, a rest, some Spanish study and writing up my journal. Then I would be ready for the second part of my day which consisted of exploring the town and visiting antiquities or other places of interest, idling my time at wayside cafés and, finally, searching for a suitable restaurant in which to take my evening meal. Food in the earlier part of the day I regarded as a necessity; in the evening it was to be savoured as a pleasure and, since the Spanish rarely eat before half past nine, I would have ample time to search for the restaurant of my choice. By the time I had crossed the Alemtejo region of Portugal to the Spanish border this daily routine had become more or less fixed.

The Bible Society paid its agents well and covered their often considerable expenses; certainly, Borrow never seemed to want for money to hire mules or guides and almost invariably stayed in the leading *posada* though in many places this meant no more than the only inn which the town boasted. I, on the other hand, enjoyed the advantage of that modern traveller's aid, the plastic card although paying with plastic cards has its drawbacks. Sometimes inns displayed Visa or other signs to attract custom only for me to discover when I presented my card for payment that the machine, *la maquina*, had broken down, was not working, was out of order—I got to know all the phrases which, no doubt, the innkeepers knew by heart. At other times a shiny new sign in the window of an inn or restaurant convinced me that at least on this occasion my card would be honoured in lieu of dwindling ready money only to discover, on presenting it, that *la maquina* had not yet been installed and the shiny new sign was merely anticipatory of convenience to come. There was, I am sure, a reluctance in at least some of the smaller inns to deal in plastic money and on one particular occasion the landlord was saved by an act of God. I had been assured the night before, though I detected a certain hesitant reserve, that my Visa card would be acceptable in payment the next morning. The day began exceptionally gloomy and a great thunderstorm erupted just as I was on the point of paying my bill. The lights went out following a power cut and with undisguised amusement at my irritation the landlord said "Alas, the power has gone, the *maquina* cannot work!" And once, towards the end of my long journey when I had offered one of my cards in payment for my supper, a solemn waiter returned to my table to inform me that my plastic card "had been eaten by the machine."

I am useless at bargaining so that on the rare occasions when I do achieve what I consider to be a bargain I am elated. I did this once in relation to a room. Prices are normally fixed and, on the whole, were remarkably cheap, but on a particular occasion along the north coast I came to an inn that looked pristine new and clearly had only just opened. I asked the diminutive little woman in reception the price of a single room. "Four thousand with bath," she said. "That is very expensive," I replied. "That is our fixed price," she said. "But you are empty, I appear to be your only customer," and I looked round the empty reception area. "We have only just opened," she replied, then "three thousand." "Done!" and I had my bargain.

I developed a special affection for the little roadside bars which were a mixture of café and pub. They were not designed for tourists and could rarely have been visited by them; rather, they were the local equivalent of an English pub. Their hosts were pleased enough to greet me as a customer in the general line of business but though reasonably friendly and sometimes talkative they did not go out of their way to treat me as anyone special. If it was my wish to sit silently, which was often the case after a long hot stretch of walking, they left me alone, but should I offer to talk they were happy to do so. These bars catered for the local village or the nearby farming community and the people who entered them always knew one another. When, as sometimes happened in mid-morning, I had the bar to myself my host or hostess would be inclined to satisfy his or her curiosity by asking my nationality and where I had come from and then I would have the chance of engaging in more lengthy conversation.

Those long walks gave me an enormous appetite as well as thirst, and thick Galician or Asturian soups were especially welcome after a long morning's trudge since they satisfied both hunger and thirst at the same time. It was the usual custom of the house to place a large tureen of soup before a diner who helped himself and more than once I demolished the entire contents of the tureen, which contained provision for three or four normal diners, much to the amusement and astonishment of the waiters. And I developed a taste for the red house wines that were served chilled and found myself quaffing the wine much as Borrow talked of quaffing ale.

დ

Few people travel on their own these days, at least as far as I can judge, and I was often subjected to a look of astonishment less because I was walking, though I did not meet any serious walkers at all until I came to the Pilgrim Way in the north, than because I was walking alone. Solitary walking is conducive to thinking and I did a great deal of thinking in Spain: the state of the human race, naturally, the pleasure of doing anything that is useless, the pointless absurdity of human beings, the cruelty of religions and, as the great and sometimes arid vistas of Spain opened out before me, I thought of the compulsions that had led this proud and arrogant people to conquer half the New World as conquistadors or endorse the dogmas of the Catholic religion with the cruelties of the Inquisition. Sometimes I just thought of my next meal and a bottle of cold wine.

Borrow, of course, had a purpose for which he was paid: to bring enlightenment to the Spanish in the form of Protestant Testaments in a land which he and the Bible Society regarded as benighted since it adhered to Roman Catholicism and followed Rome. But Borrow, bigot though he appeared in religious matters, had two other interests apart from his commitment to his Earl Street mentors in London. The first of these was the gypsies. Whenever he met them, and there were many in Spain, he became enlivened with a sense of mystery and purpose, delighting to reveal that he understood their language and ways. He questioned them as to their religion and translated part of the New Testament into Romany yet despite paying obeisance, as it were, to Biblical purposes he was interested in the gypsies as gypsies. His other interest was his compulsion to travel and to do so in a land that in his time was still one of the wildest and most dangerous in Europe. He met with robbers, there was a civil war in progress and the dangers to a foreigner travelling on his own were many and real although Borrow's natural instinct and pleasure was to enhance rather than play down the attendant dangers for to do so made for better copy.

When I set out to follow Borrow's trail I thought that the time gap of over a century and a half was not too great and at one level this was so: the lifestyle in small rural villages cannot have changed that much in the intervening years while the spectacular scenery of Spain has hardly altered at all. But in other respects the change has been enormous: television must have altered the perceptions of life rather than the lifestyles of even the most remote villages in ways that are hard to calculate for it has brought instant knowledge of events throughout a wider world—often, it has to be said, ridiculous knowledge centred upon fashion or the idiocies of soap operas—while the enormous changes in transportation, the super-highways, the cars, buses and trains, mean that strangers are no longer strange. And that, perhaps, is the greatest loss of all.

5

The Province Beyond
the Tagus

Crossing the Tagus—Costa da Caparica—Mary—Setúbal—
I begin to sketch—Vendas Novas—two gastronomes—
Montemor-O-Novo—dogs—a friendly lift—Arroyolos

AFTER completing his business in Lisbon, Borrow determined to set
up depots for Bibles in one or two provincial towns and decided to
visit the Alemtejo which, he had heard, was a most benighted region.
The Alemtejo, meaning the province beyond the Tagus, is one of the
poorer regions of Portugal and not especially picturesque. As Borrow
described it, "The greater part consists of heaths broken by knolls,
and gloomy dingles, and forests of stunted pine," which were then
infested with banditti. But if bandits are no longer to be found, much
of the description still stands although an expanding population and
the spread of agriculture have, no doubt, softened the appearance of
the region as a whole.

When Borrow went to cross the Tagus he discovered that an
adverse tide would delay the passenger boat until evening and since,
as always, he was keen to be on his way he hired a man and a boy to
take him across in their own small boat. He almost met with disaster
as the wind rose and "the waves of the noble Tagus began to be
crested with foam," so to cheer himself and show camaraderie to the
boy, who was battling with the sail, Borrow hummed a well known
song "I, who am a smuggler," which appealed to the boy who laughed

and said he would not drown them if he could help it.[1] They arrived on the southern shore of the Tagus pool in the pitch dark December night to disembark at the Aldea Gallega or Galician village as it was then called. Borrow stayed overnight in a dreadful inn and left at five the next morning on the road to Evora. His route would take him through Vendas Novas, Montemor-O-Novo and Arroyolos.

I crossed to Cacilhas, as it is now called, on the modern ferry that goes back and forth all day departing from the corner of the Praça do Comércio and, though there was little drama to my crossing, it was a miserable wet day and failing to find accommodation anywhere in Cacilhas, I was persuaded to take a bus to what I misunderstood my informant to say was a suburb of Cacilhas where hotels and inns were to be found. I ended up in the Costa da Caparica.

Now this was off my Borrow trail and not remotely the kind of place I would wish to visit. Costa da Caparica is a modern holiday resort some ten kilometres over the hills from Cacilhas on the Atlantic coast. It is a 1984-style wasteland of stark blocks of shoddily built holiday flats, rows of little bars and cafés altogether lacking in style, a seafront hidden behind sand dunes and funfairs, the whole geared to meet the minimum requirements of the lower end of the package holiday industry—a sort of miniature Portuguese Blackpool without the Tower. At least it had stopped raining so I selected a pavement table outside a small café where I could examine my map and work out where I ought to have gone.

"Good day to you, Sir, can I help you? English, I suppose?" I was startled less by her English or her assumption that I was English than by her accent which was brummagem rather than Portuguese.

"I'll have a glass of wine, please. You speak very good English," I added.

"Well, my custom comes from there; my English customers have been coming here for years now." She was plump and comfortable and disposed to talk. She brought my drink and I invited her to have one, which she declined: "Not now, thank you, love, or I'll fall asleep."

"How did you learn such good English?"

35

"This place is full of the English in the season and besides…" she hesitated with just a suggestion of delicacy.

"Besides, the English don't learn Portuguese," I added for her.

"That's right, Sir." She gave a comfortable laugh: "Not so as you would notice," she added.

"And what sort of English people do you get here?"

"Well, not your type," she said emphatically. "We don't cater for individuals here, they come in packages."

"Where do they come from, in England, I mean?"

"All over, but most of them come from your Midlands for a week or two weeks, special deals." Most of them, she added, rented apartments in the blocks of flats; the hotels were very expensive, she said, looking at my backpack.

"And what do they do during their stay?"

"Sun, sex and lager, dear," the answer came pat as though from a hoiday brochure. "Would you care for another drink?"

I left Mary—"They all call me Mary, not Maria," she told me—and went to catch a bus. Since I had made a wrong start I decided to go to Setubal for the night and then rejoin the Borrow trail the following day. Nothing would persuade me to stay in Costa da Caparica and Mary, who would have made a good English publican and had divined my thoughts, called a cheery farewell "and shake the dust off."

In Setúbal I found a pleasant *pensión* in a tiny side alley near the waterfront and had the high-ceilinged divided-off portion of what must once have been a very grand room indeed in a former merchant's house. Setúbal had been a royal residence, but most of the old city was destroyed in the earthquake of 1755 except for a fifteenth-century church and seventeenth-century castle. It had the pleasant, dilapidated appearance of a well-used commercial centre and port—it is now Portugal's third port. The evening was warm and the sun made the wet façades of the waterfront glisten in the aftermath of yet another heavy downpour. A model caravel of the kind in which Columbus had sailed to the Americas was moored conveniently in the centre of the seafront for visitors to inspect; its tiny size was its most striking feature.

I decided to take the train to Vendas Novas the next afternoon and since it rained steadily for most of the day spent the morning in a variety of cafés drinking coffee or wine. It was in Setúbal that I began to sketch. A big-boned monk looking remarkably like pictures of Friar Tuck stood talking with the proprietor at the bar and surreptitiously I sketched him, keeping my pad out of sight on my knee below the level of the table so that neither the friar nor anyone else could see what I was about. It was only a rough likeness but my first effort.

I had to change trains at Pinhal Novo and was struck by the elegant station decorations of antique blue tiles. One panel of tiles, which was about six feet long and three feet high, had the appearance of an enlarged Persian miniature except that its horsemen were not knights but nineteenth-century *vaqueros* chasing stampeding cattle. As we approached Vendas Novas I searched in vain for the royal palace which Borrow describes as "towering majestically in the distance," although on closer inspection he had discovered it to be quite uninteresting.

Apart from an impressive barracks the town of Vendas Novas offered little of interest although in my search for a place to stay I was

twice directed by the same friendly man standing in the high street near the taxi rank, first to an inn and then to a *pensión*, both of which proved to be full. On each occasion I was directed back to the taxi rank which, I was informed, was situated outside a *pensión*. On my second return my helpful informant had disappeared; he had been standing immediately in front of the *pensión* where I then obtained a room.

Watching other people eat as I dined alone became an all-absorbing occupation and that evening I was treated to a comedy of manners at a neighbouring table where two men for whom the evening meal was clearly the object of their day enjoyed a long discussion about what to eat and then repeated it, point by point, to the waiter. One of the men was of splendid girth, a highly prized customer to whom the waiter deferred with practised skill. His friend was later joined by his wife and small son who were treated to a reasonable though not excessive meal before they departed to leave the two men *tête-à-tête* or perhaps *bouche-à-bouche* for a further round of courses. When I left a fresh tablecloth was being placed before them preparatory to yet another onslaught.

Montemor-o-Novo, a former Moorish fortress town, was dramatically situated on the top of a sharp hill which overlooked the country for miles around. Borrow was pressed for time when he came to Montemor-o-Novo and though he compares the little hilltop town with Sintra and describes it as exceedingly picturesque he did not stop long enough to explore further. It is a place of steep cobbled streets and small old houses in the Moorish style and there are wonderful vistas from the ruins of the castle that commands the hilltop. The town possesses a museum of archaeology and I had all but completed an inspection of it—I had the museum to myself—when the woman curator discovered me and insisted on showing me round again.

During my walking I was becoming conscious of the large dogs which guarded lonely farms; several times one such creature had made a vicious foray in my direction. Once, years before, when walking in Turkey, I had rounded the steep shoulder of a hill to encounter a sight I shall never forget. Perhaps two hundred yards ahead of me and down the slope of the hill was a large flock of sheep tightly gathered round a solitary tree. I had heard the tinkle of their bells for some time before I caught sight of them without realising what the sound meant. Standing under the tree's shade leaning on a great staff was the shepherd, while a boy on a donkey circled the flock. Beyond the sheep the hill sloped ever more steeply to the valley far below where a line of trees marked the course of a river. It was an idyllic, Biblical scene of a kind that could hardly have changed in centuries. I continued towards the flock, enjoying the serenity of this ancient rural picture, when seven of what appeared to be the largest sheep detached themselves from the rest and came racing towards me, baying in that deep-throated way which belongs to only the most savage of dogs. This indeed was what they were: the great Anatolian shepherd dogs. They were huge with especially powerful shoulders and wore wide iron collars with two-inch iron spikes sticking out of them. These perform a dual task: they make it impossible for the dog to lay its head flat on the ground to rest so that they are always watchful with savage tempers to match; and in a fight the spikes act as a formidable addition to the dog's natural armoury of teeth and claws. They win prizes according to the number of wolves they kill.

The dogs reached the road and, trained in attack, formed a half circle round me, growling and snapping. I did not even have a walking stick on that occasion, so stood still except that I revolved slowly looking at each in turn. Saliva dripped from their large blackened teeth which their drawn back muzzles revealed. The shepherd came running up the hill; while the boy on the donkey uttered shrill cries as he urged his beast towards me. By the time they reached us the nearest and largest of the dogs was only six feet away from me and preparing to attack. I knew that once he made a dash for a bite the others would follow. I stamped my foot extra hard just as this largest, most savage dog moved nearer and it backed a pace, snarling. Then the shepherd arrived and drove his dogs back and the boy leaped off his donkey wielding a long supple stick and the dogs retreated though with great reluctance. Neither of my rescuers took the slightest notice of me except to hold the dogs back as I resumed my walk.[2]

At that time I had yet to read *The Bible in Spain* for, had I done so, I would no doubt have followed Borrow's advice for he tells us how

> *(...) an immense dog, such as those which guard the flocks in the neighbourhood against wolves, came bounding to attack me 'with eyes that glowed, and fangs that grinned'. Had I retreated, or had recourse to any other mode of defence than that which I invariably practice under such circumstances, he would probably have worried me; but I stooped till my chin nearly touched my knee, and looked him full in the eyes.*[3]

This approach may have worked for Borrow though I doubt it would have kept seven Anatolian shepherd dogs at bay for long. I hoped that on my walks I would not be obliged to put Borrow's expedient to the test.

From Montemor-o-Novo, where I had stayed in a pleasant little *pensión* in the main square, I set off to walk to Arroyolos; I intended to make a diversion to visit some Druid ruins which Borrow extols. Borrow, indeed, could wax lyrical about something of which he approved and in this case he first lists things which have crumbled to dust—Roman temples, Arian churches, Moorish mosques—before returning to the Druid ruins:

> *There it stands on the hill of winds, as strong and as freshly new as the day, perhaps thirty centuries back, when it was first raised, by means which are a mystery. Earthquakes have heaved it, but its cope stone has not fallen; rain floods have deluged it, but failed to sweep it from its station; the burning sun has flashed upon it, but neither split nor crumbled it; and time, stern old time, has rubbed it with his iron tooth, and with what effect let those who view it declare.*[4]

After such a brave exhortation I wanted to view it but, alas, I was thwarted by rain and kindness. When I set off from Montemor-o-Novo the next morning the sky was dull and heavy and I had hardly cleared the town before the rain began to fall: gently at first, then steadily and finally heavily. I had not associated Portugal with so much rain. I had covered about six kilometres and had water dripping all over me when a small red van pulled up on the other side of the road to offer me a lift. The driver was the young man from the *pensión* of the night before. He had as little English as I had Portuguese but we conversed in a mixture of tongues and I used my Spanish dictionary to help the conversation along. He was an ordinary young man, now on his way to Evora to obtain provisions for his establishment, and he asked me how long my holiday was to be. I told him, not without linguistic complications, that I was not on holiday but following a trail in order to write a book. He became intrigued and when we reached the outskirts of Arroloyos stopped at the roadside for a while so that we could continue our conversation. He was so excited by the idea, which evoked his own concealed aspirations to travel, that I felt ashamed of having dismissed him as an ordinary young man. He needed opportunity. But his act of kindness had ruined my plans. I had now arrived at Arroloyos in mid-morning instead of enjoying four hours walking in the rain and had missed the Druid ruins as well.

The rain ceased and the sun came out as I walked up the steep cobbled street into the centre of the town, which, like so many Portuguese and Spanish towns, was built on a hilltop. Like Montemor-o-Novo this, too, was crowned with a Moorish castle. Arroyolos is a pretty town of white painted houses, red tiled roofs, curving narrow streets and cobblestones. Standing on a neighbouring hill was a grim, grey stone monastery which looked deserted while from the walls of the Moorish castle I could follow the long straight road over which I had approached across miles of the undulating plain. A fitful sun appeared and disappeared behind fast moving clouds, the wind blew and the long grass that now covered the castle courtyards rustled as, slowly, I walked the circumference of the walls and looked over a lush green land. A squat, heavy-built white church occupied the summit of the keep within the castle walls, a symbol of the triumph of Christianity over Islam that is repeated through half the peninsula.

I found a *pensión* that occupied a large, grand old house; the walls of the hall and stairs were tiled to a height of four feet from the ground; such tiles, much in evidence in southern Portugal, act as a constant reminder of the lasting impact of Moorish culture. I was given a high-ceilinged spacious room which contained two large elegant canopied beds. These I regarded as something of an augury as Borrow claimed to have been provided with a two-bedded room which he was asked to share with a young Spanish gentleman who had run away from his people in order to travel, providing Borrow, who had done much the same, with the opportunity to lecture him on his wicked and foolish action. The public rooms of that *pensión*, which was the most expensive I stayed in throughout the peninsula, were like a stage set including an elegant, unused, gaming room and a hall lined with luxurious leather-bound chairs.

Borrow, in a hurry to press on with his journey, also complained of the high price he paid in Arroyolos: "At nine, after having paid a most exorbitant sum for slight accommodation, I started from Arroyolos, which is a town or large village situated on very elevated ground, and discernible far off. It can boast the remains of a large ancient and seemingly Moorish castle..."[5] Little had changed. When I left the next morning I asked my hostess whether, by chance, her establishment had been an inn a hundred and fifty years earlier, but "no" it had then been a private house.

6

The Last of Portugal

ARROYOLOS to Evora was an easy walk of twenty-two kilometres. The rain of the previous day had given way to bright sunshine and fast-moving light clouds, the road passed through gently rolling country whose undulating fields of yellow and purple flowers sparkled in the sunlight. As I passed a farm two huge dogs came racing towards me but, to my relief, were on the end of long chains so that I did not have to test Borrow's strategy of lowering my chin to my knees to outstare them. The road was quiet with little traffic although when I had covered about half the distance to Evora a small car drew up and its owner offered me a lift. He had already picked up one passenger, a young man with a rucksack, and assumed that I too wished for a lift. I declined, assuring him that I preferred to walk, and my refusal embarrassed the young man who looked as though he felt he too ought to be walking. A turn in the road brought me my first view of the cathedral whose twin towers rose black above the city of Evora clustered on its hilltop. On the outskirts of the city the road passes under the aches of an elegant Roman aqueduct but, curiously, Borrow does not mention this although he spent time in Evora whose other sights he describes in detail.

> *Evora is a small city, walled, but not regularly fortified, and could not sustain a siege of a day. It has five gates; before that to the south-west is*

43

*the principal promenade of its inhabitants; ... the houses in general are
very ancient... The two principal edifices are the See, or cathedral, and
the convent of San Francisco, in the square before the latter of which was
the posada where I had taken up my abode.*[1]

The street into the centre rose steeply from the gate through which
I entered and the walls looked magnificent whatever their capacity to
resist a siege may once have been. The cathedral, which I had seen
looming on the skyline for the last half of my walk, dominates one
of end of a long rectangular plaza. Originally built at the end of the
twelfth century but later renovated in the Gothic manner, it is a
heavy though not especially large building, its façade onto the square
signalling the certainty in its power of a Church that had no rivals.
The sides of the square were graced by elegant, mellowed frontages of
yellow stone; the tall buildings rose above the arches of arcades that
ran along either side of the plaza while black iron balconies graced
the first and second storeys of the old houses. The centre of this plaza
was covered with tables, some sheltered from the sun by large bright
sunshades, others exposed. I was thirsty and wandered through the
maze of tables searching in vain for one that was free. I must have
looked hot and tired because an elderly American sitting with his wife
indicated the spare seat at their table and invited me to join them. I
did so gratefully and we introduced ourselves.

"An Englishman, and walking! Now isn't that something, Aubrey."

"It surely is, my dear."

"And where do you say you came from now? Arroyolos! Why, that
is a most energetic way of taking a holiday. How long are you here
for?" Mrs Pride, for that was their unlikely name, turned out to be a
gently probing chatty woman who looked to her husband, Aubrey,
for confirmation of every statement she made.

"I am not on a holiday, I am following an old trail in order to
write a book."

"An old trail, to write a book! Why this is exciting, don't you think
it is exciting, Aubrey."

"It surely is, my dear; May I ask what is the nature of your trail,
Mr Arnold?" So I told them about Borrow and *The Bible in Spain*;
neither had heard of Borrow.

"This is an education. George Borrow, you say, and *The Bible in Spain*? I feel quite thrilled. I am being educated. Don't you think you are being educated, Aubrey?"

"I surely do, honey, I surely do," intoned Aubrey; then, turning to me, "And where do you go from here, Mr Arnold, what is to be your route?" So I took out my map and outlined my planned route which was greeted with suitable expressions of astonishment.

"And all on foot, Mr Arnold, are you going to walk all that way?" She noted down the name of George Borrow and *The Bible in Spain* in her diary—"I always keep a diary when we travel, don't I Aubrey?"—and assured me she would look them up when they got back home. "Won't we Aubrey?" to both of which questions he replied with his usual affirmatives. They told me where they had been in Portugal and then I excused myself so that I could find rooms but this set her off again.

"You mean you just come to a town without knowing if there is a place to stay? Why, that is certainly to take a chance, Mr Arnold. I admire you for that. We book in advance, always, don't we Aubrey?"

"We surely do, my dear, we surely do."

"Well, Mr Arnold, we shan't keep you any longer. But I have to say, you are the most interesting person we have met on our trip to Portugal. Isn't he, Aubrey?"

"He most certainly is, my dear."

"I suppose, Mr Arnold, you are an Anglican? *The Bible in Spain*! Well, just fancy that. We, of course, are Baptists, aren't we, Aubrey."

"Yes, we are Baptists, our family have always been Baptists," and Mr Pride, who had detected an expression on my face which was lost to his spouse, refrained from following up her question as to my own religious adherence at which I was pleased for they were a pleasant, harmless couple; there was more to Mr Pride than I had at first imagined, despite the primary role he seemed destined to fulfil of confirmation in support of his wife.

The word Bible can trigger very different reactions. I had put off reading *The Bible in Spain* for years simply because the word appeared in the title; Mrs Pride assumed I must be religious because I was interested in a book with such a title. When first he arrived in Evora, Borrow talked with middle-class people, probing for information about the state of religious instruction, and says: "When I spoke of religion, they exhibited the utmost apathy for the subject, and, making their bows, left me as soon as possible."[2] My sympathies lie with the people who excused themselves; the prospect of the immensely tall, black-dressed George Borrow beginning one of his interrogations about religion must have been a forbidding one.

⟡

Evora is one of those timeless cities whose layers of history give to it both a feel of longevity and a sense of time to come: it has seen much and, no doubt, will see a great deal more. Its history predates the Romans while, for them, it was an important military centre for years before and after Caesar. The city fell to the Moors at the beginning of the eighth century and they held it for 450 years before the Christians retook it in 1166 and began building the cathedral twenty years later. Apart from the aqueduct, the principal Roman remains consist of the delicately columned ruins of the Temple of Diana, attributed to that deity without any evidence. There is also a massive sixteenth-century royal church of St Francis, almost as grand as the cathedral.

When I left my American friends I found my way to the church of St Francis which occupies one side of a picturesque old square somewhat lower down the hillside than the cathedral plaza. Borrow lodged in a *posada* opposite St Francis and I hoped to discover this; instead, I found a bustling restaurant behind which was a little *pensión* where I obtained lodgings. There was a building alongside the restaurant which looked both old enough and of a design that could have been a *posada* but it was firmly closed with no indication as to its present use. Borrow describes sitting down "on a log of wood on the hearth within the immense chimney in the common apartment" of the hostelry[3] whereas my small *pensión* did not boast a common room at all.

The Roman Temple to Diana has been finely preserved and is one of the modern attractions of the city but this was not so in Borrow's time. Then, as he says: "Part of it was evidently of Roman architecture, for there was no mistaking the beautiful light pillars… but the original space between the pillars had been filled up with rubbish of a modern date, and the rest of the building was apparently of the architecture of the Middle Ages."[4] Since then, however, those additions have been stripped away and only the Roman structure remains. It was a lovely fresh evening and I sat at an open-air café by the temple for a drink while an enormous black hound, happily muzzled, came to sit beside me.

If you draw a circle on the ground round a cock and then place its beak on the line it will follow this round, mesmerised, believing itself to be imprisoned. In the square of St Francis, later that evening, I sat at one of the outer tables of a pavement restaurant over a light supper and watched two old men create a circle of expectoration round them. They had met for their regular evening's gossip and stood about twelve feet from my table, oblivious to the activity of the square as they peered at one another through rheumy eyes and talked of I know not what. Despite the warm weather they were dressed in heavy black suits and wore ancient trilby hats. Their suits were crumpled and stained, their shirts, collarless and certainly not clean, were held in place at the throat by large studs, their shoes scuffed and

long unpolished. One leaned on a stick, the other was bow-legged and they had about them the appearance of having achieved all the ageing they intended and hereafter would look the same until the day they died. Each had the silvery-grey stubble of old men on their unshaved, parchment-crinkled jaws and neither possessed more than a scattering of blackened teeth. They expectorated alternately until, little by little, they had created a defensive circle of spittle on the cobbles around

them. I judged myself to be out of spitting distance though not by a great margin and occupied my time sketching them. Engrossed in the events of their day, they were quite unaware of my interest although my waiter was not and came periodically to give approving nods over my shoulder.

Borrow spent some time in Evora and was tireless in seeking out people whose welfare he might influence. From Evora he returned to Lisbon to make further arrangements about the distribution of testaments in Portugal before returning over the same ground to make his way into Spain and on to Madrid.

When I left the city early the next morning a heavy mist hung round the walls and when I looked back after a mile or so I could see Evora rising on its hill out of a misty sea. I again found myself passing through a landscape of great fields covered in yellow and purple flowers. By noon I was walking through an undulating countryside of cork oaks while far ahead I glimpsed the conical hill crowned by the castle of Evoramonte. The old town of Evoramonte rose steeply up the hillside from the main road to the remains of yet another Moorish castle. The town only boasted one *pensión* and that, as I discovered, was two kilometres from the centre along a dirt road so I climbed the hill to inspect the castle first and then followed the dirt road through a tiny village in my search for lodgings, true to my form but not as Mrs Pride would have recommended. What I found was an old farmhouse that had been expensively renovated. I must have rung three or four times before a tall blond sleepy man, direct from his siesta, opened the door. They were full, he informed me, and the nearest accommodation was in Estremoz.   He was Norwegian and showed great surprise when he found me to be English and expressed astonishment when he learned I had walked from Evora. I was glad of that since he promptly invited me in for a drink. It was a hot day and I had walked thirty kilometres so I enjoyed the cool of their hall—his Portuguese wife joined us—and in return for his kindness I told him of my Borrow trail. By then I had worked out a form of exposition which allowed me, on each occasion that I was asked to explain about Borrow and my route, to do so with slowly improving fluency as to language, although on this occasion my Norwegian host spoke English. My intended route and the fact that I expected to walk a good part of it drew from him a heavily outdated Nordic compliment about "mad dogs and Englishmen."

There was a five o'clock bus into Estremoz so he gave me a lift back into town; there was also, I knew, something at the back of his mind and as we bumped slowly along the dirt track he asked me how old I might be. This upset me, not because I mind my age though I would prefer to be younger but rather because he appeared to assume that anyone over thirty who went walking with a backpack must be, though he did not say so, out of his mind. I answered his question although Borrow would have done no such thing. When he was living at Oulton, in extreme old age, Borrow was visited by the Vicar of Lowestoft, who wished to meet the distinguished writer and traveller. They talked amicably until, in innocence, the vicar asked Borrow his age. The old man snapped: "Sir, I tell my age to no man!" and abruptly brought the meeting to an end. After the discomforted vicar had departed Borrow retired to his summer house where he wrote a short tract entitled "People's Age".[5]

Our perceptions of places are almost invariably affected by our moods and I did not accord to Estremoz either the attention or the consideration it deserved. It was raining again. My inn was both drab and cold. And circumstances had forced me to come to the town late by bus over a dramatic road that I would much have preferred to walk. The centre of Estremoz consists of a huge square. Borrow says he took up his quarters in the principal inn, "which looks upon a large plain or market-place occupying the centre of the town, and which is so extensive that I should think ten thousand soldiers at least might perform their evolutions there with ease."[6] It is a gated city overlooked by a thirteenth-century castle and it played a significant role as a focus of resistance to Spain in the seventeenth century. Now it is renowned as the centre of the region's pottery, wines, olive oil and marble.

Borrow the linguist and philologist noticed a change in pronunciation at Estremoz and records this:

> *I now first began to observe an alteration in the language spoken; it had become less sibilant, and more guttural; this is the result of constant communication with the natives of Spain, who never condescend to speak Portuguese, even when in Portugal, but persist in the use of their own beautiful language, which, perhaps, at some future period, the Portuguese will generally adopt. This would greatly facilitate the union of the two countries, hitherto kept asunder by the natural waywardness of mankind.[7]*

Borrow's hopes seem unlikely to be realised even in the present time of European Union. I cannot pretend to have noticed such subtleties of language for I was still far too absorbed in the struggle to make myself understood at all.

❧

Elvas was the last city in Portugal in which I stayed before crossing into Spain. Founded by the Romans and repeatedly besieged over the centuries, its long history has been that of a border fortress. The city occupies the top of a great hill while on a second hill on the other side of a dramatic valley is the fort of Elvas, the city with its massive walls and the fortress together being considered impregnable. Badajoz lay a mere seventeen kilometres distant across the intervening plain. A Moorish castle dominates the citadel and from here it is possible to see many miles across the plain in all directions. The cathedral, which occupies one end of the main square, is late Gothic and has an unusual appearance with a squat pyramid-like steeple while the houses of the city rise in white layers up the steep hillside above the enormous walls and battlements. Yet the most spectacular monument that Elvas has to offer is the aqueduct. Known as the Aqueduct of Amoreiras and built between 1498 and 1622, it still brings water to the city and is considered to be a national monument. Borrow, however, compares it unfavourably with the aqueduct of Lisbon. The water, he says, must have been flowing "near a hundred feet above my head, and I was filled with wonder at the immensity of the structure which conveyed it." But, he continues,

> *There was, however, one feature which was no slight drawback to its pretensions to grandeur and magnificence: the water was supported not by gigantic single arches, like those of the aqueduct of Lisbon, which stalk over the valley like legs of Titans, but by three layers of arches, which, like three distinct aqueducts, rise above each other.*

Now, grand as is the aqueduct of Lisbon, these triple layers of arches are the principal feature of the Elvas structure and give it a unique appeal of its own. Borrow reflects further upon the expense and labour involved and how modern developments make aqueducts unnecessary: "We cannot help congratulating ourselves that we live in times when it is not necessary to exhaust the wealth of a province to supply a town on a hill with one of the first necessaries of existence."[8]

Borrow abroad was very much the English nationalist even if at home he was more than ready to criticise the government and establishment of his day; he was a nationalist, moreover, at a time when British power was respected as paramount in Europe. At Elvas he gets into an argument with a Portuguese officer who declaims against the English; after interrogating the man and making him look foolish, he apologises to his readers: "I must be permitted to add that I believe no other provocation would have elicited from me a reply so full of angry feeling: but I could not command myself when I heard my own glorious land traduced in this unmerited manner. By whom? A Portuguese! A native of a country which has twice been liberated from horrid and detestable thraldom by the hands of Englishmen."[9]

Orchards of orange trees now fill the moat outside the city walls to provide a relaxing walk, as well as trysting places, for the citizens of Elvas and I wandered by these walls for some time in the early evening before returning to the square opposite the cathedral where I sat for a drink and watched wary waiters eyeing two gypsies who took a table next to mine though they caused no trouble. I returned to the citadel and looked across the immense plains of Spain beyond Badajoz just before the sun went down.

7

A Little Spanish History: An Old Fascist

The Cid—the Romans in Spain—the Moors—Spain's century—the Carlist wars—Badajoz—a little old fascist

ALL countries love their myths though most do not bear too close an examination. The Cid is Spain's best-known hero, and so many were the legends surrounding his name that at one time it was assumed he was a purely mythical character. More than 200 ballads still exist with the Cid as the central figure. He came of a noble family of Castile and lived in the eleventh century but though he was a prominent supporter of Sancho of Castile, in fact he became the captain of a free company and offered his mercenary services to both the Spaniards and the Moors in the endless wars and faction fights of that century. Hollywood's film *El Cid* with Charlton Heston in the title role gave the legend one more modern boost when at the end it had the dead Heston placed on his horse to ride out into the sunset against the Moors—but that is how we always like our myths.

Spain has an astonishing history of warfare and bloodshed, beginning with the Carthaginian invasion in the third century BC when Hamilcar and Hasdrubal conquered the south of the peninsula. Their successes led to a clash with Rome and the Punic wars which followed finally gave the Iberian Peninsula to Rome although it was not to be totally absorbed into the Roman Empire until the time of Augustus. The Visigoths invaded Spain early in the fifth century as the Roman Empire of the West declined and collapsed, and remained the dominant power until the Moorish invasion of 711. Moors reached the Pyrenees in 718 and then invaded France to advance as far as the Loire; only after their defeat at Tours by Charles Martel in 732 did the Moors quit France. Centuries of warfare between the Spanish and the Moors followed until, gradually, Castile in the north emerged as the leading Christian power in the peninsula to spearhead the reconquest of Spain from its Moorish rulers. Sancho the Great of Navarre and his son Ferdinand I, both of whom were served by the Cid, brought about the unity of Castile, León and Asturias in the north while Ferdinand advanced south to the Tagus and threatened the Moors in Seville. The union of Spain, however, was not finally achieved until the end of the fifteenth century with the marriage of Ferdinand of Aragon and Isabella of Castile.

Once the Moors had been driven from Spain the country became the most powerful in Europe and the reign of the "Catholic" sovereigns Ferdinand and Isabella also saw Spain's monarchs assume the role of guardians of the Roman religion and champions of the Holy See, a role that reached its apotheosis under Philip II. The sixteenth century belonged to Spain: under the Emperor Charles V, Spain controlled half of Europe and was the dominant power of the age while, in an astonishingly short time, Spain's conquistadors had created a mighty empire in Central and South America, destroying the ancient Aztec and Inca empires in the process and very nearly exterminating their people as well. With the death of Philip II in 1598 Spain entered upon a period of decline and though it was involved in all the European wars of the seventeenth century it obtained few advantages from them while France rose in influence and splendour to replace Spain as Europe's leading power. Spain went to war against Revolutionary France at the end of the eighteenth century, but switched sides to have its fleet largely annihilated at Trafalgar only to be invaded three years later by Napoleon's forces in support of Joseph Bonaparte, his candidate for the Spanish throne. The bloody Peninsular War of 1808-14, which followed, saw some of the most savage fighting in Spain's long history, its atrocities being recorded in the stark cartoons of Goya.

The Spain that Borrow knew was torn by the Carlist civil war, while a second Carlist civil war of 1872-76 was to be fought by the grandson of the Don Carlos who had laid claim to the throne in the 1830s. At the end of the century Spain lost all its Caribbean colonies as well as the Philippines to the United States in a war that was an economic disaster for the country. The wonder is that Spain managed to take a rest from fighting and keep out of both the World Wars of the twentieth century although the Civil War of 1936 to 1939 produced a heavy enough toll of casualties and brutalities from both sides by way of compensation.

ℰ↷

When Borrow reached the brook which forms the border between Portugal and Spain he shouted out in ecstasy the thousand-year old battle-cry of Castile: "Santiago y Sierra España!" I walked across the border from Portugal but cannot claim to have emulated him although I had long been intrigued by Spain and felt excitement on entering it for the first time.

Badajoz has made its own contributions to the warlike history of Spain. It began as a Roman town, then grew to significance under the Moors until it was conquered in 1229 by Alfonso IX of León. Long regarded as the key to Portugal or the gateway to Spain, it was fought over brutally in both the Peninsular War of 1808-14 and the Civil War of 1936-39 when little-publicised massacres were carried out by the Nationalists. During the Peninsular War, which was still close in memory at the time Borrow visited Spain, Badajoz had been besieged by the French in 1808, 1809 and then 1811 when it surrendered to them. Wellington also besieged it three times, on the first two occasions without success. Finally, he captured it by storm on 6 April 1812, as a prelude to his advance through Spain. The storming of Badajoz was one of the bloodiest engagements of the entire war in which British casualties amounted to 72 officers and 963 men killed and 306 officers and 3,483 men wounded (casualties for the other side were not recorded). In the sack of the city which followed

In the Footsteps of George Borrow

the successful storming of the walls the British troops behaved abominably.

The Guadiana river circles much of the old city which lies on its south bank. Borrow describes hearing the singing of the washerwomen on its banks as he approached the city, the words "Guadiana, Guadiana" reverberating far and wide as they were sung by the clear strong voices of

> *many a dark-cheeked maid and matron. I thought there was some analogy between their employment and my own: I was about to tan my northern complexion by exposing myself to the hot sun of Spain, in the humble hope of being able to cleanse some of the foul stains of Popery from the minds of its children, with whom I had little acquaintance; whilst they were bronzing themselves on the banks of the river in order to make white the garments of strangers.* [1]

Borrow's simile is as suitably imaginative as his expression of repugnance for "Popery" is sufficiently extreme. His antagonism to Catholicism had its roots in his childhood, moving round England and Ireland with the army, yet expressions of anti-Popish sentiments in *The Bible in Spain* are so extreme as to raise the suspicion that they are included for the benefit of the Bible Society rather than representing his true feelings. He was not a man of half measures.

The city's principal monuments consist of the Moorish castle and some remnants of walls, and the cathedral. I decided to visit the cathedral first and asked an old man for directions. "Of course," he replied, "I will take you there myself," and though I protested that he need not come out of his way he insisted. He was a diminutive little man of no more than five feet in height and must have been well into his seventies but there was a sprightliness about him as he walked at my side.

"You are English?" he asked to which I agreed. "And how long have you been in Spain?" he asked with courteous diffidence, not wishing to appear probing but I replied readily enough. "This is my first day in Spain, I only crossed the border from Portugal this morning." "But you speak our language," and he paused in consideration, "with a fine accent," he added with a wonderful courtesy that bypassed the necessity of commenting upon its linguistic limitations. "May I ask where you learnt it?" "I worked on books and tapes in England, before I came here." My small guide nodded sagely at this as if my answer satisfied him on a point that he had at first misunderstood. Then he smiled his approval as much as to say that my smattering of "tape-learnt" Spanish pleased him. We set off to find the cathedral in the direction he had already indicated with a precise motion of his arm and hand as though giving directions in semaphore.

"I am from Castile, of course," he said as though he were stating something so blindingly obvious that words had not really been needed while the "of course" was a prelude to what followed. "I am not from Extremadura," and he shrugged his contempt, for to many Spaniards and perhaps especially Castilians Extremadura is a backward region as are its people. I had a great deal to learn about the tribal and regional subtleties of Spain and though I was quite unable to distinguish the purity of his Castilian pronunciation from that of the local citizens of Badajoz among whom my guide had elected to live, I assured him that I would be able to make such distinctions should I remain long enough in Spain. Naturally, I asked him how long he had lived in Badajoz and the Extremadura. "Many years, my work brought me here though now I am retired." I refrained from asking him why, in his retirement, he had not returned to the superior civilisation of Castile and for a while we lapsed into silence as he led me at a spanking pace along one of the city's principal streets.

But then we passed a roadside beggar. She was an old woman, sitting on a tiny stool at the edge of the pavement whining pitifully at passers-by for alms. The sight was too much for my taciturn companion and he exploded with vitriolic passion: "There were no beggars in the time of Franco, our Caudillo, but now—with all this democracy," and he fairly spat out the word, "they are back on the streets again, a disgrace to Spain." He certainly spoke from the heart, did that little old fascist, and his lips were actually trembling with the vehemence of his emotions.

For a moment I was at a loss as to how I should respond, for he was my most courteous guide, but then, with the ambiguity which I felt was fitting to the occasion, I said: "I know exactly what you mean but, unfortunately, I do not have sufficient Spanish at my command to reply adequately." He gave me a long sideways look, walked on a couple of dozen paces in silence, then said: "You do not approve, do you?" I bowed in silent assent.

We rounded a corner into the square, which contained the Town Hall and the cathedral. I thanked him and we shook hands and he started back in the direction from which we had just come. The cathedral has massive walls and appears more like a fortress than a church but, given the history of Badajoz and its sieges, perhaps that was wise.

Later, I found myself wandering through some quite dismal slums near the Moorish castle where I was accosted, first by a drunk, then by a prostitute and finally by an old woman inquiring the time. Without thinking I did what I normally do in such circumstances and held out my wrist so that she could read the hands of the watch herself, but she shook her head and shrugged to convey her helplessness for she was quite unable to tell the time.

8

Gypsies and the Road to Trujillo

Spanish gypsies—the gypsy Antonio—Mérida—Spanish courtesy—"on the business of Egypt"—the Cruce de las Herreras—La Torre de Santa Maria—an orange giant— Pizarro

FEW occasions are more satisfying than those which allow one, without effort, to upstage the obnoxious or overbearing, or change a situation by the revelation of superior knowledge which no one is in a position to deny. Once, at a literary dinner party, my claim to have read a book which had only recently been published was challenged on the grounds that I had only just returned to England from wandering in South America; I was in the happy position of being able to reply (truthfully) that I had read it going down the Essequibo in a canoe. Few situations gave Borrow more pleasure than those— which he often contrived with care—that allowed him to confound representatives of minority groups by the sudden revelation that he could speak their language. He gives a dramatic example of this in *The Gypsies of Spain*. Borrow asks for a room in an inn and the family, who are gypsies, welcome him: "'O, what a handsome face! What a royal person!' exclaimed the whole family... in Spanish but in the whining, canting tones peculiar to the Gypsies, when they are bent on victimising. 'A more ugly Busno it has never been our chance to see,' said the same voices in the next breath, speaking in the jargon of the tribe."[1] After he has allowed them to continue for a while with literal doublespeak, flattering him to his face in Spanish and then describing him in unflattering terms to each other in Romany, Borrow confounds them by addressing them in their own language.

However, David Urquhart, who stayed in the same inn a few years later and writes of it in *The Pillars of Hercules*, highlights many inaccuracies in Borrow's account to suggest what other critics of Borrow have also claimed: that he was making things up in order to dramatise both his story and his own cleverness—and this raises a question about all travellers' accounts of their adventures: how much is true and how much is invention?[2]

Borrow first fell in with Spanish gypsies in Badajoz and spent far more of his time with them than pursuing his other Bible activities although he tells us: "It was here I first preached the gospel to the gypsy people, and commenced that translation of the New Testament in the Spanish gypsy tongue, a portion of which I subsequently printed in Madrid."[3] In *The Gypsies in Spain* Borrow insists that he deals in facts rather than theories in his account of these people and argues that they were not interested in the Gospel for its own sake but rather that

> *Whatever they did for the Gospel in Spain, was done in the hope that he whom they conceived to be their brother (Borrow) had some purpose in view which was to contribute to the profit of the Cales, or Gypsies, and to terminate in the confusion and plunder of the Busne, or Gentiles.*

The gypsies helped Borrow because they thought he was one of them. But though he attributes to them a willingness to do down, often murderously, anyone who is not a gypsy, he also says, speaking of himself: "Nor has he (Borrow) ever done them injustice by attributing to them licentious habits, from which they are, perhaps, more free than any race in the creation."[4]

This view would hardly have been popular or accepted in Borrow's time or later and must have raised eyebrows at the Bible Society. Borrow spent three weeks in Badajoz and was on the point of departure when a leading gypsy, Antonio, with whom he had become well acquainted, offered to accompany him on the road to Madrid.

Though Antonio was a strange and dangerous man, Borrow accepted his offer:

> *Certainly few people in my situation would have accepted the offer of this singular gypsy. It was not, however, without its allurements for me; I was fond of adventure, and what more ready means of gratifying my love of it than by putting myself under the hands of such a guide?*[5]

He goes on to say:

> *During my stay at Badajoz I had but little intercourse with the Spaniards, my time being chiefly devoted to the gypsies, with whom, from long intercourse with various sections of their race in different parts of the world, I felt myself much more at home than with the silent, reserved men of Spain, with whom a foreigner might mingle for half a century without having half a dozen words addressed to him, unless he himself made the first advances to intimacy, which, after all, might be rejected with a shrug and a* no entiendo.[6]

It is another interesting sidelight on Borrow's extraordinary character that in his first three weeks in Spain he becomes deeply involved with the gypsies but very nearly dismisses the Spaniards among whom he has come to work. Borrow came to Mérida in the company of the gypsy Antonio who had business of his own to conduct and despite Borrow's stated love of adventure there are hints that he was less than happy about his company. They reached Mérida at dusk and Antonio left Borrow outside the town while he entered to reconnoitre, for the gypsies were having much trouble with the authorities. "On the business of Egypt, brother" was the phrase Antonio used whenever he did not wish Borrow to ask him more questions. After dark, a gypsy woman came to lead Borrow into the town where, he tells us: "During the whole time that I remained at Merida I stirred not once from the house; following the advice of Antonio, who informed me that it would not be convenient."[7] He stayed for three days in the strange house with the gypsies, so he has nothing to tell us of Mérida and its many ancient monuments.

Mérida was the capital of Roman Lusitania and has a wealth of startlingly well-preserved Roman sites whose grandest are the theatre, the amphitheatre and the bridge over the river. Like Badajoz, it is on

the Guadiana, and the ancient beauty of the many-arched Roman bridge, which once had eighty-one arches, is emphasised by the near proximity of a modern steel suspension bridge which boasts a twentieth-century elegance of its own. The grand façade of the Roman theatre must be one of the best preserved as well as the most beautiful to be found anywhere in the Roman world.

On several occasions I was obliged to ask directions and always met with remarkable courtesy and an astonishing willingness of people to walk out of their way to show me mine. Near my hostelry were the ruined arches of part of a Roman aqueduct and, though they now had more the appearance of the remains of a modern city after a blitz than anything else, they were in their way even more dramatic than the wonderfully preserved aqueducts I had seen elsewhere on my journey. The remains of a Moorish citadel take up several acres on the river bank, and deep underground, cool and strangely inviting, was a well of fresh water, emergency supplies in time of siege, which was fed by seepage from the river.

Borrow made the eighty-kilometre journey from Mérida to Trujillo on horseback in a single day, his gypsy companion on a mule, travelling over "wide plains, scantily clothed with brushwood, with here and there a melancholy village," and reached Trujillo long after dark to discover that the house of the gypsies to which Antonio had been taking him was closed.

> *"Caramba!" said he; "they are out—I feared it might be so. Now what are we to do?"*
>
> *"There can be no difficulty," said I, "with respect to what we have to do; if your friends are gone out, it is easy enough to go to a posada."*
>
> *"You know not what you say," replied the gypsy, "I dare not go to the mesuna, nor enter any house in Trujillo save this, and this is shut. Well, there is no remedy; we must move on, and, between ourselves, the sooner we leave this place the better."* [8]

Despite Borrow's weariness and unease, they left the town and continued until they eventually came upon some gypsies in a wood where they had fled from Trujillo "on the business of Egypt, brother," as Antonio tells Borrow, and they passed the night in the forest instead of back in Trujillo.

I, on the other hand, took three days to walk from Mérida to Trujillo, and it was one of the most pleasant as well as most dramatic walks I managed anywhere in Spain. I broke my watch on the first day and so was obliged to timekeep according to the sun; I suffered from the heat and found I had made a mistake in only bringing short-sleeved shirts from England, for by the time I reached Trujillo my forearms were badly blistered; and on those long roads I found myself consciously searching the wayside ahead for the next tree since to walk even four steps in the shade it cast was a relief from the burning sun.

My first stop was where the road for Trujillo left the main Mérida-Cáceres road and I stayed at the Cruce de las Herreras. It was a busy place which served both as a focal point for the nearby village of Alcuescar and as a resting place for long-distance truckers. I sat on a cool verandah and surveyed an oddly mixed scene: one great truck whose driver stopped for refreshment was filled with bellowing cattle on their way to market; another guest came from the village in a donkey cart, a third came on a mule. Then, at this odd corner where the old and the new insisted on meeting, a man rode proudly by on a magnificent stallion. A busload of teenage children on some school outing poured out to take a half-hour break for refreshment and disturbed the peace of the verandah with their excited talk and laughter although not at a neighbouring table where three elderly, demure matrons conducted a gentle discussion of I know not what apparently quite oblivious to the hubbub around them. The children left as suddenly as they had come and general peace was restored. Behind the inn the hills shimmered in the evening sunlight; in the bar television showed bullfighting from the great arena in Madrid; it was the season and I often witnessed the spectacle but though there may be a certain skill attached to killing the bulls the great heavy-bred monsters never have a chance. I always hoped that a matador would prove careless and be tossed and gored.

The next day I stopped at La Torre de Santa Maria, a sleepy little village of narrow white-washed streets, with a tiny square and an old church the four corners of whose tower provided perfect perches for stork nests. In a dim bar whose three ancient inhabitants I was careful to greet before I sought refreshment, one old man eyed me judiciously for five minutes following my arrival and then asked: "Where do you come from?" "Alcuescar," I replied densely. "And your country?" "England." "Ah, Inglaterra." He nodded sagely to himself, waiting for a minute or two while we each gravely sipped our respective drinks, then: "And where might you be going?" "Madrid." Apparently satisfied with this answer, he turned back to the bar and his drink and I relaxed over my beer. But then another thought came to him and once more he asked: "Today?" "No, I shall go to Trujillo tomorrow, and then on to Madrid, today I stay here." "That is good," he said though whether he meant because I was staying or because I was not going he did not make clear.

℞

That evening I sat outside the same bar facing the church tower. A man clattered through the square on a horse and stopped outside a house where a child placed fodder for the beast's feed in a doorside manger. A group of small children pestered me to take a photograph, which I did, and the storks on their church tower nests threw back their heads and clicked their long beaks, responding to each other's messages with their Morse-code language.

The sun was already up, bright and strong, when I set out on the third day for Trujillo. A low-lying haze spread over the fields and came halfway up the hedgerows so that I seemed to be walking through a shimmering white sea. An orange giant suddenly appeared on the road ahead, walking or, rather, meandering towards me as though he was encountering a strong undertow of current in the waist-high mist. As he lurched to one side of the road he was suddenly greeted by the thrilled barks of a tiny dog which erupted from the ditch and circled him in surprised delight. He was not, in fact, a giant at all although a trick of the sun had inflated the fluorescent orange vest that is worn by road menders to invest him with gigantic proportions until he was quite close. He greeted me as a long expected friend: "Caballero, buen dia." "Buenos dias, señor." "A donde va?" "Trujillo." "Trujillo! Hombre valiente!" and he breathed a litre of wine into my face before he reeled away in the direction of the nearest ditch, the little dog leaping up and down at his side. "Vaya Usted con Dios," I called as he settled down among the brambles.

Trujillo rises out of the plain on its dramatic hill and can be seen from miles away. The Plaza Mayor is dominated by the equestrian statue of Pizarro which occupies the upper end in front of the great church of Santa Maria. It is a wonderful square of steps and different levels, its façades of palaces in ageing yellow stone encompassing centuries of history. Yet the eyes are drawn back constantly to the great statue. Francisco Pizarro was the greatest of the conquistadors after Cortés: conqueror of Peru and founder of Lima, he crossed the Isthmus of Panama with Balboa to be among the first Europeans to see the Pacific from "a peak in Darien." Taciturn and ruthless, allegedly beginning life as a swineherd (something he shared in common with a number of ancient heroes), he now stares into the distance for all time from under his visor, the great plumes of his helmet standing up like antlers behind his head, his drawn sword held ready for battle alongside his horse's neck. Behind the church and Pizarro the town rises in a series of winding alleys and narrow streets to the Moorish citadel high above, and from that vantage point I could see in every direction over the plain and trace the road along which I had toiled in the heat of the day before it disappeared in an evening haze.

Back in Pizarro's square a tramp begged a cigarette from me while an elegant waiter hovered uneasily, not liking the tramp but fearful of telling him to go about his business, and the tramp and I formed an immediate bond of understanding in our mutual contempt for the waiter. Later still, I amused another waiter with my mispronunciation of words so I enlisted his help for an impromptu lesson in Spanish which he was pleased to impart. The storks came gliding in across the square to their nests on the surrounding buildings and then clicked their beaks to one another, the sun dropped below the distant horizon and the temperature fell sharply to herald the coming of night.

9

The Conquistador
of Jaraceijo

Jaraceijo—the national guard—Lord Palmerston—the old
"conquistador"—"I am walking"—the church—gypsies on
the heath—the pass of Miravete—across the Tagus—the
battle of Talavera

JARACEIJO rises up a steep hillside off the main highway and is dominated by a huge square church of cathedral dimensions which dwarfs the small village it serves; had the landscape been flat instead of hilly it could have been in Norfolk where the grandeur of a church when compared with the dwindling size of the community acts as a reminder that nothing stands still. The medieval wealth that built the huge churches has disappeared with the vanishing wool trade alongside the diminishing importance of Christianity whose monuments stand grand and beautiful but largely unused. We do not live in an age of faith, not at least in Europe, and it becomes increasingly difficult to envisage a time when such churches were the automatic centre of life in their communities. I walked up the narrow main street of Jaraceijo, which could not have changed much since Borrow passed through it, to the square by the great church where trestle tables were being laid out to accommodate a midday market.

Borrow came to Jaraceijo in the company of the gypsy Antonio who wished them to hurry through the little town which, he said, was a bad place for gypsies. They separated, Antonio passing through first and Borrow coming behind with the intention of buying provisions. Borrow described Jaraceijo—he did not mention the huge church—as "an old dilapidated place, consisting of little more than one street." He was challenged by a member of the national guard who asked whether he was travelling with the gypsy who had just passed through. "Do I look a person," Borrow replied, "likely to keep company with gypsies?" The guard then asked for his passport and Borrow pointed out that it was given to him by the "great Lord Palmerston, minister of England, whom you have of course heard of here; at the bottom you will see his own handwriting. Look at it and rejoice; perhaps you will never have another opportunity."[1]

Arrogance in such circumstances often pays dividends. Palmerston, "a fragment of the eighteenth century projected far into the nineteenth," was Foreign Secretary throughout the 1830s and continued a dominant figure in British politics until his death in 1865. His robust style and sense of nationalism, the good humoured contempt which he reserved for foreigners and his readiness to send a gunboat to back up British interests appealed to the insular qualities of the English of his day; he lectured foreigners and told them where they were mistaken and if this approach failed there was always the fleet, his "big stick", to be used as a final means of persuasion. When Borrow fell foul of the Spanish government in Madrid and was imprisoned he was firmly supported by Britain's ambassador on the spot and Palmerston in London.

Borrow's own sturdy nationalism as well as his readiness to tell foreigners how they should behave make him a natural representative abroad of Palmerston's England. The national guard who had approached Borrow with great suspicion was suitably mollified by this reference to Palmerston and asked, before Borrow finally left Jaraceijo, whether he could "see once more the signature of the Caballero Balmerson."

❦

There was much activity in the little square but not a great deal to buy. The market stalls either sold fruit and vegetables or second-hand clothes, so I purchased a kilo of cherries and sat on a stone bench against the wall of the church to watch the market and sketch. Two very old men, arm in arm, slowly paraded round the square, taking infinite care with each step as they advanced, the one with his walking stick in his right hand, the other with his stick in his left hand. They reminded me of the two old men of Evora except that these two were not slovenly of dress or dirty in their habits but elegantly turned out for their promenade while they walked as though Jaraceijo's square existed solely for their personal perambulations. One of this duo had a high-cheek-boned face whose skin was drawn taut over his bones: his mouth, small and straight above a pointed chin, had no softening curves to suggest either gentleness or humour while his eyes, of cold piercing blue, stared from under a broad hat brim to endow him with the unmistakable remoteness of an ancient conquistador. His companion was altogether softer, moonfaced and compliant, a Boswell listening to his Johnson. I sat by the church for an hour during which period they only made the complete circuit of the square five times, talking to one another slowly and courteously all the while, oblivious of the bustle around them, an accepted part of the community through which they passed unseeing. I was so intrigued by their sense of dignity and their obvious belief that the square existed solely for their midday exercise that I forgot my sketching in following their progress and then, on the third occasion that they passed me, ventured a greeting but the conquistador stared stonily into a distant horizon that did not admit present-day travellers and they passed by as though I did not exist.

I tried to inspect the church but it was bolted to the world so I wandered round to the far side of the square where tables extended beyond an archway from a lively bar all of whose customers appeared to be engrossed in card games. I took the last remaining free table and ordered a beer and was at once joined by a man whom earlier I had seen watching me as I sketched; now, curiosity and courtesy having battled for supremacy, the former had triumphed.

"You are visiting Spain," he began on a lightly interrogative note.

"It is my first time but, yes, I am visiting Spain."

"And you are from Germany?"

"No, not from Germany, from England."

"Ah, Inglaterra. That is interesting. You are motoring."

"No, I am not motoring."

"Not motoring, but how do you travel?" and his eyes widened.

"I am walking. At least, sometimes I walk, sometimes I take a bus or train. Tomorrow I shall walk through the pass of Miravete."

I am not certain he believed me at first. "But it is too hot to walk; there are easier ways to travel."

"Of course. But I like walking and besides," I had decided to play up to his curiosity, "I am on a trail, I shall be in Spain for three months."

My new acquaintance now became genuinely interested as opposed to merely curious and I took him through my developing exposition of Borrow and *The Bible in Spain* while my inquisitor began to wonder just what he had let himself in for; I am not sure how much he understood but it was certainly an opportunity for me to exercise my Spanish. We had a second beer together and argued as to who should pay then went our separate ways in search of our midday meals and subsequent siestas.

I returned to the square in the early evening and found that the church was now open. It is early sixteenth-century with an interior of great simplicity and a wonderful vaulted roof. I took my time examining it until I became conscious of a very old woman, bent nearly double so that the tasselled ends of the shawl which covered her head sometimes brushed the stone floor as she bobbed about her business lighting candles and making other preparations for a service later that evening. I greeted her and commented upon the great beauty of her church but she exhibited every sign of growing impatience at my slow, carefully chosen words and, as soon as I had finished, said: "Will you please leave so that I can lock up."

When Borrow finally left Jaraceijo, after exchanging more compliments with the national guard, he rode through the town onto the heath above which he described as extending for nearly three leagues (fourteen kilometres) towards a lofty eminence, naked and bare, at whose base he found the gypsy Antonio waiting for him. I left the corner of the square by the church and passed under an arch

which connected it with the priest's house to ascend a steep, narrow road out of the village onto the moor which still stretched for miles unchanged, much as it must have been in Borrow's time except that the road out of the village which I had followed soon loses itself on the heath, for a new highway now carries the great trucks as they pass on their journeys between Portugal and Madrid. Antonio was waiting for a messenger who eventually came to tell him that his whole band had been seized by the authorities, having fallen into a trap, so Borrow left him on the heath and proceeded to the pass of Miravete on his own.

I, too, saw gypsies on the heath. As I walked in the early morning I watched two battered dormobiles draw into the roadside some distance ahead of me to disgorge perhaps four families of gypsies who, by the time I came abreast of them, had already lighted a fire on which they were cooking their breakfast. Several watched stonily as I passed and though I called a greeting they made no response.

Borrow describes the view from the top of the pass of Miravete as one of the finest in the world: "Before me outstretched lay immense plains, bounded in the distance by huge mountains, whilst at the foot of the hill which I was now descending rolled the Tagus, in a deep narrow stream, between lofty banks."[2]

Now, there glittered below me a great lake or reservoir which had been formed on the river while the road twisted down the mountainside in a series of hairpin bends, each one affording me new views of what was indeed a breathtaking scene, the green of the great plain merging into the distant blue line of the mountains. That afternoon I stopped at the inn of the Torre Eiffel at the bottom of the pass. The modern road has bypassed the village of Casas de Miravete and big trucks grind their way slowly up from the Tagus below or down the zigzag road, which I had just descended while families on the way to their holidays stopped at the inn for refreshment. I idled away the afternoon on the open verandah holding periodic conversations with a friendly waiter who appeared from time to time to see to my needs while otherwise idling away his afternoon. Thunderclouds had been gathering all day until, in the early evening when they had banked up into a series of formidable black mountains, a great storm broke and the first raindrops hissed on the hot pavement before streams of water ran down the hillside.

Borrow was obliged to cross the Tagus by ferry because he "reached the river at a place where stood the remains of what once had been a magnificent bridge, which had, however, been blown up in the Peninsular War and never since repaired."[3] There was a fine old bridge of yellow stone, which I crossed but farther upstream the three rough remains of what must have been the arches of the former bridge reared their jagged ends above the water.

The road rose sharply from the river to the plain beyond where I came in sight of something very modern indeed: the large nuclear plant at Almaraz. The town lay behind it, an old church tower rising in protest amidst the new buildings which modern technology had brought to transform a quieter, gentler landscape. Some kind of demonstration was gathering outside the gates of the plant and I was treated to a ragged cheer as I trudged past. Newly laid out beds of roses with walkways and seats between them, had been arranged along the main highway the length of the little town in an effort to compensate for the harsh modernity of the new technology down the road. I sat on one of the benches to suck an orange and, on cue, an old man appeared to prune the roses near me, a security guard perhaps, set to watch the spying stranger. I reached Navalmoral just in time to cash a cheque before the banks closed and the obliging bank clerk took one look at my backpack and then, assuming that I only wanted the worst, offered me directions, unasked, to the cheapest *pensión* in town.

Talavera lies on the northern bank of the Tagus and there has been a town here since Roman times. It boasts a fine stretch of twelfth-century walls with eighteen watchtowers, two interesting churches of which one is in an attractive park that occupies the centre of the town and a fifteenth-century bridge across the river. In the park I sketched a group of elderly men playing boules. For the British, however, the name Talavera conjures up one of Wellesley's most famous and bloody battles; it is the principal battle honour of the former Northamptonshire Regiment now no longer with us and then known as the 48th. At one point during the battle the part played by the 48th was crucial as, in Napier's words, they resumed "their proud and beautiful line." Wellesley himself said: "The battle of Talavera was the hardest fought of modern times."[4] It was fought on the plain to the north of Talavera and involved the three armies of Britain and Spain on the one side, and France on the other although, in the event, the Spanish took little part. When it was over Wellesley had lost over 5,000 men, a quarter of his force, the French more than 7,000. It was after this battle that Wellesley became Viscount Wellington of Talavera.

Misunderstanding, as well as differences of temperament between Wellesley and the fierce old Spanish commander, General Cuesta, was a foretaste of greater misunderstandings to come although that is hardly surprising. The cold-blooded, methodical English and the hot-blooded, proud Spanish were—and no doubt still are—temperamentally as far apart as it is possible for two European peoples to be and the wonder is that they worked together as much as they managed to do for the remainder of the war.

10

Borrow in Toledo

Toledo's dramatic setting—Borrow in Toledo—the Burial of the Conde of Orgaz by El Greco—artists—tapas—La Plaza Santiago de los Caballeros—the Alcázar—a storm

TOLEDO occupies a dramatic rock promontory that appears to rise out of the Tagus which flows on three sides of it. The city is beautiful, full of ancient buildings and museums; it is the guardian of much history and has been declared a national monument. It is also evocative of grim and terrible aspects of Spain's long story. The interior of its immense Gothic cathedral acts as a sombre reminder of the cruelties of the Spanish Inquisition which achieved its most fearsome reputation during the fifteenth century under Torquemada. Today, the city's main square, the Plaza de Zocodover, is a magnet for visitors who congregate in it to drink coffee and decide where next to go while they study their city maps, awed by the many monuments to a glorious past which they see all round them. But for earlier generations the plaza was the scene of the *auto-da-fe*, the grim ceremony in which heretics and backsliders were put to death, and of masquerades and bullfights. Reminders of violence and warfare are part of the fabric of the city, which has been renowned for its steel blades for centuries and already had a reputation for the quality of its swords before the birth of Christ. The grim Alcázar, which dominates the Toledo skyline, was the stronghold where the Nationalists held out during the course of a desperate siege in the Civil War; now, lovingly restored, it is both a military museum and a shrine.

Livy describes Toledo as a small city fortified by location and it was to play a major role in Spain's history through Roman, Visigothic

and Moorish times. It blended uniquely within its small rock citadel the attributes of three main cultures—Christian, Islamic and Jewish. After 1560, however, when Philip II moved the capital to Madrid, the city declined in importance. Borrow said that Toledo "still possesses a great many remarkable edifices, notwithstanding that it has long since fallen into decay," and when he visited the city its population had dwindled to a mere 15,000 although it had stood as high as two or three hundred thousand in both Roman times and the Middle Ages.[1] Today, the population has risen again to about 60,000 but though the city has a number of industries, including armaments in place of the traditional sword blades, its principal business is tourism, which seems to be the dubious fate of almost every historic city in our present age.

Borrow did not visit Toledo until halfway through his five-year sojourn in Spain (1837), after he had returned to Madrid from his long trip to the north of the country, when he found that a change of government had occurred: the liberal party had been ousted to be replaced by members of the court party. (For reasons of convenience in travel, I had decided to visit Toledo before continuing to Madrid; this was my only major deviation from Borrow's Spanish itinerary.) As he records, ruefully:

> *From the present ministry I could expect but little; they consisted of men*
> *the greater part of whom had been either courtiers or employees of the*
> *deceased King Ferdinand, who were friends of absolutism, and by no*
> *means inclined to do or to favour anything calculated to give offence to*
> *the court of Rome, which they were anxious to conciliate, hoping that*
> *eventually it might be induced to recognize the young queen, not as the*
> *constitutional but as the absolute Queen Isabella the Second.*[2]

In the circumstances, Borrow decided to leave Madrid for a while and visit Toledo where, to his surprise, he found a liberal bookseller who was happy to sell his testaments and told Borrow that the clergy already hated him so much that a new offence in their eyes would make no difference.

My first object was to visit the parish church of Santo Tomé, which houses El Greco's painting, "Burial of the Conde de Orgaz". Borrow had praised it highly although John Murray, his publishers, had added a footnote to his remarks in which they quote a Professor Justi who says the painting is in El Greco's "worst manner" and then, themselves, go on to say that it "is indeed a very stiff performance," adding that his acknowledged masterpiece is the Christ on Mount Calvary in Toledo Cathedral. One detects a slight hedging of bets by the publishers who quote Justi, but then add a more non-committal appraisal of their own, leaving the final judgement to posterity.[3] Borrow, who also tells us that many of Toledo's finest works of art had been destroyed or carried off by the French during the Peninsular War, goes on to claim:

> *Perhaps the most remarkable one still remains; I allude to that which*
> *represents the burial of the Count of Orgas, the masterpiece of Domenico,*
> *the Greek, a most extraordinary genius, some of whose productions*
> *possess merit of a very high order. The picture in question is in the little*
> *parish church of San Tome, at the bottom of the aisle, on the left side of*
> *the altar. Could it be purchased, I should say it would be cheap at five*
> *thousand pounds.*[4]

That was a great deal of money for any painting in the 1830s, but when Borrow enthuses he goes all the way.

El Greco's work is certainly not to everyone's taste though there is an extraordinary fascination in his elongated figures and doleful countenances. The picture is still in the parish church although now it has been elevated to the rank of a major tourist attraction and has a chapel of its own where the stream of visitors can be controlled and stalls sell postcards and El Greco reproductions. The little chapel was so crowded when I visited it and the hucksters were so active that it was reminiscent, above all, of the moneylenders in the temple. Attendants marshalled and harried the sightseers and shouted at those who tried to take photographs with flashlights and it was almost impossible to reach the guardrail in front of the picture, which is undoubtedly a masterpiece despite the now forgotten Professor Justi.

An old beggar woman had taken up her position on the steps outside the church, confident of largesse from so steady a stream of foreigners. She sat in obliging profile while a man and a woman, artists both, sketched her ostentatiously: sometimes they held their pads at arms length, twisting them a little this way and a little that; then they peered at the heavens as though to alter the available light; and periodically they got up and stepped close to the beggar woman herself to inspect a detail of her face; the rest of the crowd was an irritation to them since thoughtless individuals insisted upon walking between the artists and the object of their attentions. The beggar

woman sat still, I presume to order, and the artists continued their self-appointed tasks and I hoped that when they had finished they would present her with suitably large donations for her patience.

I then found the Monastery of Santo Domingo el Antiguo where El Greco is buried; the church had been decorated by the artist and it is possible to peer down through a glass panel at his tomb. In astonishing contrast to the parish church of Santo Tomé, no one was there at all except for the guardian nuns.

When he was in Toledo Borrow stayed at the Posada de los Caballeros (the inn of the gentlemen), which he describes in flattering terms. It is one of the very few inns he actually names and I had hoped to locate it but the tourist office had not heard of it and no such inn was listed, so I assumed that time and decay had taken care of it. I found a pleasant place to stay in a small street just off the Plaza de Zocodover which was perfectly placed for examining the city although more than once I got lost in the maze of its winding streets. At the end of a day's exploration I came up a series of steps and then a steep incline to enter a small square where half a dozen tables had been arranged outside a bar. It had been raining for most of the afternoon so that few people were about and with the exception of a group at one table the others were all free. I was in need of refreshment and selected a table that faced down the length of the little square. A woman of severe if striking features rose from the only table that was occupied and came to serve me; she was, I think, the proprietress and later I managed to sketch her. I ordered a glass of wine and relaxed; the sun came out and with it the people and soon the other tables filled up so that the woman was obliged to

leave her friends and take up her position inside the bar, handing the drinks through a hatchway to a small belligerent man who now waited upon the tables.

I was still learning Spanish customs and though I had often been served *tapas*—snacks of olives, nuts or some other savoury trifle that came with the drink—I was not certain whether the *tapa* was automatic (paid for, as it were, by the drink) or an optional extra at the discretion of the host. The newcomers who had arrived after me had all received a dish of nuts with their drinks; I ordered a second glass of wine and noticed how, when he collected it from the proprietress at the window, she pointed to a dish of nuts and then gestured towards me. Her meaning was obvious enough and she was atoning for her failure to give me a *tapa* in the first place but the man shook his head and only brought me my glass of wine. I accepted this slight without comment but, since everyone else had been given *tapas* automatically, became increasingly irritated. By now I had drunk two glasses of wine, *sans* nuts, and felt I deserved better treatment. I beckoned the small belligerent man, I think he was the proprietor and husband of the striking-looking woman who was more than a head taller than he, and ordered a third glass of wine.

I was now feeling as angry as Borrow did if ever he believed the English were being slighted. The little belligerent man duly returned with my third glass of wine but still no *tapa*. I, meanwhile, had looked up nuts in my pocket dictionary and asked him: "Señor, why do you not also give me a dish of nuts (*tuercas*)?" and I waved a casual hand at the other tables. He, however, regarded me with astonishment, as well he might, and shrugged. "*Tuercas*," I repeated and he remained before my table as though I had gone mad. Of course, I had looked up the wrong nut and was fiercely demanding the kind which accompanies a bolt. I returned to my dictionary, rectified my absurd though understandable linguistic error, and then demanded a dish of peanuts—*cacahuetes*. Enlightenment suffused his grumpy face to be followed by a big delighted smile at my stupidity; he went to his wife, told her of our passage of misunderstanding with evident pleasure and then, in compensation for his past bad behaviour, brought me an enormous dish of nuts which he placed before me with elaborate courtesy, for there were certain depths to my host. As he placed the nuts on the table in front of me I happened to look over my shoulder and saw on the wall above my head a plaque with the name of the small square: La Plaza Santiago de los Caballeros. Astonished at the coincidence, I asked my belligerent friend whether there had ever been a *posada* of that name in the square. Now it was his turn to be astonished.

"Of course, Señor, it was famous, at the end of the square," and he pointed to the far end from where I was sitting, "But it was demolished a long time ago." He was intrigued at my question and his former unfriendly belligerence now gave way to frank curiosity: "But how did you know about an inn here?" I shrugged, a small revenge: "An ancestor of mine stayed there 150 years ago," I replied with suitable *hauteur*. Back at his window he talked to his partner with lively animation that put his earlier surly behaviour to shame.

The Alcázar, huge and grim on the skyline, is a reminder of recent brutal history. There was a fortress here as early as the third century but the Roman one was destroyed by the Visigoths while the present structure was begun in 1531. It is a massive square building that was partly destroyed during the Spanish Civil War though it has been restored. Today, this fortress houses a military museum which includes what must be one of the best collections of model soldiers to be found anywhere; case after case of parading ranks of lead soldiers in the uniforms of several centuries. But the lower part of the fortress, the cellars and dungeons, has been preserved as it was during the siege of the Civil War to become a Nationalist shrine to those who defended the Alcázar in 1936 in what has been described as one of the most heroic episodes of that war. The chambers have been kept exactly as they were at the time of the siege and include the corner of a cellar where one of the besieged women gave birth during a bombardment. I was reminded of the perfectly preserved ruins of the Residency in Lucknow where Indian guides show visitors where one of the English Mem'Sahibs gave birth during the siege of the Indian Mutiny.

I was awakened in the middle of the night by an eerie high whine and it took me a moment to realise what was happening: a brilliantly fierce storm was disturbing the night and sheets of rain were lashing almost horizontally across the ancient rooftops of Toledo which were illuminated by continuous flashes of lightning. As Borrow tells us, "The city, standing on a rocky mountain, has no wells," so that rainwater has to be collected in great tanks. The scene was an unsettling one: constant sheet lightning, horizontal rain driven by the whining wind and rivers of water rushing down high gables to pour in great jets into the narrow streets and alleyways far below, for I was on the top floor of my hotel. I hoped that the summer storm was doing its duty by the city tanks.

11

Madrid and
the Spaniards

*History—Borrow's comparisons—Mendizábal—Borrow and
the Bible Society—the Retiro—the Puerta del Sol—Borrow's
imprisonment—the lower classes of Spain*

MADRID was originally a Moorish fortress and was only brought
under Christian control in 1083. Visitors to modern Spain, though
they may inspect the monuments which have been left behind by the
Moors, some of them like the Alhambra at Granada of world renown,
probably do not also understand the extent to which Spanish culture
is a mixture, following centuries in which Moors and Christians lived
side by side, sometimes fighting, sometimes tolerating one another
in uneasy truce. The Moors were only finally expelled from Granada
and Spain in 1492, the year Columbus sailed for the New World,
and only then did their long period of hegemony in Spain come to
a physical end though their influence in art, culture and language as
well as their astonishing architecture has remained to the present.

Madrid was not an important place until Philip II decided to move
his capital there in the mid-sixteenth century when it began to grow
rapidly. The choice of Madrid was for geographic reasons rather
than for any other advantages the site offered for it is situated in the
very centre of the peninsula—though Toledo which is a mere sixty-
five kilometres to its south is only a little less central. Borrow was
to make Madrid the centre of his operations for the greater part of

his five years in Spain and by the time he came to describe the city his view of the ordinary people of Spain had changed markedly from the negative attitude he displayed when first he entered the country through Badajoz. Not one to minimise his achievements, Borrow begins his description of the Spanish capital with reference to his own wide travels.

> *I have visited most of the principal capitals of the world, but upon the whole none has ever so interested me as this city of Madrid, in which I now found myself. I will not dwell upon its streets, its edifices, its public squares, its fountains, though some of these are remarkable enough; but Petersburg has finer streets, Paris and Edinburgh more stately edifices, London far nobler squares, whilst Shiraz can boast of more costly fountains, though not cooler waters. But the population! Within a mud wall scarcely one league and a half in circuit, are contained two hundred thousand human beings, certainly forming the most extraordinary vital mass to be found in the entire world; and be it always remembered that this mass is strictly Spanish.*[1]

One cannot help thinking, though this may appear as heresy to some of Borrow's admirers, that had the Bible Society sent him to another country—Italy, for example, or China—he would have enthused in exactly the same way about its capital city.

Madrid is an elegant, spacious city though by its very nature as a huge capital, now with more than three million people, less obviously Spanish than Salamanca or Toledo. The remoteness of the city meant that it only grew to its present size after the coming of the railways; it sits in a barren province, a dry plain that grows wheat, vines and olives and at a height of 640 metres (2,100 feet) is one of Europe's most elevated as well as hottest capital cities.

Borrow came to Madrid during a civil war with the intention of undermining the Roman Catholic faith of the overwhelming majority of the population by distributing Protestant Testaments on behalf of the British Bible Society; he knew no one in Madrid and had no introductions although he was to receive firm support from the British ambassador, George Villiers, later Earl of Clarendon. With his usual persistence he soon obtained an interview with the Spanish prime minister, Mendizábal, whom he describes in detail including the fact that he was a huge man somewhat larger than Borrow who was above six foot two inches. Mendizábal was not well disposed towards the Bible Society. "I found him, as I had been informed, a bitter enemy of the Bible Society, of which he spoke in terms of hatred and contempt." At least, Mendizábal promised that at the end of a few months, when (he hoped) the country would be more tranquil, Borrow could then print the Scriptures. But as Borrow was leaving his presence, Mendizábal said: "Yours is not the first application I have had: ever since I have held the reins of government I have been pestered in this manner by English, calling themselves Evangelical Christians, who have of late come flocking over into Spain."[2]

It was hardly an auspicious start but not one to daunt Borrow. His account of how he established his own shop in Madrid to sell Testaments—because no bookseller was willing to sell them on his behalf—and his description of the ways in which the priestly party in the capital attacked and vilified him is presented with gusto and Borrow's usual sense of panache. Accused of consorting with gypsies and being a sorcerer, both accusations which must have given him considerable pleasure, Borrow says: "Why should I be ashamed of their company when my Master mingled with publicans and thieves? Many of the gypsy race came frequently to visit me; received instruction, and heard parts of the Gospel read to them in their own language, and when they were hungry and faint, I gave them to eat and drink."[3]

There are splendid, and surely deliberate, echoes of the New Testament in this passage as well as a substantial hint of the pride which the Rev. Jowett had detected in Borrow when he first applied to work for the Bible Society. What must have been meat and drink to Borrow was the fact that in Madrid, as he tells us, "Several of the ultra-popish bishops, then resident in Madrid, had denounced the Bible, the Bible Society, and myself." Taking on the Catholic Church in Spain gave Borrow more satisfaction, at least to judge by the raciness of his accounts, than anything else. The Bible Society had provided him with the bona fides, as it were, to be himself: to preach didactically, to be conspicuous, to arouse enmity and to be seen back in England as a Protestant champion as he took on the forces of the ancient Spanish-Catholic enemy. He was never to have such an opportunity again. On a visit to London from Spain in 1836 Borrow wrote a report of his labours in Spain and compared the mind of the Spaniard to a garden run to waste; it was for the Bible Society to cultivate it and "purge it of the rank and bitter weeds."[4]

The most interesting as well as most elegant of Madrid's attractions are the magnificent Prado Gallery where Velázquez and Goya reign supreme, the Retiro Park which is a match for London's much-vaunted Hyde Park, and the Royal Palace, which in point of heavy grandeur is among Europe's most dazzling royal residences. I visited these and other sights while also searching out Borrow's Madrid.

Parks in summer are places for reflection and the Retiro, like all good parks, offers a wide range of distractions: a lake stocked with fish and offering boating for the incompetent whose main role is to highlight the skills of a few athletic youths who pilot their way effortlessly between the hopeless and the inept; endless vendors of refreshments; an avenue of stalls selling a range of books, Spanish and foreign, or offering appalling reproductions of paintings; the suitably named Velázquez Palace which houses exhibitions— it was photography on this occasion; and the Crystal Palace. This last named might have been copied from the vast Victorian masterpiece of 1851 but if so it has achieved all the charms of a miniature replica that is able to hide among the trees and overlook a sparkling pond fed by perpetual fountains. There I watched a father

provide his two small sons with breadcrumbs to feed the ducks but, armed with the absolute perversity of their kind, the children insisted upon throwing the crumbs at the greedy pigeons which swooped from all directions to obtain their largesse while the father, whose passion was clearly ducks, restrained with difficulty his anger at the obtuse wilfulness of his tiny offspring.

I had found a small *pensión* just off the Plaza Mayor whose owners seemed delighted to have me: business was slack, I surmised, and, as they told me with courteous flattery that made me feel my outlay of 1,400 pesetas was well spent, they rarely had English visitors. The Plaza Mayor is a grand rectangular square of eighteenth-century design similar to the Praça do Comercio of Lisbon; it is entered by archways of which there are seven while a colonnaded covered way, in which every kind of huckster operates upon the unwary tourist, surrounds it. On Sundays this is given over to vendors of coins and stamps for which the Plaza is famous. Originally, for the setting is one of spaciousness and splendour, it was designed for royal entertainments.

Borrow described the Puerta del Sol as "The most central point of Madrid, into which four or five of the principal streets debouch, and which is, at all times of the year, the great place of assemblage for the idlers of the capital, poor or rich." This it still remains thought it is perhaps less sleazy than Piccadilly Circus and less menacing in general appearance than Times Square.

When Borrow first visited Madrid he lodged at 3 Calle de la Zarza, or Street of the Bramble, "a dark, dirty street, which, however, was close to the Puerto del Sol,"[5] but neither reference to maps nor inquiries at the tourist office or of policemen produced any result so it must have given way to modern improvements. Later, he took lodgings in the Calle Santiago though the place where he lodged is now an uninterestingly uniform modern block.

℘

Much of Borrow's time in Madrid was spent dealing with hostile authorities and, as he says, in January 1838 "a swoop was made upon me by my enemies, in the shape of a peremptory prohibition from the political governor of Madrid to sell any more New Testaments."[6] He received much support from the British ambassador, George Villiers, who presented to Count Ofalia, the new prime minister, a memorial by Borrow describing the Bible Society and its intentions in Spain. On reading it, Ofalia said: "What a pity that this is a Protestant society, and that all its members are not Catholics!"[7] This did not prevent the authorities from finding a pretext to send Borrow to prison and though he was only to be incarcerated for three weeks he made the most of it as the subtitle of *The Bible in Spain* suggests.

Borrow passed the greater part of his time in Spain at Madrid but made almost no contact with the upper classes whom he dismisses in a couple of lines: "The truth is I have little to say about them; I mingled but little in their society, and what I saw of them by no means tended to exalt them in my imagination." Borrow, however, waxes lyrical about the lower classes and perhaps, given his interest in gypsies and the rough life, this is not surprising. Thus, in Madrid, he says: "I would sooner talk of the lower class, not only of Madrid, but of all Spain. The Spaniard of the lower class has much more interest for me, whether *manolo*, labourer, or muleteer. He is not a common being; he is an extraordinary man."[8]

Certainly the ordinary Spaniard, the Spaniard of the streets, has an independence close to arrogance mixed with a compensating courtesy that gives him an appeal which at its best is charming though, when he wishes to be surly or unfriendly, such a man can be very surly indeed.

12

Cádiz and the South Coast

Cádiz and the Carlists—Borrow and the lower classes—the British Legion in Spain—an odd place to stay—a wonderful old city—Algeciras—cheated of Tangier

BORROW returned to England briefly in 1836 to consult with the Bible Society and plan his Biblical campaign in Spain; it was agreed that he would print the New Testament "with as little delay as possible" once back in Madrid. On his return to Spain Borrow sailed direct to Cádiz, although the ship called at Lisbon on the way, and planned to travel overland at once through Andalusia to Madrid even though the Carlists under their leader Gómez were ravaging the country through which he had to pass. (In 1838 Borrow again returned to Spain through Cádiz after another visit to England and on this second occasion visited Gibraltar and other places along the coast before making for Madrid; I have combined these various excursions as though part of a single journey.)

On his arrival at Cádiz in late 1836, Borrow found great confusion reigning in the city, which was then threatened by armed bands of the Carlists who had recently been in occupation in the course of the civil war. He tells us that he took up his abode at the French Hotel in the Calle de la Niveria; the hotel was very full apparently because of the attractions of its cuisine. Borrow then reveals two interesting aspects of his character. First, when called upon by some of the company, as a newly arrived stranger, to give his opinion of what France and England might do about the war, he replies that he does not know but "that it would be as well if the Spaniards would exert themselves more, and call less upon Jupiter." But having thrown out this belligerent and characteristic response, virtually a challenge to the company, Borrow adds, almost as though he regretted his rashness or was fearful of its repercussions, "As I did not wish to engage in any political conversation, I instantly quitted the house, and sought those parts of the town where the lower classes principally reside."[1]

These, however, he found to be ignorant on the subject of religion.

Did Borrow seek the lower classes simply in order to proselytise on behalf of the Bible Society; or did he prefer their company whether or not they were remotely interested in his Testaments? All the evidence from his own writings would suggest that he preferred their company anyway and then justified to the Bible Society spending his time working amongst them rather than other classes in Spain on the general grounds that they were more in need of instruction and would provide more fruitful possibilities for conversion.

Meanwhile, England, under Palmerston's control of foreign policy, supported the government of Queen Isabella or, rather, of her mother Christina, the regent, and opposed the Carlist pretenders. It is interesting and also a trifle odd that Borrow, who often has occasion to mention the war in the pages of *The Bible in Spain* and is ready enough to extol British military efforts abroad, never mentions the British Legion in Spain. In 1835 Palmerston had sanctioned the enlisting of an army of 10,000 men in England under the command of Colonel, later Sir, de Lacy Evans which landed at San Sebastián in August of that year to assist the regency against the Carlists in the north-west. Later, reinforcements were landed at Santander. Perhaps Borrow says nothing of the expedition since it was a failure, principally because it was scandalously neglected by the government it had come to assist, for within six months of its arrival nearly 5,000 members or half the Legion had died of privation or fever or had been invalided home. The remainder stayed on in Spain for another two years before they too returned home, having meanwhile failed to obtain from the Spanish government any of the assistance which had been promised.

℃⊃

The establishment where I lodged was distinctly odd: not an inn or *pensión* but simply *camas* or rooms in a tall, dilapidated old house built round a courtyard that had once been open to the sky though now it was roofed in. A balcony on each floor overlooked the courtyard below. The rooms were small, containing a minimum of furniture and that of the cheapest, most rickety kind as well as a tiny corner washbasin, a courtesy nod in the direction of cleanliness supplied only with cold water, while the locks on the doors were so flimsy that a ten-year-old child would have no difficulty in forcing them and, as if to emphasise the insecurity and provide an incompetent ten-year-old with an alternative, the skylight over the door would not shut and was large enough to admit an agile thief. Despite these drawbacks, I had left my pack in such a room on arrival while I went to seek supper and enjoy the balmy sea breezes of late evening. My night, however, was disturbed by constant comings and goings and gently murmured conversations rising from the different landings.

Cádiz is a wonderful compact old city of straight narrow streets and little squares and massive ramparts facing the encircling sea, for it is built on a peninsula which permits only one narrow approach from the landward side. Cádiz was founded by the Phoenicians about 1100 BC and named Gades after it fell to the Romans. Now it is the capital of Andalusia. Its period of greatest glory coincided with the Spanish American Empire when it became the headquarters of the Spanish treasure fleets; it never really recovered from the loss of the colonies in the Americas and by the time Borrow visited it the city was in general decline. Even so, he described it as a lively place with a population of 80,000 and containing some shops in the style of Paris or London. As he says of it:

> *The town… is of modern construction, and very unlike any other town*
> *which is to be found in the Peninsula, being built with great regularity*

and symmetry. The streets are numerous, and intersect each other, for the most part at right angles. They are very narrow in comparison to the height of the houses, so that they are almost impervious to the rays of the sun, except when at its midday altitude."²

This description still applies to Cádiz today.

It is a most pleasant city in which to stroll and even in hot weather is cooled by sea breezes. The esplanade along the Atlantic-facing ramparts has been laid out in elegant gardens with exotic trees and tiled seats for use of promenaders. Restaurants serve a variety of snails, and notices among the flowerbeds warn people not to gather the snails for fear of poisonous varieties although I suspect that these, nonetheless, were gathered by the gardeners for sale to the restaurants.

Borrow took ship from Cádiz to Gibraltar, his vessel stopping briefly at Algeciras in order to drop off the governor who hated all things Moorish. It is no longer possible to do this journey by ship so I travelled by bus along the coast road, switch-backing up and down spectacular hills that crowd the coast, some of them crowned with a forest of giant single propeller windmills, the new (old) technology to harness wind power. Algeciras just misses being part of the Costa del Sol.

It was on the south coast that I became conscious of the constant changes in accent from one province of Spain to another. In Algeciras over a long leisurely lunch I listened in shamelessly to an animated, dramatic argument between four men at the next table and though my limited Spanish crippled my capacity to understand what the fast-flowing argument was about the change of accents since I had left Madrid and the Extremadura completed my discomfiture so that I understood almost nothing at all. I wanted to visit Tangier from Algeciras (Borrow went to Tangier just before his final return to England, his trip having nothing to do with his Bible activities), and booked a trip on a hovercraft for the next morning. I then idled much of the day in Algeciras, which has the dilapidated charm of a minor port and resort that, as yet, has not been elevated to real significance by the ubiquitous tourist industry.

The next morning I had to report at the jetty for my Tangier ferry at eight so I paid the rather sulky young man in my small *pensión* a further 1,000 pesetas to keep my room for another night and then went to the jetty only to discover a group of disgruntled German and American tourists who had just been told the trip had been cancelled. When I went to the agency to retrieve my money the woman first claimed that I had purchased an open ticket; then suggested that I hold onto it and visit Tangier the following day; and finally, with great reluctance, opened her cash box to return my money but attempted to short change me. When I pointed out her error and requested the full payment her look of defeated malevolence drew a laugh from several Spanish men waiting their turn to do business with her. I had not been a good start to her day. Cheated of Tangier, I decided to take the next bus to La Linea for Gibraltar and back at my *pensión* the sulky young man, who must have had some designs upon my room, grinned with pleasure and sudden friendliness when I cancelled my reservation and asked for the return of my 1,000 pesetas, which he gave me with alacrity.

13

Gibraltar: Lion Couchant

Borrow the patriot—the Barbary apes—a tourist—a cup of "English" tea—on the threshold of the Third World—"It does make you feel good"

BORROW was a strangely mixed character of many moods. Gibraltar brought out his sense of Britishness, and the cosmopolitan multi-tongued Borrow is temporarily replaced by the patronising nationalist who looks with pride upon the British soldiers on the Rock and compares their bearing with that of their Spanish counterparts to the detriment of the latter. He came to Gibraltar by boat towards the end of the day and had to get ashore before the evening gun was fired, after which no one was permitted to land. He managed this and, once his passport had been inspected, passed under the low archway which tunnels beneath the ramparts to the town.

> Beneath this archway paced, with measured tread, tall red-coated sentinels with shouldered guns. There was no stopping, no sauntering in these men. There was no laughter, no exchange of light conversation with the passers-by, but their bearing was that of British soldiers, conscious of the duties of their station. What a difference between them and the listless loiterers who stand at guard at the gate of a Spanish garrisoned town.[1]

The sight of these soldiers, no doubt, reminded Borrow nostalgically of his boyhood when he had moved from town to town with his soldier father.

The Battle of Trafalgar ensured British world naval supremacy through to 1914, and by then the Rock had become as much a part of British mythology as the Battle of Hastings. It was not to be given up, ever! The Rock certainly looks impressive from Algeciras: a *lion couchant* facing Spain and since, over the centuries, the British have made much of their lion image it is understandable that their continued control of Gibraltar irritates patriotic Spaniards.

As Borrow proceeded up Gibraltar's principal street he says he was almost deafened by "the noise and bustle which reigned around." After he had settled in his inn and eaten, he heard martial music in the square outside and went down to watch a military band beat retreat. The sight and sounds once more affected his sense of nationalism and he indulges in a soliloquy about his country: "O England! long, long may it be ere the sun of glory sink beneath the wave of darkness!... Of all fates, may it please the Lord to preserve thee from a disgraceful and slow decay; becoming, ere extinct, a scorn and a mockery for those selfsame foes who now, though they envy and abhor thee, still fear thee, nay, even against their will, honour and respect thee!"[2] There is considerably more in this vein and Borrow ends the passage by claiming that his soliloquy was "part of a broken prayer for my native land, which, after my usual thanksgiving, I breathed to the Almighty ere retiring to rest that Sunday night at Gibraltar."[3]

Borrow's musings upon his native land in such a fashion will grate upon modern sensibilities; at the same time his patriotism, ingrained through his boyhood background as a soldier's son, is always brought out by contact with British soldiers. His reference to his usual thanksgiving and the Almighty would, no doubt, have amused Harriet Martineau! Borrow inspected the excavations in the Rock and is shown round by an English soldier, which causes him to reflect once more, this time on how the sons of rural England make the best soldiers. The Rock aroused all his sense of patriotism.

Apart from its many Anglo-Spanish historical connections, Gibraltar has some unique attractions of its own. There are more than 500 species of flowering plants on the Rock and one, the candytuft, is to be found nowhere else. Its mammals include the rabbit and fox and the famous Barbary ape, the only wild monkey to be found in Europe. British myth-makers decided that the apes were essential to the Empire and that should they ever become extinct Britain would then lose Gibraltar and so, during the Second World War, Winston Churchill, imperial myth-maker extraordinary, decreed that the supply of apes should be replenished to ensure that this awful prediction would not be fulfilled. Gibraltarians, though they claim to be British, are in fact of greatly mixed stock, mainly of Genoese, British, Spanish, Maltese and Portuguese descent.

そ

I crossed from Spain into Gibraltar over the airport runway towards the sheer northern face of the Rock to make my way through the main street of the old town which was bustling with as much activity as Borrow had noted: every shop was geared to the throngs of visitors and displayed all those pleasant but useless items people persuade themselves to buy when on holiday—jewellery, watches, duty-free liquor, expensive clothes, ornaments and useless knick-knacks which they subsequently give away as presents. In the less fashionable parts of the town very ordinary, rather dilapidated post-1945 apartment blocks, which had been built to house service families, now bear forlorn testimony to an already receding military past. There were also numerous signs advertising an "English pub" or "fish and chips".

I decided to stay in the Queen's Hotel rather than search for more modest accommodation and was signed in by a superior receptionist who cast a doubtful eye on my backpack as, no doubt, he pondered my financial status. This caused me to look again at the prominently displayed sign on the wall "Management reserves the right of admission," which I had last come across in white-dominated Southern Africa. The receptionist spoke the curiously accented English of a native-born Gibraltarian or Rock "lizard". I paid four pounds to ascend the cable railway and was rewarded with a stunning view of Algeciras across the bay while below me enormous container ships lay at anchor. There is a sheer drop on the Mediterranean side of the Rock, which should also have afforded me another spectacular view except that the Rock was shrouded in fast moving clouds that only allowed intermittent glimpses of the shoreline which lay almost vertically at my feet. Then I descended to the halfway point to visit the nature reserve and make acquaintance with the Barbary apes, a number of which, possibly the entire population, were dutifully performing for their visitors.

I had not imagined that the Rock, whose name implies barrenness, would have such lush vegetation on its Atlantic side but since it does the apes should have no problem surviving and, no doubt, will outlast the British presence. There is a lookout post near the entrance to the nature reserve which has been carefully marked to show that Queen Elizabeth II and the Duke of Edinburgh stood here and looked across the bay on their visit to Gibraltar in 1954.

I spent the day being a tourist in what must be one of the most consciously "British" places anywhere in the world. I enjoyed the prehistoric caves with their dripping stalactites and stalagmites and their "cave people" arranged in homely recesses: light classical music was piped to us as we inspected the huge caves, for this was superior, educational tourism. Then I took lunch at a small café on a platform, which afforded a magnificent view across to Algeciras over the sea, and treated myself to a traditional English lunch (there were no

alternatives) of steak and kidney pie and chips—from the microwave. Following an afternoon spent exploring I sought a traditional cup of English tea and, in a manner of speaking, I got one. Having passed numerous signs extolling the merits of English pubs, I discovered a solitary sign in a side street, which announced teas served, and so took a seat at a pavement table although no one else was sitting outside. I was at once transported to provincial England of half a century earlier. First I was left to sit in solitude without service. Then a somewhat slovenly girl appeared to take my order, intimating by a body language peculiar to her type that it would have been more convenient all round had I taken a place inside the café so that she did not need to come outside. I ordered a pot of tea and settled down for another wait of fifteen minutes. When my quintessentially English afternoon refreshment finally arrived it came in that variety of steel pot with a flap lid that never pours properly. The white mug-like cup was only just clean while the powdered milk gave to the tea an unmistakable wartime flavour of Britain at bay. I went back to my hotel to do some writing and found myself comparing unfavourably its general level of cleanliness for which I was paying thirty-three pounds with the far cleaner little room of the night before in Algeciras for which I had only paid five.

As I wandered in the old town looking for an eating place for my evening meal I came into a tiny square which boasted three undistinguished looking restaurants. Two small girls fell in beside me demanding, "Where you eat? That café is a good one." "Or that one." "No, that one is better," and following each suggestion they giggled at each other and at me. "You must choose," they insisted and they pursued me with the persistence of child touts in a Third World country, a thought which startled me at first until I realised that the Third World was just across the Straits and its people waiting to come across.

My final impression of the Rock was touchingly old-fashioned. "It is so English, my dear. I feel that here, on the Rock, we are on our soil again." Her companion nodded, understandingly: "It does make you feel good." I overheard this little gem of appreciation from two middle-aged middle-class English ladies while making my way through the centre of Gibraltar as I returned to Spain. Their comments came straight from the pages of Agatha Christie.

14

The Road to Seville

*La Linea—help from an idler—the Guadalquivir—pigeons
in Sanlúcar—a famous bathing resort—leaping shrimps*

I WAS happy to be back in Spain once more. Across the border in
La Linea I had a coffee and in the process of giving my order and
responding to the waiter again became aware of the constant changes
in regional accents. Pronunciations I thought I had mastered must be
tackled afresh. I sat on the waterfront for a while, the *lion couchant*
reclining on my left, and then set off to explore the town.

As I often discovered, Spanish towns which at first appeared
uninteresting, almost bleak, would later reveal old quarters of great
charm that had been assiduously tucked away in corners. This was
the case in La Linea. I began by walking along dull wide streets of
little architectural merit or attraction and had all but written the
town off when I turned into a small alleyway to get lost in a maze
of little streets. In a tiny market of half-a-dozen fruit stalls I asked a
man where I could find the centre, the old centre of La Linea. The
man was an idler, a passer of time for whom time meant little. He
was leaning against a wall watching the fruit stalls in a detached sort
of way, which clearly implied that whether or not they sold their
produce was of no concern to him. But he liked watching and now,
just as readily, he insisted upon accompanying me to the plaza that
had successfully eluded any searching of mine and was at the centre
of these small jumbled streets. There were tables and people drinking
and I invited him to take some refreshment with me but, No, and he
thanked me and said he was happy to show a stranger the way. There
was just a hint of reproof that I might have thought he was helping

me for a reward, so we shook hands ceremonially and he departed, presumably to resume his loitering.

I caught a bus to Cádiz and on to Sanlúcar de Barrameda at the mouth of the Guadalquivir. The Guadalquivir rates very nearly a column in the *Encyclopaedia Britannica* and I had not realised just how important a river it claims to be. The Great River of the Moors, it flows west across southern Spain for four hundred miles to drain a region half the size of England and passes through one of the richest areas of plant and animal life in Europe and, with irrigation in its wide and fertile plain, it supports the abundant vineyards and olive groves of Andalusia. I was not actually apprised of all this information when I reached Sanlúcar and looked instead upon the river through the eyes of George Borrow who said it lacked attraction despite its historic importance, that its banks were low, that there were no trees, that the country through which it runs was flat and uninteresting, the water turbid and muddy and in colour "closely resembling the contents of a duck-pool," while the average width is between 150 and 200 metres. And yet, the Guadalquivir acted as a highway for Romans, Vandals and Arabs while the conquistadors sailed down it from Seville on their way to conquer the New World.

Borrow travelled from Cádiz to Seville by a small steamer which regularly made the journey along the coast and up the river and though I had already failed to find sea transport from Cádiz to Gibraltar I still hoped—though, I confess, without much conviction—that I might be able to travel up the Guadalquivir by some form of boat. But when I inquired in the tourist office about a boat I was faced with a kind of blank, incredulous astonishment. "But there are no boats going up the river. Why do you want a boat? There are plenty of buses."

"But there used to be a boat," I said.

"There has never been a boat," I was assured in the kind of voice that began to suggest I was a foreign troublemaker.

"There certainly used to be," I insisted with such assurance on my part that the tourist official with whom I was conducting this now useless conversation looked quite startled.

"When was there a boat?" she demanded sharply.

"In 1836," I replied smugly.

ℰℛ

Sanlúcar is not on the main tourist routes and, in consequence, has retained a great deal of charm that has not been preserved, as it were, for visitors. I spent the evening first drinking and then eating at a corner of its elegant main square where I watched people congregate for their usual evening meetings, aperitifs and gossip. In cities round the world the authorities have banned the feeding of pigeons on the grounds that they are a pest and that their droppings damage public buildings. Such bans are ignored with the contempt they deserve. That evening in Sanlúcar, whose square had a large resident population of pigeons, I watched five bird fanciers arrive with their bags of stale bread, which they scattered before an expectant flock of fat waddling pigeons. The scattering took some time and each dispenser of largesse followed his or her particular ritual.

As Borrow tells us, airing his encyclopaedic knowledge of literature as he does so, the *playa* or beach of Sanlúcar is famous "in the ancient novels of Spain, of that class called Picaresque, or those devoted to the adventures of notorious scoundrels..." and was a rendezvous for ruffians, *contrabandistas*, and vagabonds of every description..." Sanlúcar itself "was always noted for the thievish propensity of its inhabitants—the worst in all Andalusia."[1]

Sanlúcar is also a famous bathing resort although no one was bathing in the Guadalquivir that evening. Borrow describes how he was met by a lively spectacle:

> *The shore was covered with a multitude of females either dressing or undressing themselves, while (I speak within bounds) hundreds were in the water, sporting and playing: some were close to the beach, stretched at their full length on the sand and pebbles, allowing the little billows to dash over their heads and bossoms; whilst others were swimming boldly out into the firth.*[2]

The men, he tells us, were bathing further along the beach. The beach to which he alludes is on the estuary of the river which at this point widens into the Bay of Cádiz.

Sanlúcar, which is home of Manzanilla wine, lies back from the river and rises up a hill with its castle over on the left. Like almost every town I visited in Spain it had a Roman foundation before becoming a Moorish settlement and then being taken by the Spaniards in the thirteenth century. Columbus sailed from it on his third and last voyage to the New World as did Magellan when he set off to circumnavigate the globe.

One of the narrow streets leading off the square and up the hill had been turned into a lively market the following morning and was crowded with early shoppers. It had fruit and vegetables and meat and fish as well as stalls of leather goods and ornaments and the mere sight of some of the fruit in season made my mouth water. I peered into boxes of tiny grey shrimps to realise that they were still alive for the surface of shrimps was in constant flickering motion and every once in a while, with a convulsion of its muscles, one of the more vigorous shrimps would leap high from the mass in a fruitless attempt to escape its coming fate. The bus stop was in a square so small that the big bus could only just manoeuvre its way round with inches to spare. The countryside between Sanlúcar and Seville through which the Guadalquivir meanders for a hundred kilometres bears out Borrow's description: it is flat and uninteresting.

15

Shimmering Seville

A tout—the cathedral—the Giralda and a beggar woman—
Seville oranges—the Paseo de las Delicias—Borrow in
Seville—instructions to Mrs Clarke—Borrow and the Bible
Society—an enchanting little square—Italica—in Borrow's
day and now—the Emperor Hadrian

SEVILLE has grown from the 90,000 population in Borrow's day to
more than 660,000 today to make it Spain's fourth city. Outside the
tourist office I was buttonholed by a small balding man whose weak
eyes peered at me through thick glasses as he thrust a grubby card
into my hand: "You want cheap lodgings, good ones, right in the
centre of the city?" "What price?" "Only 1,500 pesetas, close to the
cathedral and the Alcázar." Perhaps, for once, I would not spend a
weary hour searching for lodgings in the heat of the day so I agreed
to follow him. He led me past the cathedral, beside the Alcázar
and then through a maze of narrow streets and tiny alleyways in
the old quarter of the city. I tried to pick out landmarks for my
future guidance and confidently memorised features that gave an
appearance of being unique until I found them repeated round the
next corner and gave up.

The landlord of the *pensión* was a squat fat man of slow movement
and cunning visage who at my appearance behind his tout at once
displayed a broad professional smile of welcome. The 1,500-peseta
room, which I had been promised, unfortunately, had just been let
but he could manage a double at 2,000! At my silence he continued
blandly, a routine he had long perfected: "You can move to a single
room at 1,500 pesetas tomorrow, then the two nights will only cost

you 3,500." He beamed. I accepted. I had come too far, it was very hot and though I knew I had been conned it was still remarkably cheap. My little guide required drinking money for his services—for coffee, he said—so the cheap room would not be quite such a bargain after all.

Seville Cathedral is the largest Gothic building, as well as being one of the biggest cathedrals, in the world; inside it is gloomy, stark and immense. As Borrow says:

> *It is utterly impossible to wander through the long aisles, and to raise one's eyes to the richly inlaid roof, supported by colossal pillars, without experiencing sensations of sacred awe and deep astonishment. It is true that the interior, like those of the generality of Spanish cathedrals, is somewhat dark and gloomy; yet it loses nothing by this gloom, which, on the contrary, rather increases the solemnity of the effect. Notre Dame of Paris is a noble building, yet to him who has seen the Spanish cathedrals, and particularly this of Seville, it almost appears trivial and mean, and more like a town-hall than a temple of the Eternal.*[1]

Alongside the cathedral stands the Giralda, the great square tower or campanile with huge bells which originally formed part of the grand mosque of Seville. It stands 85 metres high and is ascended by a vaulted pathway or inclined plane up which Ferdinand VII is

said to have ridden to the top on his horse. As I approached the Giralda I was accosted by a smartly dressed woman who asked which language I spoke and what I was looking for, "since you look lost," she said. I indicated the Giralda and assured her that I was not lost only to discover her real purpose which was to beg.

Now there are beggars and beggars and I prefer the straightforward whining or shouting or arrogant or miserable cringing beggar to the smarmy superior kind who come at

you from an angle and pretend not to be beggars at all. Her line was a charity, she was begging on behalf of the desperate of the world though I have forgotten which particular group, but I resented her approach and told her so: "Don't ask if I am lost when clearly I am not," I said "but beg from the beginning." She turned angrily away and I ascended the Giralda to stare across distant vistas beyond shimmering Seville, and examine the giant bells housed in its open belfry or look straight below me at the elegantly symmetrical rows of orange trees in the ancient garden of the old mosque.

The other great splendour of Seville is the Alcázar or Moorish palace of intricately tiled walls and a succession of magnificent halls and courtyards. Its lush green gardens, overlooked by different levels of balconies and a covered walk along the top of the walls, are a hidden delight, a true oasis in the centre of scorching Seville. A long time ago, before air freight meant that every kind of fruit or vegetable can be found on sale in England all through the year, there were seasons, and there used to be a season of a few short weeks when Seville oranges suddenly appeared in the shops and markets. Now, as I wandered round the Arabian gardens of the Alcázar, I was able to pick up fallen oranges: not any old Seville orange but oranges from the very heart of the city, the Moorish pleasure gardens. But, alas, they were dry and pithy, from old ornamental trees and not remotely suitable for eating.

According to Borrow, Seville was "surrounded with high Moorish walls, in a good state of preservation, and built of such durable materials that it is probable they will for many centuries still bid defiance to the encroachments of time."[2] He was being optimistic for most of the walls have disappeared although there is an impressive stretch on one side of the city and a noble gateway, and I was foolish enough to circle what would once have been the entire walled city on the afternoon of an exceptionally hot day. I visited the Paseo de las Delicias (The Delights), which in Borrow's time was outside the city but has now been engulfed by it. Borrow describes this as the favourite promenade of the Sevillians

and there one occasionally sees assembled whatever the town produces of beauty and gallantry. There wander the black-eyed Andalusian dames and damsels, clad in their graceful silken mantillas; and there gallops the Andalusian cavalier, on his long-tailed thick-maned steed of Moorish ancestry. As the sun is descending, it is enchanting to glance in the direction of the city; the prospect is inexpressibly beautiful. Yonder, in the distance, high and enormous, stands the Golden Tower, now used as a toll-house, but the principal bulwark of the city in the time of the Moors. It stands on the shore of the river, like a giant keeping watch, and is the first edifice which attracts the eye of the voyager as he moves up the stream to Seville.[3]

When Borrow came to Seville for the last time during his travels in Spain, which was from May to December 1839, there are hints at least that perhaps Isopel Berners in the Dingle had been correct when she said she thought he was mad. He had no friends there but soon gathered round him several curious characters of the kind he always managed to attract. These included a gigantic Greek from Cephalonia, an aged professor of music and a Greek bricklayer who had excellent contacts with the lower classes. Then Borrow hired a huge house for himself and his servant Antonio and their horses in a solitary part of the town where he lived in great seclusion spending much of his time in study or dreamy meditation. He was to complain to the Bible Society that he did not have Bibles to distribute as opposed to Testaments although by this time his employers appeared to be losing patience with him. For one thing, it seems there was a reason other than his need for seclusion which had led Borrow to hire the large house. While in Spain Borrow had been in regular correspondence with the widow, Mrs Clarke, of Oulton. Complications had arisen about her estate in Norfolk, and her legal advisers suggested that she should disappear for a time. Nothing loath, it would seem, she wrote to Borrow to say she intended to take up her abode for a while in Seville. Borrow wrote back to give her instructions as to what she needed to bring and these have an interesting imbalance about them:

> *Bring with you, therefore, your clothes, plenty of bed linen, etc, half-a-dozen blankets, two dozen knives and forks, a mirror or two, twelve silver table spoons, and a large one for soup, tea things and urn (for the Spaniards never drink tea), a few books but not too many,—and you will have occasion for nothing more, or, if you have, you can purchase it here as cheap as in England.*

Mrs Clarke arrived with her twenty-year-old daughter Henrietta to share the big house with Borrow in Seville—although she is not mentioned by Borrow in *The Bible in Spain.*

By this time, however, Borrow was facing increasing difficulties with the Spanish authorities and was again briefly imprisoned; in part because, for political reasons, Lord Palmerston had sent a circular to all British consuls in Spain forbidding them "to afford the slightest countenance to religious agents"; and, in part, because by then he was far too eccentric and notorious a figure to escape their attention or that of the Catholic clergy despite his secluded house. In addition, he was now falling out of favour with the Bible Society, not least, perhaps, because they had taken exception to Mrs Clarke and her daughter staying in the same house as their agent. By this time, moreover, the Secretary of the Bible Society, Rev. Brandram, was complaining that his distribution of Testaments had been small.

This complaint goes to the heart of Borrow's activities. In a letter that must seem naïve, though not to Borrow, he wrote to Brandram first to say that he had been the zealous servant of the Bible Society in Spain but then continues to demonstrate how many other things he had also managed to do:

> *I have the materials of a curious book of travels in Spain; I have enough metrical translations from all languages, especially the Celtic and Sclavonic, to fill a dozen volumes; and I have formed a vocabulary of the Spanish Gypsy tongue, and also a collection of the sayings and poetry of the Gitanos, with introductory essays. Perhaps some of these literary labours might be turned to account. I wish to obtain honourably and respectably the means of visiting China or particular parts of Africa.*

Such a letter was hardly an answer to Brandram's claim that he had only distributed a small number of Testaments. In Seville prison Borrow found himself in the company of thieves, murderers and embezzlers and, possibly unwisely, wrote to say as much to the Bible Society.

Borrow and Mrs Clarke now became engaged (November 1839) though they did not marry until April 1840 back in England. Their relationship has always been a matter of some mystery and Borrow's first biographer, Dr W. J. Knapp, suggests that it was a marriage of convenience: Mrs Clarke needed a man to arrange her affairs, Borrow needed a secure income. What does seem likely is that the widow wanted Borrow more than he desired her but he got his income for the rest of his life.

⌘

That evening I discovered an enchanting little square in which to eat and drink. It was an ordinary working square, so that prices were ordinary and working too, although the fact that the square had four rival restaurants, or rather cafés, possibly had something to do with it. Most of the open centre of the square was taken up with tables belonging to these four establishments and they gradually filled up as the evening progressed. There was a sort of dilapidation about that square—half the lamps in the centre did not work—and from the windows and balconies above the residents would peer down to see what was going on, sit in their windows to enjoy the scene below or call down to acquaintances. Most of the patrons at the tables were Spaniards. Groups of tourists did appear from time to time but most of these, after a cursory inspection, continued on their way, no doubt in search of a grander venue. However, a German couple came to sit at the table next to mine. The tables were covered in red or blue or yellow or green chequered cloths, the colours denoting the cafés to which they belonged. I had ordered a dish of tiny snails but the waiter handed them to the Germans by mistake. They ate them with relish and then, as they got up to leave, the man turned to me and said: "We took, perhaps, your food?" and gave me a courteous little bow. The British, who insist the Germans have no sense of humour, are quite wrong.

The lights above the door of my café fused: a ladder was produced and three men, each, perhaps, possessed of a particular skill in the electrical line, climbed up in turn to inspect the fuse box and climbed down again. Then they held a consultation. One went into the bar to use the telephone, another mounted the ladder for a second time to inspect the contents of the fuse box all over again and then all three retired to the bar for a drink. A new man, equipped with a toolbox, now arrived and speedily repaired the fuse while the first three looked on nodding their approval at his efficiency. Then all four repaired to the bar for more wine.

At the tables the groups kept changing while inside the bar the tension built up as a soccer match vital to Seville's honour was followed on television. By then it was approaching eleven o'clock and was quite dark yet families accompanied by small children continued to join their friends while the children at once made the square their playground, disappearing happily between the tables and only occasionally being sought by parents who made these perfunctory searches more for show than out of anxiety. A tiny child appeared alongside my table and we had a grave conversation before he passed on to the next table—no parents claimed him—and beggars made periodic circuits of the tables while a man came to sell balloons, since by then the children had multiplied. Three young bloods on motorcycles arrived noisily at a corner of the square where they were joined by three pretty girls while a solitary old man, sitting alone, leered at the girls with so evil an eye that the people at the next table to mine began to laugh and then found they could not stop. Now a man sauntered jauntily into the square to play the guitar, wandering among the tables strumming his instrument in the manner of a troubadour except that he could not act and had no ear for music; his playing was execrable so that even such a relaxed and tolerant crowd as that one became restless. When his performance was over the troubadour looked round in expectation of applause but, receiving none, gravely clapped himself. When at last I found my way back to my *pensión* the door was bolted from within and I was obliged to batter at it for ten minutes to arouse my squat and sleepy host. On the morning, as I had guessed, my host told me with regret that the single room he had promised me had not been vacated but—and he shrugged his shoulders and beamed, knowing I would be sensible about it.

I spent the day visiting the Roman remains of Italica just beyond Sante Ponce, which is nine kilometres outside modern Seville. Borrow says he walked there but I took a bus as the whole area has been built up and walking would be no pleasure. Italica was founded by Scipio for his wounded veterans after his victory over the Carthaginians in 206 BCE. It is one of the most important Roman sites in Spain, the birthplace of two out of four of the great emperors who ruled Rome for the magical eighty years in the second century that constitute Gibbon's "golden age of Rome". The two born at Italica are Trajan and Hadrian: Trajan was the last emperor in Rome's long history who pursued a forward policy, adding Dacia (Romania) to the empire and then, having conquered Ctesiphon and reached the Persian Gulf, is reported to have wept because he was too old to follow Alexander's path to India. He was succeeded by Hadrian, that most enigmatic of Roman emperors, who spent his restless life moving constantly from one end of his vast domains to the other to maintain order, review the legions, build new monuments and ensure the stability of the civilised world. When he built his wall in the farthest northern part of his province of Britannia he signalled, though he must have been unaware of the fact, the beginning of the decline of the apparently impregnable empire over which he reigned, for the law of empires is unalterable: expand or retract but do not stand still. Hadrian raised Italica to colonial status in tribute to his adopted father, Trajan.

In Borrow's time Italica was deserted and wild and he gives a wonderful description of the ruins of the amphitheatre:

> *On all sides are to be seen the time-worn broken granite benches, from whence myriads of human beings once gazed down on the area below, where the gladiators shouted, and the lion and the leopard yelled: all round, beneath these flights of benches, are vaulted excavations from whence the combatants, part human, part bestial, darted forth by their several doors. I spent many hours in this singular place, forcing my way through the wild fennel and brushwood into the caverns, now the haunts of adders and other reptiles, whose hissings I heard.[6]*

As he leaves the ruined amphitheatre Borrow finds an enormous vulture feasting on the carcase of a horse.

On my visit, however, order prevailed. There was a toll gate and keeper, and crowds of schoolchildren in groups were being educated, when they were unable to escape the attention of their teachers, while more earnest students looked at mosaics, and tourists took pictures and guardians of this now lucrative attraction hovered about to see all was well. Italica covers more than fifty hectares and the main street is two kilometres long and more than fifteen metres wide, supposedly the widest street in the whole empire. It had magnificent porticoed houses, two public baths, a theatre, a hotel and a gymnasium which were more splendid than Pompeii. The huge amphitheatre which had been built to seat 25,000 was the fourth largest in the entire empire, but though I sat on one of its upper benches I found it hard to travel back 2000 years in time; there were too many reminders of the present as a constant parade of sightseers passed below me: school groups had to be called to order and tourists endlessly clicked their cameras and teenage lovers posed dramatically for their friends.

When he was dying in agony Hadrian composed five incomparable lines of poetry:

> *Warming, wand'ring little sprite*

Body's guest and company,
Whither now take your flight,
Cold and comfortless and white,
Leaving all your jollity.[7]

Anyone who can manage that on a desperate deathbed deserves the obeisance of posterity; he was the greatest figure to come out of ancient Spain.

16

Pedro the Cruel

*Pedro the Cruel—an elegant pensión—Carmona's
impregnable position—King Kong and brandy—a ladies'
riding school*

ON the morning of my departure from Seville I met my little room
tout of two days earlier leading a young couple through the maze of
tiny streets and alleys by the Alcázar and he smiled at me happily,
for his day was off to a good start. Perhaps they would settle for my
double bed at 4,000 pesetas.

Pedro the Cruel, also called the Just, ruled Castile and León from
1350 to 1369 when he was killed in an unfair fight by his half-
brother against whom he had battled for most of his life. He liked to
relax in the Alcázar of Seville and it is a curious as well as revealing
fact of history that some of its most ferocious captains have also
most enjoyed the luxury of elegant palaces. Perhaps it is a question
of contrasts: cruelty and rapine matched by luxury and beauty.
Carmona, my next stopping place on the great road to Madrid, is
particularly associated with Pedro, a figure about whom myths have
been created, and though he may well have been more just than
cruel, it is his alleged cruelty which appealed to the balladeers and
myth-makers. Sir Walter Scott—and not at his best—produces the
following quatrain on Pedro's death:

> *Thus with mortal gasp and quiver*
> *While the blood in bubbles well'd*
> *Fled the fiercest soul that ever*
> *In a Christian bosom dwell'd.*[1]

Just how to differentiate between brutality in a brutal age, for which the English were then renowned on the continent, and cruelty for which Pedro was constantly condemned by his enemies, is no easy matter. In 1370, a year after Pedro's death, the Black Prince was responsible for the capture of Limoges which was followed by a terrible massacre of its inhabitants. Yet in his lifetime, despite the blot of Limoges, the Black Prince was regarded as the epitome of medieval chivalry while Pedro, who was condemned in his lifetime for cruelty, later came to be viewed as a strong dispenser of justice.

က

The road to Carmona leads up a steep hill to a strong Moorish gateway which guards the entrance to the old town, a place of narrow alleys and curving bright white walls with the azure blue sky captured in strips between and above them. I settled for an elegant old *pensión* just outside this gateway; my room contained a three-foot thick embrasure at head height with a small window at the end of it on a level with the pavement of a narrow lane outside so that, with an effort, I could glimpse the feet of people ascending or descending this steep hill. My door opened onto the traditional courtyard round which the house had been built, and seats invited the guests to relax there except for the presence of an ancient concierge or guardian who sat all day in her high-backed chair, dressed entirely in black, a large bunch of keys at her waist, scrupulously surveying everyone who entered or left. She never smiled, she never appeared to relax, she did not nod off and if, as appearances suggested, she was the mother of the hostess who was herself a comfortable grandmother, she must have been well into her eighties. Her forbidding presence in the courtyard was offset by that of a young man in a wheelchair, a severely afflicted paraplegic, whose lolling head nodded constant encouragement to all who appeared.

"Perhaps in the whole of Spain," Borrow tells us, "there is scarcely a finer Moorish monument of antiquity than the eastern side of this town of Carmona, which occupies the brow of a lofty hill, and frowns over an extensive vega or plain, which extends for leagues unplanted and uncultivated, producing nothing but brushwood and carrasco. Here rise tall and dusky walls, with square towers at short distances, of so massive a structure that they would seem to bid defiance alike to the tooth of time and the hand of man."[2]

Carmona had been the military key to Seville and only fell to the Christians after a long and desperate siege. When I found my way to the eastern ramparts the plain below was rugged and rock-strewn, much as Borrow must have seen it, fading into the hazy shimmering distance of the late afternoon.

Carmona is a film-set of a town whose narrow streets of white painted houses twist into small squares while great studded doors guard the ancient palaces of nobles. I only saw one of these doors open, and since a man and woman were entering I made the mistake of a typical tourist and went to follow them, assuming that one palace at least was on show to an inquiring public, but the woman turned to murmur that it was their home. The town appears largely untouched by time except for cars and tourists, and with regard to these latter it clearly only encourages the upper end of the trade for it boasts one five-star hotel, one four-star hotel and a *parador*.

I wanted to find out the times of buses to Córdoba in the morning and was directed back to the bar where I had alighted earlier in the day. The clientele of that bar was made up exclusively of old men: a celebration of some kind was in progress and everyone was drinking brandy. Behind the bar, perched on a high stool, was a fat girl staring with rapt attention at the corner above her head where *King Kong* flickered back and forth across the screen. I approached the bar opposite the girl and inquired, politely I hoped, but raising my voice to make myself heard over the general din, the times of buses to Córdoba in the morning. I felt half ashamed of breaking in upon such concentration. I need not have worried. There was no answer, no movement, no indication that she had heard me. I tried again, my voice a decibel sharper. The same negative result. I tried a third time. Still no response. A freshly opened bottle of brandy was now coming along the bar, one old man at a time, and the nearest ancient sitting up to the bar next to the space I had occupied gave me a careful look; he had, I believe, been trying to decide whether I was German,

American, Scandinavian or Italian and now he went into action on my behalf. He leant forward and rapped sharply with his knuckles on the bar beneath the fat girl's nose. Startled away from *King Kong* she looked round. "This Caballero"—and he indicated me with a polite flourish—"requires your attention." Once more I put my question and, after some disentangling, discovered that the Córdoba bus went at eight thirty in the morning. By this time the brandy bottle had reached the old man beside me: first he filled his own glass; then he stretched over the bar and brought back a clean glass which he placed in front of me and filled to the brim with brandy. Gratefully I toasted him: "Salud—but I am English," I said and he gave a slow smile in delighted acknowledgement that I had guessed correctly his failure to place my nationality.

A tree-lined promenade stretched away from the main street of Carmona like a huge ship's deck, its western side falling sharply down to the base of the great escarpment that rises once more to be crowned by old Carmona. Through a hedge on the side facing high Carmona I found a tiny bar where I took a table overlooking the plain. Beside me was a low hedge and then a sheer drop of twenty feet to a road which wound steeply down the hill; beyond that, across some rough ground and trees, rose the sheer escarpment on whose precipitous edge abutted the old town, red roofs crowding white walls.

As I sat staring across the great plain that undulated into the misty blue towards Córdoba, I became aware of the familiar blowing and champing of horses and on looking over the hedge to the road below discovered that a riding school for young ladies had appeared: ten young ladies in ages ranging from six to sixteen, dressed in the height of riding fashion, always conscious of their pose and poise, were about to be put through their paces. They were under the eagle eye and stern direction of a large man of military aspect, dressed in hunting uniform though his coat was black, and in appearance not unlike a choleric British sergeant-major; he was assisted by four young grooms who had dismounted from their horses and were walking among the young ladies, adjusting stirrups or holding the horses' heads for the youngest and smallest of their charges. Upper-class young ladies learning to ride, or young ladies who think they are upper-class which is much the same thing, are similar all the world over and these could as easily have been part of the rural background in Leicestershire or Maryland but they were Spanish and this was Carmona. As I watched I became conscious of someone standing beside me and turned to find one of the two men from the only other table that was occupied peering over my shoulders to watch. "Elegante," he murmured with a wonderful inflection to his voice that defied analysis so that I was not certain whether he was mocking or sober, impressed or amused. After further cavorting and posturing the "sergeant-major" gave a word of command and they set off at a walk down the hill.

I took one last impression of Carmona with me the next morning. I had already paid my bill the night before so had only to deposit my key and depart which I did at a quarter to eight; yet the ancient "concierge" was already in place. I greeted her and then handed her my key and, to my astonishment, what I had thought of as her inflexible grimness gave way to a token smile: not quite a real smile but a gesture of the lips in that direction. The bus stop bar was already doing a thriving early morning trade: still old men; coffee and aperitifs; and dominoes. The big bus arrived on time and I was on my way to fabled Córdoba.

17

Córdoba within its Moorish Walls

The Jewish quarter—the Moorish walls—the cathedral-mosque—compared with Sancta Sofia—ambivalent Borrow—the British criminal classes

THERE is a marvellous scenic view of Córdoba from across the Guadalquivir by the ancient, many-arched bridge: the squat mass of the great mosque with the later baroque tower of the cathedral, which enveloped the original minaret, rising behind it, dominates the city skyline and though it is not especially tall its immensity succeeds in dwarfing everything else. Also across the bridge stands the monumental gate erected by Philip II and to the left of it the Alcázar. The river was high and lush vegetation covered the islets in mid-stream while the Moorish walls with their crenellated battlements had the unreal appearance of picture-book castles.

Borrow begins by being almost totally dismissive of the city except for its situation and the cathedral-mosque. "Little can be said with respect to the town of Cordova, which is a mean, dark, gloomy place, full of narrow streets and alleys, without squares or public buildings worthy of attention, save and except its far-famed cathedral; its situation, however, is beautiful and picturesque."[1]

Much, of course, depends upon the eye of the beholder, and the mean and narrow streets and alleys that so signally failed to attract Borrow are in fact the enchanting white-painted and flower-bedecked

Jewish quarter, which to the modern visitor at least forms one of the principal attractions of the city. The quarter extends all round the mosque and simply to wander about in it and peer through doors into courtyards that are cooled by fountains or enter one of the tiny bars can be an engrossing morning's occupation.

Borrow continues his description of the city: "The town or city is surrounded on all sides by lofty Moorish walls, which may measure about three-quarters of a league in circumference; unlike Seville, and most other towns in Spain, it has no suburbs." That last statement is no longer true, and though the lofty Moorish walls look impressive from across the Guadalquivir, to the west, north and east the old city is engulfed by its growing modern counterpart which now merges into extensive suburbs, for present-day Córdoba has a population of about 300,000.

Although my first objective was the mosque I did not hurry but wandered through the city where the fancy took me, past eleven elegant Roman columns forming three sides of what had once been a temple which rose stark and beautiful against a cloud-bedecked blue sky and through the lanes and alleys so easily dismissed by Borrow that were now crowded with the early summer tourists until I came to the great jewel of Córdoba: the *mezquita-catedral* or combined mosque and cathedral.

Much has been written about this astonishing building which is unique in a double sense: first, for its Moorish architecture which Borrow describes as follows: "In shape is was quadrangular, with a low roof, supported by an infinity of small and delicately rounded marble pillars, many of which still remain, and present at first sight the appearance of a marble grove." And second, because of the sixteenth-century Christian cathedral that was built in the centre of it after the Moors had been expelled. Only in Istanbul has a comparable process taken place: there the great Christian church of Justinian, Sancta (later Hagia) Sofia, was converted by the Ottoman Turks under Mehmet II the Conqueror into a mosque: the Ottomans, however, did not spoil the interior except, as Gibbon tells us, "the walls, which were covered with images and mosaics, were washed and purified, and restored to a state of naked simplicity," although, outside, minarets were later added. It was the lifelong ambition of Sinan, the most celebrated of Ottoman architects who served Mehmet II and adorned Istanbul with his finest creations, to build something as beautiful as Sancta Sofia.

It is interesting and strangely symbolic that two of the world's most impressive religious monuments—the mosque in Córdoba and Sancta Sofia in Istanbul—each served both Christianity and Islam in turn though in the former case the Moors originally agreed to take only half of the existing Christian church, allowing the Christians to continue using the other half alongside them, and only later took over the entire site for their great mosque, while in Istanbul the Turks at once converted Sancta Sofia into a mosque.

Borrow describes the unimaginative partial conversion of Córdoba's mosque in terms that reveal the catholic range of his tastes despite his apparent strict adherence to the Protestant faith.

As it at present exists, the temple appears to belong partly to Mahomet, and partly to the Nazarene; and though this jumbling together of massive Gothic architecture with the light and delicate style of the Arabians produces an effect somewhat bizarre, it still remains a magnificent and glorious edifice...[2]

The most famous judgement of all, much quoted yet worthy of repetition, comes from the greatest Christian monarch of the age in which the cathedral was added, the Emperor Charles V who was not pleased by the conversion and said: "You have destroyed something unique to build something commonplace." Luckily for posterity, they had only destroyed a portion of the original and what is left of the mosque, which is the greater part, entirely surrounds and encloses the cathedral.

Despite a constant flow of visitors I was able to lose myself in the forest of marble pillars that extends all round the cathedral, which occupies a central position in the mosque but covers no more than a fifth of the entire site whose vastness is rendered less obvious by the low roof so that, should the rest of the pillars be removed, four more comparable sized cathedrals could be erected on the remains of the original ground plan.

Virginia Woolf wrote: "*The Bible in Spain*, for instance, gives a clear portrait both of Borrow and of Spain, but it would be hard to say where Spain ends and Borrow begins."[3] By the time I reached Córdoba I had become increasingly bemused by Borrow's ambivalence: was he really the stern, bigoted Protestant dispenser of Testaments whom the Bible Society imagined they had sent to Spain; or was his hatred of the papacy at least as much coloured by his early upbringing as the son of an English soldier and a part of that English heritage which saw the Pope as the Scarlet Woman of Rome rather than from any clear conviction that the

Protestant message was the only one? Gypsies, the low life, travel and the very un-Christian sin of pride in his philological and linguistic achievements seem more than to offset the small total of Testaments he managed to dispose of during five years in Spain. Sometimes, as the reader follows Borrow through Spain in the pages of his book, it is as though he realised he ought to include another passage relating to his missionary activities so as to reassure the Bible Society back in England.

ల

The Sierra Morena hills rise just outside the town and Borrow describes them as planted to the top with olive trees; he walked up them more than once during his stay in the city. Now, unfortunately, urban sprawl has made its way up the slopes. The Guadalquivir is crossed by one of the finest Romano-Moorish bridges anywhere in Spain, its ends guarded by redoubtable gateways, the river acting as a wide moat on the southern side of the city. To the left of the bridge as one crosses into the city is the Alcázar, but though it is grand enough it cannot compete either as to architecture or beauty with the great mosque.

That evening I sat outside a restaurant in the main square of the modern part of the city and enjoyed a meal of bulls' tails. It was a busy, noisy square and a constant parade of people passing by enlivened my meal. On one side of me there was a large garish pelican belonging to the next-door shop and designed for the pleasure of small children who could sit on it and have a rocking ride at a few pesetas a time, but though the entire evening passed without the pelican attracting a single customer it never ceased its high-pitched mechanical squeaking which, after a while, I came to accept as a novel form of background music. The table on my other side was empty when I arrived but was to be occupied by two Englishmen. They were men in their mid-thirties, large and strong-bodied whose athletic muscularity was now inclining to the thickness which is brought on by too much good living rather than exercise. They had rough, indeterminate accents, complexions long darkened by the Spanish sun and the easy-going bonhomie of fixers, the kind who knew just when to bribe and when to be threatening, assured of their own capacity to get away with whatever particular nastiness they were up to at the moment. It was a noisy square, the buses stopped right in front of the restaurant, half the traffic of Córdoba came through it and a constant stream of pedestrians loitered past or stopped in groups on the pavement to chat so that, even straining, I could only catch snatches of their conversation and odd snatches they were. "Three years now, I'd like to return but…"; "keep some stashed away, you never know, they might change the law"; "that damned CID bastard, working with the Spanish police, I suppose"; "we knew each other, of course"; "don't be fooled, they watch us." Members of the British criminal fraternity in exile, they were, and I would have liked to hear more.

It was an exceptionally warm night and quite a few of the women who promenaded slowly past held fans; several of these women were short and squat, angularly bulky rather than fat and they reminded me, irresistibly, of paintings by Velázquez whose works contain more than a mere token or representative scattering of dwarves. When, finally, I settled my bill, the proprietor of the pelican came out to close shop and at last deactivated his gruesome toy. The two

Englishmen were still discussing successes and failures in the fraud and embezzlement line and I was tempted to murmur something about criminal elements as I passed them but they were both considerably bigger than me, so I held my peace.

18

Small Towns on the Road to Aranjuez

Andújar's Roman gate—the victory of Bailén—the defile of Despeñaperros—the blind girl of Manzanares—the Spanish Versailles

I now passed through a series of small towns on the great trunk road to Madrid—Andújar, Bailén, La Carolina, Manzanares, Aranjuez. Borrow passes over his journey from Córdoba to Madrid with curious despatch although the places he visited had much of interest and on other occasions might, just as easily, have led him to provide lengthy descriptions. In fact, he says: "Leaving at our right the mountains of Jaen, we passed through Andújar and Bailen, and on the third day reached Carolina, a small but beautiful town on the skirts of the Sierra Morena, inhabited by the descendants of German colonists."[1]

Andújar is a medium-sized town of no obvious attractions and I only spent an afternoon there. Yet, the town had been besieged by Scipio Africanus in 206 BC and possessed one dramatic reminder of its ancient history in the form of an isolated Roman arch. In my wanderings I then saw some of the old houses that date from the fifteenth and sixteenth centuries before I continued on my way to Bailén.

The outskirts of Bailén are not prepossessing: it is the centre of a ceramics industry and ugly factories sprawled along the side of the road although, once I had walked into the centre from the

bus station, the town became more interesting. I took a room at the Hotel Cuatro Caminos, which was an elegant, old-fashioned establishment. Then I went in search of monuments and discovered a grand parade—the Paseo de las Palmiras—which was clearly Bailén's principal promenade where the more elderly members of the community took a solemn evening stroll; symmetrical rows of pollarded palms lined either side of the broad avenue like sentinels while the far end away from the town centre was occupied by a soaring, futuristic monument. This celebrated the fact that Bailén stands at a crossroads—hence the name of my inn—and, more important to patriotism, was the site of the first Spanish victory over the French in 1808 at the beginning of the Peninsular War. A French army of 18,000 soldiers under Dupont was surrounded by General Castaños and forced to surrender. It was such a brilliant victory that for the rest of the war Spanish commanders were tempted to repeat the same tactics whenever they faced the French, no matter what the circumstances or the lay of the land, leading Wellington on various occasions to say: "Now this is not a battle of Baylen: don't attempt to make it a battle of Baylen."[2]

Carolina is dissected by dead straight, narrow streets at right angles to one another and from a central point it is possible to see for half a mile in either direction without curve or impediment until the town begins to falter away. Yet, despite such geometrical precision, I did discover a charming little square whose entrance was guarded by a twin-towered gateway. The square boasted a number of cafés but the one I decided to patronise had menus in French rather than German for the town's founding fathers.

Not far from Carolina is the defile of Despeñaperros which even in quiet times according to Borrow, "has an evil name, on account of the robberies which are continually being perpetrated within its recesses."[3] When he passed through it with his servant Borrow claimed that the pass was swarming with banditti—although he did not meet any—and though he said he expected to be robbed, he was attended with his usual good luck and did not see even a single individual in the pass although occasionally hearing "whistles and loud cries". There is nothing like passing close to danger but not actually having to suffer any of its ill effects, and throughout *The Bible in Spain* Borrow is always close to war and robbers and drama though where the reality left off and his imaginings began is hard to say.

The journey through the Desfiladero de Despeñaperros was certainly spectacular. It is still possible to imagine the howls of wolves and men—the fierce robbers of Borrow's time—and especially in winter, but now the great highway splits into two roads, one for the traffic in either direction, and these are often separated from each other by several hundred metres of wild, gorse- and shrub-covered hillside.

❧

I reached Manzanares in the middle of an exceptionally hot day, and while Borrow describes it as a large village it may now be described as a small town. Borrow recounts how he met a ragged blind girl in Manzanares and the encounter is one of the more bizarre episodes in his story.

> *I was standing in the market-place conversing with a curate, when a frightful ragged object presented itself; it was a girl about eighteen or*

nineteen, perfectly blind, a white film being spread over her huge staring eyes. Her countenance was as yellow as that of a Mulatto.[4]

Borrow thinks she is a gypsy and addresses her in Gitano, but though she understands she replies that she can use a better language and then proceeds to speak in exceedingly good Latin, which, she says, she had been taught by a Jesuit. The two of them converse in Latin while a crowd gathers to applaud the girl, although they cannot understand a word that is being said, because she could answer the Englishman. When she learns that he is English she says she has always loved Britain, "which was once the nursery of saints and sages," and she goes on to mention Bede, Alcuin, Columbus and Thomas of Canterbury. But such good times had passed "since the reappearance of Semiramis (Elizabeth)." The crowd make a collection for her and Borrow goes on his way.

This passage reveals a great deal about Borrow. First, he is the centre of attention. Second, he demonstrates, as he never tires of doing, his familiarity and fluency with languages. Third, and what is much more interesting, he suggests through the instrument of the blind girl that there was a golden age in Britain in the days when the country adhered to the Catholic faith but that this had passed when the country turned Protestant under Elizabeth whom she likens to Semiramis the ancient Assyrian queen sometimes confused with the goddess of love and war. It is idle to speculate but interesting to wonder just what the more perceptive members of the Bible Society made of that and other odd Borrow passages. Was he just having fun; or was he suggesting a personal affinity with the religion whose Pope he constantly derides?

I decided not to stay in Manzanares but to make straight for Aranjuez, a name which I experienced particular difficulty pronouncing. I went to a travel agent to find out train times and gave the girl enormous pleasure as I stumbled, hopelessly, over the name Aranjuez and when at last I thought I had finally mastered the pronunciation correctly and tried it out I merely sent her off once more in peals of laughter.

I had time to kill before my train, so relaxed over a slow lunch in a pleasant little restaurant until I was the sole remaining diner. My host now decided upon conversation.

"You are on holiday in Spain?"

"Not a holiday; I am following a trail."

"What do you mean, a trail?"

"I am following the road taken by an Englishman a hundred and fifty years ago."

"And what was this Englishman doing on his trail?"

"He was selling Protestant Bibles."

Nonplussed by this reply, my host paused, then switched his line of questioning. "Where have you been?"

I shrugged: Lisbon, Evora, Badajoz, Toledo, Madrid, Cádiz— Gibraltar, "although that was a diversion," but he did not bat an eyelid or rise to my bait as I had hoped. "Seville, Córdoba," and I paused to take a sip of wine.

"And this Englishman sold Protestant Bibles?"

"Sometimes. Sometimes he gave them away. The authorities and the priests did not like what he was doing, of course."

"And what was his name, this man with his Bibles?"

"George Borrow; he was famous. You put him in prison."

He rubbed his hands at that. "And why did we put him in prison, what crimes had he committed?"

"Selling Protestant Bibles—in Catholic Spain."

My host laughed at this but we were entering deep theological waters, which, clearly, he wished to avoid, so he changed the subject and asked me where I was going next. I produced my map and we pored over it, tracing the rest of my planned route in the north of the country. "If you do all that, Señor, you will have seen more of Spain than I have." He brought a bottle of wine and two fresh glasses and we toasted George Boor—ow.

When finally I stepped out of the cool of the little restaurant into the street the heat rose up from the pavement to assault me and I made my way with careful slowness towards the railway station. It was a slow train and stopped seven times before we reached Aranjuez; the land through which we passed was mainly flat though I did see the occasional windmill standing stark on a hillock or hump of land for we were now in La Mancha. The station at Aranjuez is large and ornate, if also fading, for it has seen better days. The approach to Aranjuez had not been impressive; we had skirted dilapidated housing and what appeared to be a deserted and collapsing factory so that I was quite unprepared for what was to come. From the station I walked down a dark avenue of great overhanging trees whose shade provided welcome coolness; this led directly to the rear façade of the eighteenth-century royal palace, which has been described as the Spanish Versailles. The town lies in the Tagus valley with hills rising sharply to one side of it.

Borrow's description of Aranjuez might have been written for a travel guide:

> *A lovely spot is Aranjuez, though in desolation: here the Tagus flows through a delicious valley, perhaps the most fertile in Spain; and here upsprang, in Spain's better days, a little city, with a small but beautiful palace, shaded by enormous trees, where royalty delighted to forget its cares.*[5]

Today Aranjuez is a major tourist attraction, not least because it is in easy reach of Madrid. It became a royal summer residence in the eighteenth century and the palace, which is a storehouse of treasures, was completed in 1758. The town lay on the other side of the great façade to which I had come as I approached from the station. It was an attractive town whose main street consisted of an immensely broad tree-lined avenue that led away from the palace gates and formal gardens. This was crowded with visitors and lined with restaurants. Borrow, indulging his romanticism, recounts how Ferdinand VII spent his latter days surrounded by lovely Señoras and Andalusian bull-fighters but, as he writes,

> *When the sensual king went to his dread account, royalty deserted it, and it soon fell into decay. Intriguing courtiers no longer crowd its halls; its spacious circus, where Manchegan bulls once roared in rage and agony, is now closed, and the light tinkling of guitars is no longer heard amidst its groves and gardens.*[6]

That picture of decay has been reversed though not by royalty returning to its palace. The bullring, which I visited, was far from crumbling and clearly in present-day use and the crowds, though not courtiers, were certainly bringing a measure of prosperity to the town.

19

Power and Perception

*El Escorial—a monument to power—Protestant England
and Catholic Spain—Philip II—Guadarrama—a strange
English woman—the Royal Theatre of Charles III*

OF fifty-seven chapters in *The Bible in Spain*, covering five years in
the country, Borrow devotes no fewer than fifteen to his journey to
the north. There, admittedly, he sold relatively few Testaments for
the simple reason that he did not have them to sell although when
he reaches Oviedo, as a sort of compensation, he tells the remarkable
story, almost certainly a figment of his imagination, of the Ten
Gentlemen of Oviedo who congratulate him on his Bible distributing
activities. It is as though, having travelled his wonderful route from
Madrid to Salamanca to La Coruña, to Vigo to Cape Finisterre and
then along the north coast to Oviedo, he suddenly recalled the Bible
Society back in London and thought he had better show that his
efforts—largely *sans* Bibles—were nonetheless bearing fruit.

On leaving Aranjuez I went straight through Madrid to El Escorial,
in readiness to tackle the major walking part of my journey. Borrow
did not visit El Escorial but rode forth from Madrid with his servant
Antonio "by the gate of San Vincente, directing our course to the
lofty mountains which separate Old from New Castile. That night
we rested at Guadarrama, a large village at their foot, distant from
Madrid about seven leagues."[1]

El Escorial is some forty kilometres from Madrid and I decided to
visit Guadarrama from there. Madrid has the immense advantage of
the Guadarrama mountains so that, within a few miles of the capital,
it is possible to enjoy spectacular scenery and cool breezes even in the

height of summer as the road rises sharply through the mountains and these provide a dramatic backdrop for the great monastic palace of Philip II.

Uncompromising, grim, massive and grey, the Escorial is one of the greatest monuments to power in Europe. It is an astonishing place: perfect in its architectural symmetry, forbidding and formidable in size, it was created for Philip II, who might well be dubbed the gloomy monarch, when Spain was the dominant power in Europe and her empire in the Americas had already been expanded to its greatest extent. The grey-stone symmetry of that great pile is awe-inspiring, its huge façades unrelieved by any breaks in their patterns of endless rectangular, prison-like windows, the immensity of the whole structure suggesting a world within that had little need of, or interest in, the brighter, more seductive but less enduring life outside its gloomy portals.

Philip wanted not just a monastery but a royal pantheon where all the monarchs of Spain would be buried, and the twenty-four marble tombs of kings in the deep vault are indeed one of its most impressive offerings to posterity. Although the Escorial was begun by the architect Juan Bautista de Toledo, he died in 1567 and it was his successor, Juan de Herrera, who stamped upon it the style and gloom that have made it unique. It is the scale as well as the grim greyness of the granite that make the whole so impressively forbidding. The library which Philip founded contains some of the most beautiful illuminated manuscripts in the world as well as 40,000 books, while the king's own modest royal apartments are in marked contrast to the far more opulent royal chambers of other European monarchs, perhaps a conscious message, a deliberate snub, that power did not need trappings although it could as easily be argued that the message of the apartments is contradicted, rather than supported, by the vast austerity of the monastery that surrounds them. When he was dying Philip II, who had his coffin placed in his room as a reminder of mortality and what was to come, had himself carried in a litter to the Escorial from Madrid so that he could be interred in his gloomy masterpiece.

There are wonderful partisan English sketches of Philip in James Froude's twelve-volume *History of England,* which in fact only covers the short period from the fall of Wolsey to the Spanish Armada. Froude saw the sixteenth century as the period when the forces of liberty that had been released in England by the Reformation were struggling against the forces of darkness as represented by the

Roman Catholic Church which, for that period, was synonymous with Philip's Spain. Though his history is often questionable, Froude's sense of the rightness of Protestant England as opposed to the menace of Catholic Spain strikes a nationalist chord that made his work immensely popular. He conveys this sense of a menaced England through his portrait of Philip, who came to England in 1554 when still a prince to marry Queen Mary while the Pope and his legate and the Emperor Charles V argued as to how England could be brought back into the Catholic fold. This was not to be and thirty years later Philip II as he had then become sent his Armada against Elizabeth's England. When the news of its terrible destruction came filtering back to Spain, piecemeal, one disaster after another, Philip was so affected that "he shut himself up in the Escurial, and no one dared to speak to him," and the honour of its destruction—*Toda la gloria se da a Drake*—belonged to Drake.[2]

It is possible to spend hours in the apartments of the palace, which houses some of Spain's greatest paintings including El Greco's Martyrdom of St Maurice and Velázquez' gloomy yet appropriate portrait of Philip II, dressed all in black. The king's aesthetic face is stern and strained for he had become weighed down by the problems of his immense empire. He worked tirelessly, alone in his small office, reading endless memoranda about every problem of his extensive dominions as though he alone could solve them. He rarely took advice and always championed the Catholic Church, so much so that even the Vatican which ought to have welcomed such support from the greatest monarch of Europe often found it impossible to distinguish between the interests of the Church and the interests of Spain, which he appeared to treat as one. His Protestant enemies represented him as bigoted and cruel yet this is unfair; for example, after the Spanish victory over the French at St Quentin in 1557 the young Philip is said to have developed a permanent aversion to war. He was, however, deeply suspicious of even his closest confidants and implicated in at least one murder, that of Juan de Escobedo, the secretary of Don John of Austria.

G. K. Chesterton, that most exuberant of English writers, provides a cruelly partisan "Protestant" view of Philip in his poem "Lepanto", which was published in 1911, eleven years before Chesterton himself became a convert to the Roman Catholic Church:

> *King Philip's in his closet with the Fleece about his neck.*
>
> ...
>
> *The walls are hung with velvet that is black and soft as sin,*
> *And little dwarfs creep out of it and little dwarfs creep in.*
> *He holds a crystal phial that has colours like the moon,*
> *He touches, and it tingles, and he trembles very soon,*

And his face is as a fungus of a leprous white and grey,
Like plants in the high houses that are shuttered from the day,
And death is in the phial, and the end of noble work...

ოჳ

The next day, which was shining and beautiful, I walked the short
distance to Guadarrama, which lies a mere ten kilometres from El
Escorial. I had only a light pack and cherries to eat along the way as
I was returning for another night at El Escorial but the sight of the
mountains and woods under a brilliant sun was a wonderful contrast
to my meditations upon power the day before in Philip's great palace.

I overtook a group of walkers, the first I met in Spain, as they
headed for Guadarrama, and since they were widely spread out in
ones, twos and threes I thought I might have company for the entire
length of my short walk. They were a mixed lot, young and old,
men and women who greeted me in friendly if also curious fashion
surprised it seems, at the appearance of a solitary foreigner out
walking. To my relief they soon turned off at a campsite and I had
the road to myself once more.

Guadarrama appeared still to be no more than a large village at the
foot of the mountains, little more than a built up area at a crossroads.
On the other side of this mountain range, which acts as a natural
barrier running across the centre of Spain, lies Old Castile. There was
little of interest to keep me in Guadarrama and so, after a coffee, I
walked back to El Escorial.

Apart from the vast patio or parade in front of the Escorial Palace
the little town boasts several small, quaint squares in which ordinary
mortals can sit without feeling dwarfed by such sober magnificence.
That evening I sat at the side of a square which sloped quite sharply
downwards from its upper reaches towards the Escorial below to sip
wine and watch the people gather for their evening's aperitifs.

Arches came down over the pavement on either side of the square
and across from where I was sitting my attention was caught by a
woman who came meandering slowly, without apparent purpose,
between the pillars while she tilted her head back to catch the late

sun. This action, which I think was unpremeditated, had a quite different effect so that she appeared to be consciously inspecting the people at each table she passed, and doing so moreover, down a long straight nose to convey an impression of remote hauteur. I was intrigued and watched her progress down to the bottom of the square where she made her way slowly across and then began to ascend on my side. Possibly she was a beggar, I thought, but if so she was hardly pursuing her calling with any prospect of success, so perhaps this was her day off. She was a striking woman, willowy thin, her only garment a long loose dress that fell well below her knees, bare legs and sandals beneath. Her hair was a dark sandy colour, long and straight, and reached below her shoulders, her thin face, despite her efforts to catch the sun, was unnaturally pale, high-cheekboned, the normal tautness of the skin enhanced by fasting. She had cloudy grey-blue eyes, a full sensuous mouth that was at odds with the rest of her features and the wonderful straight nose down which she looked with such arrogant assurance. From across the square she had appeared no more than twenty-five or thirty, but close up I saw she could not be less than forty and might be older although her features had an ageless quality that rendered any judgement difficult. I thought of her as an older version of Borrow's young prophetess at Manzanares though there was nothing wrong with her sight and, as she approached, half expected her to address me in Latin. She passed my table, wrapped in her personal remoteness, but then looked back quickly, startled as one is when something suddenly registers. She walked up to my table.

"English, of course," she said without any interrogative inflection in her voice.

"Naturally, how did you know?"

"You are unmistakable."

"But I am often taken for a Scandinavian or a German," I said.

"But how absurd!" and she laughed softly, a curious lilt to her voice; "those who think that cannot have any perception—or judgement," she added. Her voice was pure Bloomsbury and her features, I realised, were not unlike pictures of Virginia Woolf. I waved her to a seat. "English of course," I said.

"May I?" and she joined me.

I signalled to a waiter: "A glass of wine?"

She turned her gaze upon the people at the nearby tables who, understandably, had been intrigued by her performance as well as her appearance, and now under her flickering yet casual gaze they withdrew their attention uneasily while giving me covert glances instead. The glass of wine came and she sipped it appreciatively. Briefly, the thought again crossed my mind that she wished to beg but I dismissed it at once; begging was not her way though acceptance, as of right, of anything that would assist her progress in whatever direction that might take her was another matter.

"You are not an ordinary tourist," she said in her strange lilting voice, "what are you?" Amused by a curiosity which also flattered, I replied to a question that normally I would have taken to be an impertinence: "I like perceptive people; I am a traveller."

"And where do you travel, what is your trail?"

"I am on the Borrow trail."

"George Borrow, *The Bible in Spain*. What a wonderful thing to do. But," after a pause that might equally have been a drawl, "you don't look a Bible person to me."

"No indeed, but why should I be a Bible person to follow such a trail?" I had had this conversation before with the American couple in Evora. "I just like trails."

"Yes, of course" she said.

Even after this short conversation, which had begun so unusually, I was aware of a dwindling interest, as thought the effort of making contact with me had already become a burden to her.

"And you?" I asked, but I knew at once that my question was a mistake and provided her with the cue she needed: she wanted to return to whatever private world she inhabited that the sight of me, for whatever reminder of the past I had evoked, had so briefly interrupted. She shook her head, finished her glass of wine and came, or rather flowed, to her feet in a single extraordinarily graceful movement: "It was a pleasure to meet you," she spoke lightly, as though she had been my hostess at a superior London party and then, without a backward glance, she resumed her slow erratic walk round the square. The meeting left me with a sense of sadness: for whatever reason, the sight of me had brought her back briefly to some part of a world from which she had escaped but now, like a wild animal, she had feared to be trapped and had withdrawn at once at my question. The temperature dropped sharply, affected by the chill air descending from the mountains, and I moved inside the restaurant behind me for my supper. My strange interlocutor in her flimsy dress was then sitting on a low wall at the top of the square, staring wide-eyed yet unseeing over the busy scene below her.

There is a charming little late eighteenth-century theatre in the centre of Escorial, the Royal Theatre of Charles III, all pale blue and gilt, elegant tiers of boxes, the whole intimate and welcoming and after supper I went to a piano recital by a young pianist, Felipe Ramirez, who gave a sparkling performance of Scarlatti, Brahms, Liszt, Chopin, Szymanowsky and Prokofieff.

20

Inquisitor and Saint

*Beyond the Guadarramas—cyclists—bungee jumpers—the
square of Navalperal—Sunday evening relaxation—endless
vistas—the walls of Avila—Torquemada—Pope Alexander
VI—St Teresa of Avila*

THE next day presented me with a series of images as I began some
serious walking, thirty-five kilometres of high passes and stunning
views that unfolded sharp and clear from hilltops under the brilliant
sun only to merge into a distant grey-blue haze, and being taken
unawares by silent cyclists on their low slung bicycles as they came
up the hill behind me, and watching with a sense of awe as young
bungee jumpers hurled themselves into the depths of a great gorge
from the high bridge I crossed a hundred and fifty metres above the
sparkling stream which twisted and turned among its rocks below me.
And so on that long and dramatic walk there opened out before me a
panorama of Old Castile.

I walked out of Escorial early that morning along a tree-lined
avenue of grand houses sheltered behind high walls; most of them
kept what clearly were ferocious guard dogs so that my passage along
the otherwise deserted and silent road was marked by the deep-
throated growls and warning barks of these vicious Cerberuses which
ran furiously among the bushes behind their walls to see me on my
way. Then I came into open country and the road rose through
rounded, ancient hills, which reminded me of Scotland. When I
reached the head of the valley after about eight kilometres I was able
to look back to the great black mass of the Escorial Palace far below

me with the blue Guadarramas stretching behind and beyond it as far as the eye could see.

It was on this walk that I first became aware of cyclists as a recurring feature of the highways. They came in groups wearing bright-coloured silk shirts and shorts, helmeted, with water bottle fixed to their handlebars, small packs on their backs, sometimes in a tight group, at other times widely dispersed in twos and threes. Perhaps the leader would stop to check that the weaker or slower members of the group were not falling too far behind but as a rule they were so intent upon the physical act of cycling that they had no energy to spare even, as I discovered, for greetings. If I saw them coming towards me I would always wave or call a salutation. If they came from behind they would be upon me before I was aware of their passage and though I would then call a greeting they were often unable to do more than grunt an acknowledgement, while some were so fixed upon their task as not even to glance across the road at me, begrudging even that amount of effort for, as I soon learnt, they were not just cycling but following a designated route, aiming for particular checkpoints within specified times. In any case, though I met or was passed by cyclists on many different stretches of road, I was most usually taken by surprise going up hills when they came behind me and only a faint click at the last moment would cause me to turn my head just as a group of cyclists levelled with me as they puffed and sweated their way up a steep incline. Occasionally I was embarrassed by their silent arrival since on those long lonely walks it was my habit to hold conversations with myself and I considered it an invasion of my privacy if I had just reached a particular point in my argument only to find an unlooked for interloper silently passing by, cycling for a moment at my side to snatch, as it were, a fragment of my discussion away from me.

That first pass was at a height of 1,236 metres; then I commenced a long descent down one side of a green valley speckled with small red-roofed villages far below me. Huge guardian dogs watched me speculatively from lonely farms and then a great pine forest rose up on one side of the road before I came to the bottom of the long descent through the little village of La Paradilla and across the gorge of the Cofio where the bungee jumpers were performing. After that I had to rise again and the ascent seemed much longer than the earlier ascent as it was noon and the midday sun was blazing overhead. It must have been about three o'clock when I finally walked off the road for about a kilometre into Navalperal de Pinares.

There is a small square in the centre of Navalperal and one end of this is occupied by an inn. I am not certain whether Navalperal should be described as a large village or a small town. It had a railway station, it is true, but then every village the length of the valley had a stop or halt. There were a few shops and a church and playing fields and the whole was quite extensive but in the end I decided it was a village. It was certainly not on any tourist route. The bar and restaurant of the inn were crowded and the air of greater than normal relaxation reminded me it was Sunday. There was a pool table in the firm occupation of four youths and several card games in progress and the usual group of devotees glued to the television set and a boisterous

crowd three deep at the bar and all were Spanish. I asked for a room, and a great Hercules of a young man led me through the bar and upstairs to the first floor where he handed me over to two women, a mother and daughter, who settled me into a pleasant room with a balcony.

"You are walking?" inquired the younger woman.

"Yes, from El Escorial," I replied.

"Holy Mary," said the older woman, "now that is a walk!"

Later, when I descended to the bar, it was just as packed as before but the noise level had increased by a substantial number of decibels as the drinkers were getting into their Sunday evening stride. I took my drink outside to sit with my back to the inn: one side of the square was occupied by a small unpretentious town hall, the other side boasted a couple of dilapidated buildings and at the far end was a café. A small wall enclosed the centre of the square, which contained a fountain; the wall had been constructed by a thoughtful architect to the correct height to act as a seat and much of it was occupied, for the Sunday evening promenaders were now out in force. A foursome played cards at the table next to mine, a family group sat on the other side of me while a constant stream of people came to the inn, which was clearly the undisputed centre of social life for the village. An elderly man of somewhat dishevelled appearance walked across the little square clapping his hands. No one took any notice. The huge young man from behind the bar came outside from time to time to see that all was well, moving among the tables with the slow relaxed assurance of one who knew he could cope with anything and anybody. The square filled with people who paraded slowly round it or sat on the little wall to gossip with their friends and watch the children play. The clapping man returned to clap his way back across the square in the direction from which he had first appeared. No one took any notice.

I decided to explore the village though there was not a great deal to explore. I inspected the little railway station and was watched gloomily by an immense dog behind the high iron railings of a big house near the church; a notice on the gate informed me that the dog was unchained and he padded silently by my side as I passed his railings. The church occupied high ground from which it was possible to oversee the whole village. I found my way to a small park that was crowded with evening strollers and boys playing football, and another immense dog on a leash made a *de rigueur* lunge at me as I passed. Back at the inn I resumed my place outside to watch the square and do some sketching. The clapping man made another appearance and was ignored as before. I noticed that there was not a great deal of money in evidence, and though families or groups ordered refreshments they did so sparingly and then nursed a single drink, often a soft drink, for the rest of the evening. In any case, the drink was the excuse for sitting with friends rather than the reason for coming out. By nine o'clock when tiredness from my walk as well as hunger suggested I should go in search of food the square was humming with activity, working up to the climax of its role as the Sunday evening centre for fashionable Navalperal de Pinares. Four small boys played a ferocious game of football with a coke can in the middle of the square but though their nuisance value was clearly high no one scolded them or seemed remotely to mind. The church bell tolled, deep and melodious, and at half past nine I went into the dining room where I was the only living-in eating-in customer and ate in solitary state: soup, a steak, a *flan*, an extra egg compliments of the house because she thought I needed it, a bottle of wine and coffee. Then I settled my bill ready for an early morning start and slept like a log all night.

∞

There is nothing like walking in the early morning when no one is about and a haze lies over the land and there is a bite in the air, which is fresh and clear before the sun has warmed it too much. I rose steadily until I came to the pass of Alto Valdelavia at 1,448 metres and then walked for half the morning across the top of the hills to enjoy green-to-blue-to-grey vistas stretching into such distances that it was not possible to be certain just where the land gave way to the sky. Valleys dropped away steeply from the ridge I walked and periodically the railway would emerge far below me from one of its many tunnels, sometimes to be carried by high viaducts that would have brought joy to Borrow's heart. The middle part of my walk that day was across the high mass of the hills. I came to another pass at 1,334 metres and then to the "gates" of the old Camino Real or Royal Highway before I began the long descent onto the plain, which is dominated by the ancient walled city of Avila.

The road ran straight for ten kilometres across the high plain to Avila, which stood on a hill that appeared to gather the plain to it from all sides. On the skyline of the hilltop a huge church or cathedral rose to dominate the rest of the town. I never seemed to get any closer on that last stretch of the highway, but that is a phenomenon which often occurs when one is walking towards a town on a dead-straight road. But at last I rose steeply into Avila and, for once, asked a man to direct me to an inn. He looked at my backpack and my perspiring face, for the hill into the town had taken its final toll, and gave me directions to "some cheap rooms, only 200 pesetas a night." At this ridiculous sum I raised an eyebrow.

"Yes, yes, only 200, not 2,000," he insisted so I thanked him for his kindness and started off in the direction he had indicated; this brought me to a very poor section of the town from which I retraced my steps and went searching on my own. But, as Borrow said of a similar occasion, if you travel on a mule you ought not to give yourself airs!

I had approached Avila from the south-east to enter the modern part of the city and did not at once recall what I knew of it so that it was only after wandering and asking directions of a policeman that I came to the old city of St Teresa. The walls alone are worth a visit: they date from the twelfth century and their circumference of 2,500 metres, which includes eighty-eight round towers, completely encircles the medieval city. They are regarded as the finest walls in all Spain. At 1,128 metres Avila is the highest city in Spain and has lofty mountain ranges to the east and south of it. Romans, Visigoths, Moors and Christians have each left their mark but its fame rests upon two contrasting Christian figures, the grim fifteenth-century Dominican Torquemada, the first Grand Inquisitor of Spain, who died at Avila in 1498 and is buried in the city, and the sixteenth-century ascetic nun and mystic, St Teresa of Avila, who was born there in 1515.

They are an astonishing pair from the Catholic hierarchy of Spain: both obsessed with sin, the one burned heretics, the other prayed for them in poverty. Torquemada was born at Valladolid in 1420 and joined the Dominican Order. A nationalist religious fanatic, he saw Jews and Moors—both those who had converted to Roman Catholicism and those who had retained their own faiths—as a threat to Spain and before he died had played a major part in forcing 170,000 Jews to leave Spain for ever. He became Grand Inquisitor in 1483, first for Castile and León, and then for Aragon, Catalonia, Valencia and Majorca, and travelled the country establishing tribunals to examine suspected heretics, producing a twenty-eight article guide for inquisitors to help them judge crimes of heresy, apostasy, witchcraft, bigamy, usury and blasphemy. Over the years these tribunals handled 100,000 suspects of whom 2,000 were burnt at the stake while others were fined or in other ways forced to do penance while six to seven thousand are said to have been burnt in effigy,[1] which, at least, was better than being burnt in person. Torquemada was also credited with burning 6,000 volumes in one day at Seville.[2] His harshness proved too much even for that fanatical age: ascetic in his private life but ready to use torture on others, he became a symbol of cruelty, bigotry and fanaticism. In 1494 when he was seventy-four and still going strong, outrage at his methods led Valencia-born Pope Alexander VI to appoint four assistant inquisitors to restrain him.

It was fitting that this most worldly of Popes, the corrupt pleasure-loving Borgia patron of the arts, who possessed in high degree an ingrained understanding of the natural wickedness of mankind, the antithesis in almost every respect to the fanatical Grand Inquisitor, should have been called upon to restrain the grim septuagenarian Torquemada. There is a wonderful representation of Pope Alexander, a side view of his fat face and hooked nose, as he poses, trying unsuccessfully to look devout, hands elegantly together for public relations purposes, the suspicion of an amused smile on his lips and at the corner of his one visible eye as he reflects upon the absurdity of the situation in which he finds himself, which appears on a fresco of Pinturicchio in the Vatican. It is in total contrast to the grim, heavy-jowelled face of Torquemada, unsmiling and relentless as no doubt he thinks of further measures to purify both the Church of heretics and Spain of the foreigner, for he was also a leading proponent of the final attack upon Granada and the expulsion of the Moors.

St Teresa of Avila was born seventeen years after Torquemada's death, and in 1535 she entered the Carmelite Convent of the Incarnation in Avila. She was often ill and became a mystic who believed in mental prayer. In 1555 she experienced some form of religious awakening and embarked upon reforming the Carmelite Order, making it revert to austerity and contemplation. She insisted upon total withdrawal so that nuns could meditate upon divine law and work for the reparation of mankind through prayer and penance. Not surprisingly, she met with much worldly opposition from inside and outside the Church since she wished to found convents without endowments, insisting instead that the nuns of her order lived in poverty and depended upon public alms. She founded sixteen convents throughout Spain and eventually, with help from Philip II, obtained independent control over her order. Her mystical and saintly impact—if poverty and contemplation are the true marks of saintliness—was certainly in marked contrast to the brutal readiness to persecute that was Torquemada's hallmark, yet both, in their different ways, were fanatics.

The old city of Avila, inside its ancient walls, is an intriguing place to wander through and, as with other Spanish cities, impresses upon the modern mind the all-pervasive, dominant presence of a Church that was as great or greater than the secular state. Whenever I became aware of this religious power, as I often did through Spain, I breathed a sigh of intense relief that I lived in a modern secular society.

21

The Dwarf of Chaherrero

*The road to Salamanca—a conversation in Aveinte—a bar
full of old men—the inn—a game of cards—the dwarf of
Chaherrero*

I DEPARTED on the opposite side of Avila from that which I had
entered, past medieval walls and rounded towers of a splendour and
degree of preservation that can rarely be equalled; only the absence
of medieval men-at-arms standing in the embrasures kept me in the
twentieth century. Rising behind them, inside the city, was an elegant
little arch perched on the top of four columns, which served no
conceivable purpose that I could discern though it was topped by an
enormous stork's nest. I crossed the ancient bridge over the Adaja and
took the Salamanca road. A short distance along this road a lookout
platform provided a perfect vantage point to observe the city encased
in its walls; it was an overcast day, however, so that the ancient city
looked grim and defensive, the grey of the walls matching the grey of
the clouds.

My plan that day was to walk a mere twenty-two kilometres to the
small town of San Pedro del Aveinte, and though at first it looked
like rain and I was to experience a number of showers the breeze was
bracing and cool to make it perfect walking weather. I rose through
oak forests, breasted long hills to see great horizons stretching before
me or looked down on little red-roofed hamlets nestling in the steep

valleys below. As usual the day produced its quota of dogs: sometimes on long chains at the gates of farms, sometimes unchained and ready to walk parallel with me until I had passed their territory. There was a fair amount of traffic on the road though not enough to make walking uncomfortable but I met no people at all—neither walking nor cycling or even leaning over gates.

At the small village of Aveinte, about eighteen kilometres from Avila, I entered a tiny village shop to buy bread and cheese.

"We have no bread, but does the Señor wish to eat it now?" She was a friendly woman and had already produced a beer for me. I did want to eat it now, I told her, so she asked me to wait and disappeared into her living quarters at the back of the shop to return with her own fresh bread. So I sat at a tiny rickety table at the side of the shop and ate the bread with cheese and drank my beer. I do not think this was her normal custom but her hospitality was certainly welcome. Then, delicately, not to appear intrusive, she asked: "Has the Señor come far?"

"From Avila," I told her.

"And before that?"

"From El Escorial."

"And where are you going?"

"Salamanca," I said.

"And then?"

She had a happy sense of humour and we played a game: gradually I extended my trip backwards to Lisbon, mentioning the places I had already passed through and, alternately, took her forwards as well— Salamanca to La Coruña, Cape Finisterre and along the north coast.

"Why?" she wanted to know, which I had guessed would come next, so I explained about George Borrow but aided, or rather hindered, by my inadequate Spanish, she got lost in the intricacies of his Bible peddling activities. And then her husband came into the shop and I was obliged to go over my route again. When finally I left they both sent me on my way with good wishes for my "long journey through Spain."

The inn at San Pedro del Aveinte was full and I was faced instead, quite late in the day, with the need to walk another twelve kilometres to the next inn so that what I had intended as a relatively short walk became a long one. I was now passing through wheat country, and vast undulating fields of yellow wheat, ripe for harvesting, bent and rippled before the breeze whose direction could be followed to the far horizon as the yellow shades changed to mark its progress. Tiny hamlets rose out of the sea of yellow, red roofs above white walls that gleamed in the sunlight, while behind them forbidding storm clouds piled up to the heavens.

☙

Chaherrero was a tiny village to one side of the road with a half square opening onto the highway. I saw no sign of the inn but an old man whom I asked directed me down a small lane. The little village street appeared neglected as though all modern developments had bypassed it, keeping carefully to the main highway instead. Ahead of me two men greeted each other and entered what might be an inn though, if so, it was on a very modest scale. Then, there came tottering towards me an ancient one-eyed man whose heavy walking stick clearly served him better than his frail bandy legs. I greeted him and pointed at the building ahead: "Hostal?" "Si, si," he croaked and waved me into it.

The interior was in semi-darkness; a bar occupied one side of the long low-ceilinged room while several tables filled the centre. At one of these four old men played dominoes while at another two equally aged citizens of Chaherrero sat smoking, their drinks in front of them. My appearance, pack still on my back, brought the game and the talk to an abrupt end, the sudden silence causing a startled host to appear from a back room. "Señor?" he inquired, surprise and curiosity mingling equally. I asked if this establishment was the inn but, no, it was only a bar and he directed me to the inn, which was back on the main road on the other side of the village. I could have reached it by keeping to the highway along which I had walked all day instead of passing through the village at all, but then I should have missed that odd little bar of old men.

The inn was modern and bright and not very busy and I came down from my room to find the bar empty of customers. The host who had registered me was a thickset, surly man of indeterminate late middle age. He was now sitting at a table with another man of similar general appearance and disposition and a third, very old man whose square bald head was balanced with thin-rimmed glasses in front and a fringe of hair like the thinning remains of a monk's tonsure at the back, who turned out to be the host's father. They were absorbed in a game of cards. I asked the thin listless looking girl behind the counter for red wine and she brought a bottle of chilled wine and a dish of olives to my table. I relaxed over the wine, smoked a cigar, ate olives and wrote up my notes while I watched the game of cards at the nearby table.

I became totally engrossed in that game of cards although I had no idea what they were playing. The speed with which they handled the pasteboards showed they had been at it together for years; they must have dealt three or four hands and played them before I really took much notice. It was the shouting that drew my attention to them. I think three or four shouts had registered before I looked up to see why these were delivered with such monotonous yet sharp regularity by the host and directed at the old man, his father. He scolded him for making wrong leads and the old man loved it. He would take no notice when his son shouted at him and they would continue playing until the host roared at his father again. The third player never acknowledged by so much as a twitch that any shouting took place at all, regarding it as a purely family matter beyond his scope. Then a fourth man, another regular crony, joined them to take the vacant place at the card table. The old man had hooked his walking stick over the back of the free chair and the newcomer removed this and hooked it instead on the back of the old man's chair although the latter did not see what had been done.

They played on; the host shouted at his father; the old man won two rounds in a row, so perhaps the shouting was to put him off his winning streak. At one point, according to the rules of the game, the old man was obliged to sit out a round and while this was being played he looked for his walking stick. It was no longer where he had left it and, greatly agitated, he began a peering search until he felt it behind him, hooked over the back of his own chair. Then he relaxed, but first he had to know. Later, I realised that the old man liked being shouted at and braced his ancient shoulders every time his son berated him, an occurrence which was both frequent and regular. Perhaps he was deaf and this was his son's means of communication, a reminder that he was part of the group.

I had been so absorbed in this little scene, drawn to it by the repeated roars of a son at a father, that I had not noticed the arrival of other customers. Now, however, I saw that the bar had been filling up. Behind me, over my left shoulder was a large comfortable upholstered bucket seat standing more or less on its own in the centre of an otherwise empty floor space except for a small table alongside it. The chair was set squarely in front of the television screen which was situated high on the wall; it had been empty when I arrived but was now occupied by a man who had sunk down into the depths of his seat to enjoy the television so that only part of his head appeared above the back of the chair. A motorcycle helmet was on the table beside him. Something about the solitary television watcher drew my attention to him. His head was large with a high brow and a beautifully hooked nose, from my semi-rear view, and it was covered with a shock of white hair. The side of his face had the appearance of an ancient leathery piece of seamed parchment while a cobweb of wrinkles emerged from his eye like the delta of a vast river. He was, I realised, a very old man. My sudden fascination drew his attention to me and he turned his head sharply, birdlike, to reveal startlingly clear beady black eyes which took me in at a glance. Then he nodded, a quick intelligent acknowledgement of my interest, before turning his attention back to the television which was showing an entirely forgettable soap opera. Now a small hand appeared over the side of the chair to grip the arm. It was such a small hand that for a moment I thought he had a child on his lap, hidden from my view by the wing of the chair, but it was his own hand and with it he heaved himself forward as he laughed in a curious high falsetto that came oddly from his big head. He again turned sharply towards me and laughed his high squeak and pointed at the television with his other diminutive little hand as though to inquire why I was not also following the programme. There was a grotesqueness about him, but even then I did not fathom exactly what was bothering me except to realise that no one else at all was paying any attention to the television: it was as if by common consent everyone had left it for his sole entertainment. More shouting from the card table, prolonged this time for some reason, announced a change in that quarter and I looked to see the host get up to attend to his business while his two cronies embarked upon a game with the ancient one, but now without any shouting.

It was time for me to have some supper and I had to pass close to the chair of the solitary television viewer and only then did I see that he was a dwarf: his little legs dangled in front of the bucket chair, his feet well clear of the floor, while his diminutive body was a desperately inadequate match for his noble head. He looked up as I passed and gave a sharp little nod that conveyed his understanding of my understanding: now that I could see that he was a dwarf, he seemed to say, all was explained. It was eerie. I could not help wondering whether he had a dwarf motorcycle waiting to take him home or whether the crash helmet denoted that someone else had brought him there.

I strolled outside before eating to admire a deepening purple sky at the far end of a vast sea of yellow wheat and felt the chill bite of the air for we were at a height of about one thousand metres. Round the back of the inn I disturbed an immense guard dog whose heavy black jowls contrasted with its coat of white fluffy hair. It rumbled a deep-throated growl at me and remained standing at the end of its chain until I had turned the corner of the inn out of its sight.

22

Alba de Tormes and the Dukes

Peñaranda—children at play—a dog makes its kill—the third Duke of Alba—purity of faith—times past

PEÑARANDA lies off the main highway, the approach lined with factories, the skyline dominated by huge grain elevators. Borrow has little to say about his journey from Guadarrama to Salamanca: "No adventure worth relating occurred during this journey. We sold a few Testaments in the villages through which we passed, more especially at Penaranda." What struck me about Peñaranda was the midday absence of people. I entered a square where two small boys were playing and a group of older girls sat talking. In a second square there was a touch more life, but only a touch, though it was elegant enough with stone columns along the sides supporting the upper storeys of the houses to provide a covered walkway. Later that evening I came across a working-class tenement square, all white paint and uniform sameness, the first-floor flats connected by a continuous balcony, the whole ensemble not unlike a set of Peabody Trust tenements in London. I sat outside a bar on one side of this square where I could catch the evening sun, for in the shade it was already becoming cool, and watched about twenty children, aged from ten to fourteen, play a game which required two of them to go off and hide in an obvious spot while the rest linked hands and then came to hunt them as they chanted a song: it was a curiously old-fashioned game, almost a ritual, of the kind that might be found in a book of social history describing

154

the simple pastimes of the young in an earlier age; there was about it a pre-pubescent innocence.

I was away early the next morning, the road straight and deserted, again passing through endless wheat fields. Most of the villages were off to the side of the road and had lovely names—Nava de Sotrobal, Coca de Alba, Peñarandilla, Garcihernandez—and a gentle breeze took the edge from the sun's heat. I watched a magnificent black dog make its hunting kill in a field of stubble: elegant and strong, shiny jet, like a giant whippet with a lithe graceful body and long pointed nose, it stood motionless and took no notice whatever of my approach along the road. I was fifty metres distant when, as though suddenly galvanised, it leapt high in the air, its body a perfect arch, its tail pointing straight to heaven, to land three metres away burying its nose in the stubble. After a long moment it brought its head erect from the ground with the limp body of a rabbit hanging from its jaws. Only then did it give me a sidelong glance, I swear almost of amusement—"you leave me alone and I'll do the same"—before it loped off to the side of the field to find some shade in which to enjoy its feast.

❧

The great wheat plain drops suddenly and sharply into the valley of the Tormes where the old medieval town of Alba de Tormes nestles out of sight. Whatever its past splendours, today Alba de Tormes exists for the wheat farmers and much of the modern part of the town is given over to garages and factories to repair tractors or combine harvesters. I descended through the old town, past a great church, to cross the river by an ancient, many-arched bridge to the Hostal América. The banks of the river were clogged with reeds while little islands in mid-stream were green with lush vegetation.

A massive tower, deserted and forlorn, rises stark and solitary from the centre of the town, with nothing to say what it may once have been. It was the great keep of the castle of the Dukes of Alba, now all that remained of their former grandeur, time and change having destroyed the rest. I did not know what it was at first and when I inquired of the girl in reception at the Hostal América, who was both intelligent and helpful, she shrugged dismissively and was only able to say that it belonged to "times past." Thus much for renown! The Albas are one of the oldest and grandest families of Spain, and the third Duke of Alba, Philip II's captain and counsellor, was the foremost soldier of his age. Devout and ruthless, he epitomised in his person the contradictions of a Spain where temporal and spiritual power were inextricably intertwined. Luis de Camões, the national poet of Portugal, who was the third Duke's contemporary, could write of Spain as it extended its sway over the New World: "And had there been more world they would have reached it" (shades of Marlowe's dying Tamerlaine).[1] In 1580, the year Camões died, Alba led a Spanish army in the most brilliant military campaign of his life to conquer Portugal before he, too, died in 1582.

The union of the Iberian Peninsula marked the apogee of Spain's golden century, and not a little of the achievement belonged to Alba who, like all great men, was a mass of contradictions. He had already distinguished himself in the field by the age of seventeen. His victory at Mühlberg in 1547 over the German Protestant Princes raised Charles V to the pinnacle of his power. His defeat of the French in Italy at the end of the 1550s ensured Spanish dominance over France for another half century, while his rapid conquest of Portugal at the end of his life was his crowning achievement. But there was a darker side to his character as well as an astonishing religious subservience. In Protestant countries his name would be recalled with revulsion for his harshness in dealing with the revolt in the Netherlands where Philip II sent him as governor in 1567; there he "drowned the revolt in blood" to make his name a byword for Spanish cruelty. Yet the Pope—any Pope—filled him, it is said, with respect, fear and trembling, and when he entered Rome at the head of a victorious army in 1557, he humbly kissed the Pope's foot and implored his pardon.[2] Possibly no other incident in sixteenth-century Spanish history puts into more stark relief the contrast between Spanish power and religious piety. For Spain the century has been described as a time of purity of faith when the utter ruthlessness of her great military captains—Alba in Europe, Cortés and Pizarro in the New World—was matched by their total, dedicated religious belief.

The seventeenth Duke of Alba was a prominent Nationalist during the Spanish Civil War and served as Spain's ambassador in London during World War II. But the girl of the Hostal América in Alba de Tormes could only dismiss the grim keep of the old castle as something belonging to "times past." Yet there was a justice in her indifference, too, for Charles V, whom the third Duke of Alba served so well as a young man, allowed all men to wear swords "that the people might be able to defend itself against the nobles," and such a democratic attitude made the Spanish monarchy immensely popular.[3]

The other claim to fame of Alba de Tormes is as the resting place of St Teresa of Avila. I visited the abbey and shrine where she is buried and peered at her effigy through a glass panel while a fat avuncular priest showed a group of talkative nuns round the church: he was a showman, they were tourists.

23

Salamanca: An Irish Dimension

The Great Desert—golden Salamanca—past glories—a bigot and an Orangeman—Ireland and Spain—a Jesuitical problem—the Irish College—Borrow and the Spanish clergy—dancing in the Plaza Mayor—the Dominicas-Dueñas—a gypsy family

IN the eighth century, during the time of Abd al-Rahman I, the great plain between the Guadarramas and Salamanca was as bare as the steppes of North Africa and was called "the Great Desert". Now it is given over to wheat. When I left Alba de Tormes the next morning a thick mist lay along the river and crept over the opposite bank and up the streets of the town so that the grim keep of the Dukes of Alba rose black and forbidding from an engulfing white sea while wispy streamers of mist pulled away from the buttresses like flags. The road to Salamanca mounted steeply from the Tormes valley onto the surrounding plain and when I looked back I could still only distinguish the upper parts of the town, etched in clear outline by the bright sun of early morning, as they rose out of the shimmering white blanket of mist. The countryside gradually changed from wheat to gently rolling green hills to which scattered trees and little copses now gave a park-like appearance. Each time I topped a rise I sought the great tower and dome of Salamanca's cathedral in the distance.

Borrow, who approached Salamanca along the direct road from Peñaranda, says:

About noon of the third day, on reaching the brow of a hillock, we saw a huge dome before us, upon which the fierce rays of the sun striking, produced the appearance of burnished gold. It belonged to the cathedral of Salamanca, and we flattered ourselves that we were already at our journey's end; we were deceived, however, being still four leagues distant from the town, whose churches and convents, towering up in gigantic masses, can be distinguished at an immense distance, flattering the traveller with an idea of propinquity which does not in reality exist.[1]

The final stretch of my road allowed Salamanca to open out before me while deceiving me into thinking I should walk straight into the city and up to the sandstone-gold cathedral on the skyline. But the Tormes river runs to the south of Salamanca and I had to deviate and walk beside its bank for three kilometres before reaching the bridge that crossed into the city.

Borrow found Salamanca a melancholy town. "The days of its collegiate glory are long since past by, never more to return," he says, and then indulges in one of his periodic excesses of philistinism: "a circumstance, however, which is little to be regretted; for what benefit

159

did the world ever derive from scholastic philosophy? And for that alone was Salamanca ever famous."[2] That is somewhat rich to come from the "Gypsy, the Scholar and the Gentleman"; it is, moreover, a bitter remark for, clearly, he is thinking back to the long years of study, during his "veiled period", when neither fame nor action came his way. Borrow often indulges his contrary nature. He goes on to describe near silent halls, grass growing in the courtyards, and says that the former student population of 8,000 was equivalent to the whole population of the city when he visited it.

Today tourism if nothing else has revitalised this charming city while both its university and churches appear to have come to life again. Having denigrated scholarship, Borrow praised Salamanca's architecture:

> *Yet, with all its melancholy, what an interesting, nay, what a magnificent place is Salamanca! How glorious are its churches, how stupendous are its deserted convents, and with what sublime but sullen grandeur do its huge and crumbling walls, which crown the precipitous banks of the Tormes, look down upon the lovely river and its venerable bridge.*[3]

ℯℳ

When Napoleon escaped from Elba to send alarms throughout Europe, Borrow's father, who had just retired from the army, was recalled to the colours to drill new levies ready to fight the Corsican "ogre" once more but, after the Emperor's final defeat at Waterloo, the corps was sent to Ireland where, in 1815 at the age of twelve, Borrow found himself stationed with his father in Clonmel. They lodged with "a bigot and an Orangeman" whom Borrow describes as a fair specimen "of a most remarkable body of men, who during two centuries have fought a good fight in Ireland in the cause of civilization and religious truth." In *Lavengro* Borrow pays tribute to the Irish seminary he attends at Clonmel which their landlord describes as "no Papist school, though there may be a Papist or two there." There, true to his nature, he makes friends with one of the only three Papist boys, some four years older than himself, who is miserable because he has no cards to play with out of lessons. He answers Borrow's question about his father being a farmer by telling him that he, too, would have been a farmer like his brother had not his uncle told his father "to send me to school, to learn Greek letters, that I might be made a saggart of and sent to Paris and Salamanca." Borrow, who possesses a pack of playing cards, bargains with the boy Murtagh and gives him the cards in exchange for being taught Irish: "before Christmas, Murtagh was playing at cards with his brother Denis, and I could speak a considerable quantity of broken Irish."[4] In Salamanca Borrow sought the Irish College with an introduction to its principal:

> *My sojourn at Salamanca was rendered particularly pleasant by the kind attentions and continual acts of hospitality which I experienced from the inmates of the Irish College... It will be long before I forget these Irish, more especially their head, Dr. Gartland, a genuine scion of the good Hibernian tree, an accomplished scholar, and a courteous and high-minded gentleman. Though fully aware who I was, he held out the hand of friendship to the wandering heretic missionary.*[5]

Catholic Spain and Catholic Ireland meet in Salamanca while Protestant Borrow, who defends the bigoted Orangeman fighting for civilisation and religious truth, nonetheless seems more at home with the Catholic Irish, and especially those of the lower orders, than their Protestant counterparts. The Irish-Spanish connection was strong long before the stormy period when Queen Elizabeth I consolidated English power in Ireland and the rebels against the colonial invader looked to Spain for succour. Spanish wine was drunk in the large houses of Ireland from the fourteenth century onwards, and by the fifteenth century Galway was said to surpass Limerick for the extent of its commerce with both France and Spain. Galway boasted handsome buildings of stone erected by Spanish merchants with the arms of the founders above the portals and in the south numbers of young Irishmen were so "Spaniolized" that they spoke Spanish as well as they did Irish. Numbers of Spaniards had settled in Cork, Waterford and Limerick. When England under Henry VIII became Protestant, Ireland remained overwhelmingly Catholic, and as the

English attempted to spread the Reformation in Ireland so Catholic leagues were formed in response. The result was endless intrigues with Spain by the Irish opponents of Queen Elizabeth such as Hugh Roe O'Donnell. In 1579, nearly a decade before the Armada, a Spanish army of 30,000 men was rumoured to be on the way to Ireland to assist a rising of the whole country against Elizabeth and there were recurring fears through Elizabeth's reign of a Spanish landing in Ireland which the people would welcome—although for most of this period would-be rebels received repeated promises of Spanish support but not much help in reality. And during the last years of Elizabeth's reign, after the Armada, the towns of Ireland stood solid for the Crown though they wanted to be able to carry on their traditional commerce with Spain.

As always, an alliance between a weaker and a stronger nation—in this case between Ireland and the greatest power in Europe—is not what it seems: while the Irish expected Spain to help them drive the English out of their country, Spain was only concerned to use threats of intervention that would tie up Elizabeth's forces so that she could not send troops to fight the Spanish in Flanders. And since Catholic Irishmen, nonetheless, served in Elizabeth's armies an intriguing theological question arose. In May 1602 a special ecclesiastical council met at Salamanca to consider the difficult question of the position of Irish Catholic soldiers fighting in the armies of Queen Elizabeth against adherents of a cause that was expressly sanctioned by the Pope. The council found the issue very difficult. It recognised the right of the Queen to command the obedience of such soldiers fighting rebels against the Queen herself, but they were exhorted not to use their obedience to their sovereign to fight against the spread of the Catholic faith. Just how ordinary soldiers were to resolve this truly Jesuitical problem was passed over.[6]

Many Irishmen at this time took service and rose to favour under the banners of Spain, and the Irish regiment of Tyrone's second son, Colonel Henry O'Neill, served Spain in the Low Countries early in the seventeenth century although by the middle of the century, with the rise of France, they were more likely to seek service with the French instead. At the end of the sixteenth and beginning of the seventeenth centuries a number of Irish Catholic colleges were founded on the continent to provide an education for Irish youths, which they could no longer obtain in Ireland. That at Salamanca was one of the most popular and enduring of these; it was founded by Philip II in 1591 after Stephen White had presented some Irish students to him at Valladolid and prayed him to found a college at Salamanca for "these poor exiles from Ireland."[7] The college became a favourite resort of Irish pupils and included some illustrious students such as Colonel Henry O'Neill, while other Irish colleges were started at Madrid, Alcalá, Seville and Santiago. Irish youths became a well-known sight in Salamanca and were referred to in *Gil Blas* as *figures Hibernoises*; they were "always ready to discuss the most abstruse questions of metaphysics with any comer."[8] But all was not what it seemed at Salamanca—or the college had jealous enemies—for also in 1602 complaints from Irish Catholics were made to Philip III that the president of the Irish College, Thomas White SJ, taught its Irish students obedience to the Queen although the college was supported by the King and bishops of Spain. White, moreover, refused to take pupils from Ulster and Connaught because they were in arms against the throne. The complainants begged that the Irish president of the college should be removed and replaced by a Spanish rector.

Borrow compares the attitude towards himself from the Irish in Salamanca with that of the local Spanish clergy, "who, in their ugly shovel hats and long cloaks, glared at me askance as I passed by their whispering groups beneath the piazzas of the Plaza."[9] No doubt Borrow made a point of passing such "whispering groups", for drama as well as attention were always his meat and drink. I should have liked to visit the Irish College but, alas, it closed in 1936 after three and a half centuries. Borrow spent time in Salamanca organising the sale of testaments through its leading bookseller, one Blanco.

Christian sculptors worked the marble of the doorway of the old cathedral of Salamanca as the Moors worked plaster, anxious to rival the arabesque of their predecessors, and they left no part of the surface without ornamentation. Hernán Cortés, the conqueror of Mexico, was a student at Salamanca. Wellington defeated Marmont outside Salamanca in 1812. The historical records of the city are endless.

I made my way to the Plaza Mayor, an imposing square of wonderfully rich warm sandstone façades, where some dancers in brilliant red dresses were performing to music for the benefit of the people who thronged the plaza, and I joined the crowd to watch them. I took out my camera, which was a vintage Leica, and almost at once became conscious of someone at my shoulder. I turned to look into the handsome face of an engaging young man who smiled charmingly as though my arrival in Salamanca's main square had made his day.

"Ah, a Leica," he said: "Alemán?"

"Nein, nein," I replied.

Momentarily wrong-footed he tried again: "Vous-êtes français?" he asked in passable French.

"Mais non, Monsieur, je ne suis pas français."

"Italiano?" and there was now a rising note to his voice, an edge of frustration, so I gave my most non-committal Latin shrug. I was not Italian either.

"English, you must be English" he said.

"Si, si, soy Inglés." And I turned back to take another photograph of the dancers. He moved with me. He was handsome, clean, well-

dressed, polished in the matter of languages—at least to a necessary working level for his trade—and, I was convinced, a crook. He aimed to snatch my camera and I wished to get rid of him so, American style, I held out my hand and said: "Nice meeting you," which took him off guard. We shook hands and I moved away.

The sixteenth-century cloisters of the Dominicas-Dueñas have an upper cloister each of whose pillars is embellished with wonderfully carved capitals of distorted figures, human beings in the hell they have earned by their lack of faith on earth. Rising behind one corner of the cloisters against a clear azure sky was the tower of the cathedral as though it grew from the cloisters themselves. I spent an hour sketching and was only disturbed once by other visitors. It is strange how in a great tourist centre one can yet find an oasis of peace that somehow has managed to escape the general inspection.

Salamanca also possesses the little church of St Thomas-à-Becket, the first ever built to commemorate him; it dates from 1175, only five years after his murder, and presents an exterior of pure Norman architecture. Under the walls of the Ursuline Convent I watched a tired gypsy family: an old man, the head of the family, aged before his time, who was drunk and alternately stretched himself on the grass to sleep or sat up to shout abuse; a woman of powerful frame and strong limbs, his wife, who watched over him and instructed the two young members of the group, her daughter and son-in-law. I was sitting somewhat higher up and sketched the woman and was amazed as I often am at their self-contained lack of interest in the world around them, for at no time did they look towards me or wonder what I might be doing.

24

Borrow's Religiosity

*Borrow fascinated by gypsies—attitude to religion—
equivocation—admires Society of Jesus—William Taylor
of Norwich—Harriet Martineau—early failures—assumed
religiosity—mock Christian humility—fame in Norwich—
Spain—Borrow and the inquisitor*

IN the opening paragraph of *The Gypsies of Spain* Borrow says, simply and eloquently, "Throughout my life the Gypsy race has always had a peculiar interest for me. Indeed I can remember no period when the mere mention of the name Gypsy did not awaken within me feelings hard to be described. I cannot account for this—I merely state a fact."[1]

There is an authenticity about this statement that requires no elaboration; one knows that the gypsies were of profound importance to Borrow and whenever he describes them or his encounters with them—even if he depicts their bad habits or deplores their lack of religion—he speaks from the heart. Gypsies appear and reappear in *Lavengro*, *The Romany Rye* and *The Bible in Spain*, while *The Gypsies of Spain* is entirely devoted to them. For Borrow the romance of these strange, wild people, his kinship with their apartness from the world around them, which perhaps was their greatest source of appeal, his deep acquaintance with them and their ways and the fact that the world was aware of his unique understanding of gypsies—for in his own moody way he was proud of his fame—form the most important and exciting thread of his entire life.

In a letter to John Murray, while he was in the middle of correcting the proofs of *The Bible in Spain*, which he had promised to return at speed, Borrow writes the following marvellously eccentric and revealing explanation for his delay:

> *During the last week I have been chiefly engaged in horsebreaking. A most magnificent animal has found his way to this neighbourhood—a half-bred Arabian he is at present in the hands of a low horse-dealer; he can be bought for eight pounds, but no person will have him; it is said that he kills everybody who mounts him. I have been charming him, and have so far succeeded that at present he does not fling me more than once in five minutes. What a contemptible trade is the Author's compared to that of the jockey.*[2]

This, too, reveals the authentic Borrow: his gypsy-like love and mastery of horses and his determination to parade this particular and unusual side of his character as well as his downgrading of the writer's art to his publisher just as the book which he was correcting was about to make him famous; Borrow, if nothing else, was a superlative showman.

Nowhere in his writing does Borrow reveal a comparable feeling for religion. He demonstrates intensity, but that is not the same thing at all. He employs the piety of language expected of religious people— after he had learnt or assumed it for the benefit of his paymasters, the Bible Society—and he reveals a remarkable vitriol, real or assumed, whenever he speaks of the Pope and the falsities of Catholicism, but both stances have about them an odour of hypocrisy, an aggressive overstatement that is often highly amusing and, perhaps, was meant to be just that, though only for the discerning. Over religious matters, there is always a sense that he is playing to the gallery. In *The Bible in Spain* Borrow recounts how at Córdoba, when he is staying in an inn run by a fiercely pro-Carlist landlord, his Genoese servant, who had accompanied him from Seville in order to take the horses back, tells him that "the knave of the landlord told me that you had confessed yourself to be of the same politics as himself," something the Genoese clearly does not believe. But to this Borrow replies: "'My good man,' said I, 'I am invariably of the politics of the people at whose table I sit, or beneath whose roof I sleep; at least I never say anything which can lead them to suspect the contrary; by pursuing which system I have more than once escaped a bloody pillow, and having the wine I drank spiced with sublimate.'"3

This is a perfectly Jesuitical explanation of his behaviour and there is a good deal of the Jesuit in Borrow who clearly revels in the evasion or half-truth, as at Jaraceijo when he is challenged by a member of the national guard and asked whether he has been travelling in the company of the gypsy Antonio who had just passed through the little town ahead of Borrow, to which he replies: "Do I look a person likely to keep company with gypsies?"

As his biographer, Herbert Jenkins, says of Borrow: "He was not a profound admirer of the Society of Jesus for nothing, and although he would scorn to exercise tact in regard to his own concerns, he was fully prepared to make use of it in connection with those of the Bible Society. He was a Jesuit at heart..." Jenkins, one suspects, has got it wrong: why should not Borrow also "exercise tact" in relation to his own affairs as well as those relating to the Bible Society?

When he was a young man Borrow was a member of the literary circle which gathered round William Taylor of Norwich, the German language enthusiast and friend of Southey, around whom a certain aura of scandal developed in his old age. He drank too much, he encouraged young men with what the genteel society that Borrow so disliked would regard as preposterous ideas without any sense of proportion, putting accepted truths in a new light that was ingenious and stimulating rather than convincing. His critics, in the delicate language of the day, accused Taylor of initiating young men in the habits of conviviality; they also feared the influence upon the young of his erratic opinions. All this would have been meat and drink to an eighteen-year-old Borrow whose nature was to rebel against normal, genteel society and perhaps especially that of the provincial Norwich in which he then lived, and Taylor was just the sort of person to appeal to him. Taylor taught Borrow German and found that his pupil learned it with extraordinary rapidity. It is highly likely that Borrow's friendship with Taylor led him to consider literature as a profession.

Another member of Taylor's circle at this time was the redoubtable and extraordinarily strong-willed Harriet Martineau. She was the classic feminist of her day. She was born at Norwich in 1802, and thus was a year older than Borrow; like him she was a precocious early reader and in her biography tells us that at seven she happened to open *Paradise Lost* and soon knew it by heart. The Martineau family belonged to the Taylor coterie and Harriet must have met Borrow when they were both still teenagers—he approximately eighteen, she a year older, and it is interesting to speculate what happened between them, for both by then were likely to have outshone their contemporaries in their wide if eclectic literary knowledge and both were of a deeply serious nature at heart and neither had much time for the conventions of the day.

Knapp, Borrow's first biographer, claimed that Borrow was not a lady's man, an assertion that has been echoed by most others who have studied him since, and it is at least likely that Borrow and Martineau clashed when they met in Taylor's circle and possible that they clashed at two levels: they may well have attempted to outshine one another in demonstrations of their literary knowledge, a possibility that fits with their two characters, while Harriet, who never married, may have been physically attracted to Borrow and then repelled by him. Something like this would help explain the extraordinary vitriol with which Harriet later dismisses Borrow in her autobiography. In a passage about William Taylor she writes as follows:

> But matters grew worse in his old age, when his habits of intemperance
> kept him out of the sight of ladies, and he got round him a set of ignorant
> and conceited young men, who thought they could set the world right
> by their destructive propensities. One of his chief favourites was George
> Borrow, as George Borrow has himself given the world to understand.
> When this polyglot gentleman appeared before the public as a devout
> agent of the Bible Society in foreign parts, there was one burst of laughter
> from all who remembered the old Norwich days.[4]

If George Borrow was conceited so, too, was Harriet Martineau as anyone who has read her autobiography cannot fail to see. She wrote it in 1855, when she thought she was dying—though she went on to live another twenty years—so that she had plenty of time for reflection about the Norwich days she describes. Shortly after that time she became a literary lion while Borrow disappeared into his "veiled period"; thus Harriet, almost overnight, developed into a major literary success while Borrow, as far as the world was concerned, apparently faded away until his reappearance working for the Bible Society.

Borrow's defenders tend to dismiss the Martineau statement about him, describing her as an unreliable witness, but this is not sufficient ground for doing so, and the "burst of laughter" when he appeared as an agent of the Bible Society may well have been justified. This does not detract from Borrow but makes him still more interesting as a study than he is already. Herbert Jenkins says that those who remembered Borrow as one of William Taylor's "harum scarum" young men, who at one time intended to "abuse religion and get prosecuted," naturally adopted a similar amused reaction to that of Harriet Martineau. He goes on, however, to defend Borrow's later change of views and to argue that the views someone holds at the age of twenty are not necessarily those he holds at thirty. And then, in a revealing passage, Jenkins says: "Perhaps the chief cause of the change in Borrow's views was that he had touched the depths of failure. Here was an opening that promised much. He was a diplomatist when it suited his purpose, and if the old poison were not quite gone out of his system, he would hide his wounds or allow the secretaries to bandage them with mild reproof."[5]

Jenkins himself is now being Jesuitical. He leaves it open as to whether Borrow had become a genuine convert to religion or had merely adopted—as a necessary act of diplomacy because he needed a job—the trappings of religion that were essential if he was to seize the opportunity of employment offered by the Bible Society, which would allow him to do the two things he most enjoyed and was best at—travel and languages. If George Borrow decided to put on a cloak of religion then, Jesuit-like, he would do it magnificently.

The disappointments of Borrow's early life, his failure to succeed as a writer, his subsequent refusal ever to speak of the "veiled period" in which he implies adventure and travel and philological learning but in which, in all probability, much of the time may have been spent at his wits' end to survive provide an obvious background for claiming that he turned to religion. Equally, however, such a background could induce him to pretend to religion if by doing so he could escape from a dead-end existence—if that in fact was the case—and embark upon an exciting job or series of jobs that used his peculiar talents to the full. Certainly, the early racy style of his letters to the Bible Society, and the enthusiasm with which he tells the Rev. Brandram of his interest in gypsies and readiness to convert them, suggest an enormous sense of relief that employment is on the horizon but do not necessarily also suggest that he is seriously—as opposed to conventionally—religious. His background and the fact that the last name his father mentioned when he died in Borrow's arms was that of Christ make subsequent assumptions about his religiosity seem natural enough once he had taken employment with the Bible Society.

Moreover, in two letters to his mother written in June 1834 from Russia, Borrow says he believes the Bible Society will continue to employ him and adds that "I shall endeavour, moreover, to get ordained." In the second letter he adds the more revealing passage (already quoted in Chapter Two): "I have of late led an active life, and dread the thought of having nothing to do except studying as formerly..." A little later, in the same letter, he adds: "However, I hope God will find me something on which I can employ myself with credit and profit. I should like very much to get into the Church, though I suppose that, like all other professions, it is overstocked."[6] Those sentiments sound pious enough but it should be remembered that by then Borrow had learnt the language of Earl Street (the Bible Society) and that he was writing to the mother he adored and would certainly not wish to offend by any suggestion of religious impropriety. It is interesting that the previous year (1833) Borrow had written to his mother from Russia, when his older, soldier brother was about to return home, to say: "Should John return home by no means let him go near the Bible Society, for he would not do for them."

Borrow thought the world of his elder brother but clearly believed that John would be unlikely to behave with the kind of decorum that the Bible Society expected. Might he also have thought that John, inadvertently no doubt, would reveal more about Borrow himself than he would like the Bible Society to know? After the early exchange of correspondence between Borrow and the Bible Society, when he spoke of being "useful to the deity" to earn a reproof from Jowett, the Literary Superintendant of the Society, Jenkins says, "Borrow had yet to learn the idiom of Earl Street, which he showed himself most anxious to acquire."[7]

He set about learning it quickly enough and clearly enjoyed employing it as well. In a letter to the Rev. Jowett of August 1833, when he was on his way to St Petersburg, Borrow demonstrates that he has learnt the lesson implicit in Jowett's earlier disapproval of his racy style. Thus, he writes, "My next letter, provided it pleases the Almighty to vouchsafe me a happy arrival, will be from the Russian capital." Or, he adds, "by a fervent request that you will not forget me in your prayers."[8]

In a long letter from St Petersburg of October 1834, Borrow describes in detail what he has been obliged to do in the preceding two and a half months that precluded him from correspondence: it is essentially an account of all the difficulties of getting the Manchu Testaments printed in Russia. Early in the letter he writes: "Now, and only now, when by the blessing of God I have surmounted all my troubles and difficulties, I will tell, and were I not a Christian I should be proud to tell, what I have been engaged upon and accomplished during the last ten weeks." There is an element of tongue-in-cheek humour about this passage, with its reference to absent pride, as Borrow no doubt recalls the reproof he had received from Jowett about his earlier reference to the Deity. At the end of the same long letter he says:

> *Commend me to our most respected Committee. Assure them that in whatever I have done or left undone, I have been influenced by a desire to promote the glory of the Trinity and to give my employers ultimate and permanent satisfaction. If I have erred, it has been a defect of judgement, and I ask pardon of God and them.[9]*

Either doing or not doing, Borrow, apparently, was promoting the glory of the Trinity. One detects a certain restrained amusement on his part, possibly even a challenge that he knew would not be taken up: if Earl Street required evidence of his Christian piety he was more than happy to provide it.

Meanwhile, back in Norwich, his name was highly praised at meetings of the Bible Society and his letters were circulated among its members so that he was beginning to achieve a little of the fame he craved and, no doubt, it was at this point that Harriet Martineau and others who had lost sight of Borrow now enjoyed their laughter at his sudden reappearance in a new-found religious character. Borrow hoped that the Bible Society would send him to China and wrote to Jowett in May 1835 to say, "I again repeat that I am at command." His mother, however, was deeply disturbed by the thought of him disappearing into the land of the Tartars, and in any case nothing came of this. But if he had learnt the language of Earl Street, Borrow also urgently wanted a new job once his labours in St Petersburg came to an end. In a further communication with the Bible Society, he said: "I am a person full of faults and weaknesses, as I am every day reminded by bitter experience, but I am certain that my zeal and fidelity towards those who put confidence in me are not to be shaken."[10]

On his return to Norwich after his work in St Petersburg Borrow had the opportunity to rest and reflect; instead he became restless and wrote to Jowett that he was weary of doing nothing and sighing for employment. He then received a letter from the Rev. Brandram to say the Bible Society had resolved to send him to Portugal and Spain. Brandram, however, goes on to express doubts as to whether Borrow ought to go to the Iberian Peninsula at that particular time because of its disturbed political state and concludes by asking Borrow to "favour us with your thoughts." Borrow does so by return of post. "As you ask me to favour you with my thoughts, I certainly will; for I have thought much upon the matters in question, and the result I will communicate to you in a very few words. I decidedly approve (and so do all the religious friends whom I have communicated it to) of the plan of a journey to Portugal..."[11] Since Borrow replied in such haste it is interesting though fruitless to speculate as to who were all these religious friends of his in Norwich whom he was able to consult at such short notice.

And so he went to Portugal and Spain, an enterprise which enabled him subsequently to write his masterpiece. *The Bible in Spain* is not the book of a missionary. It is the highly coloured, exciting work of an adventurer, the astonishing account of his travels through Spain that were made possible because Borrow was distributing Protestant Testaments. His most interesting encounters, as he describes them, are with people who are not to be converted from their Catholic ways such as the old man in Córdoba who turns out to have been an inquisitor. As Borrow says to this priest: "Nothing could afford me greater pleasure than to find myself conversing with a father formerly attached to the holy house of Cordova." And the ancient inquisitor returns the compliment when he says: "I believe you to be one of us—a missionary priest." In Salamanca it is the Irish fathers who extend particular hospitality to Borrow although he also tells us how he prepared a bulletin to be published by the bookshop that is to sell his Testaments in which he says, "the New Testament was the only guide to salvation."

25

The Trojan Horse

Medina del Campo—Catherine of Aragon—the Elephant and Castle—the comuneros—Valladolid—asking directions—the English school—the Trojan Horse

FROM Salamanca Borrow turned north-east and headed for Medina del Campo and Valladolid, stopping briefly at the little village of Pitiegua where he had an introduction to the local priest from the Irish Fathers in Salamanca, and then staying overnight in Pedroso. He found that Medina del Campo gave much evidence of former grandeur but a grandeur that had decayed away so long in the past that its present inhabitants were quite unaware of it. He describes it as "formerly one of the principal cities of Spain, though at present an inconsiderable place. Immense ruins surround it in every direction, attesting the former grandeur of this 'city of the plain'."[1]

Modern guidebooks describe Medina del Campo, first and foremost, as a major railway junction! On my approach into the town I first passed a large church and then a very old brick-built covered market. I always enjoyed visiting such markets and would spend time wandering through them; their architecture is often unusual while the bustle and noise of crowded activity was in perfect and lively contrast to the churches and other monuments which I visited. This one, however, was empty, the day's business over, and its sole occupant now was an ancient crone engaged in cleaning up. She gave me a look of astonishment as I wandered round her domain of rotting cabbages and fish heads which she was then sluicing into gutters.

The Plaza Mayor is a lovely wide square of low façades except for one corner, which is occupied by a massive red-brick church set off by a tower of unusual shape. There was also an old gateway into the square but many of the buildings of Borrow's time must since have been pulled down, as he described black buildings of great antiquity that rose round the square; these had disappeared and apart from the church and town hall I did not see any other buildings to fit his description. In 1489, however, Medina del Campo was in its late medieval glory and provided the setting for a treaty between England and Spain under whose terms the Infanta Catherine, the youngest daughter of Ferdinand and Isabella, was to marry Arthur, the eldest son of Henry VII. The usual arguments about the treaty followed and it had to be renegotiated in 1496; Catherine married Prince Arthur in 1501 but he died the following year. Later she married Henry VIII and was to be much loved by the English people while her daughter, Mary, became Queen of England, although in 1533 Henry had Archbishop Cranmer annul their marriage. But this treaty of 1489 gave Londoners the Elephant and Castle, an original hostelry being named the Infanta of Castile after the proposed wife of the heir to the English throne. In due course the name was mangled and corrupted by the English whose contempt for anything foreign, then and today, matches their inability to pronounce foreign names.

The castle is massive, battlemented, with towers and a grim keep surrounded by a huge empty moat; its walls appear to be pockmarked with cannon ball shot. Medina del Campo was brutally sacked by Cardinal Adrian who was one of the new appointments of Charles of Habsburg. The town had declared for the *comuneros* who had risen in revolt against the king. When King Ferdinand died in 1516 the Spanish crown—or rather the crowns of the kingdoms he had controlled—passed to his grandson Charles I, at that time the ruler of the Netherlands and only sixteen years old. A year and a half was to pass before Charles arrived in Spain—when he came to the wrong port of entry by mistake—and by then his new Spanish subjects were both restive and resentful, an attitude that was not improved by Charles who spoke no Spanish, was personally unprepossessing and was surrounded by foreign advisers. Within two years he was elected Holy Roman Emperor (as Charles V) with the result that his chancellor demanded another round of taxes from Spain's cities and towns, on top of the round that had just been raised from them for the new monarch. He obtained the money, though only with difficulty, and Charles left his new kingdom to be crowned Emperor while the cities of Spain rose in the revolt of the *comuneros*. Toledo led the revolt and the cities and towns proclaimed a league and claimed they were the kingdom and that the Cortes could assemble to discuss the welfare of the realm without the king. The *comuneros* considered dethroning Charles in favour of his mother, Joan the Mad. Although the nobles did not join the *comuneros*, they deeply resented the appointment by the new king of various foreigners to high positions with the result that they made no attempt to check the revolt until it became too revolutionary and threatened their own interests. Then, however, in the way of nobles everywhere, whose only principle is the perpetuation of their own privileges, they raised an army and defeated the *comuneros* at the battle of Villalar in 1521. It had, nonetheless, been a dangerous revolt which might have turned into a full revolution, and Medina del Campo where Queen Isabella I of Castile had died—she was known as Isabella the Catholic for her piety and orthodoxy—lost forever its place as a leading city of Spain.

Near the castle are the remains of what must once have been massive town walls or ramparts, now entirely overgrown and partly hidden in park-like woods; these, no doubt, were part of the immense ruins to which Borrow refers. Wandering through the trees among these remains I came upon a scene of modern sensuality: a young man, stripped to his jeans to display an astonishingly well-developed torso, was stretching back on the bonnet of a car while four attendant girls pandered to his ego. The four girls were so engaged with the physical attributes of the young man and he was so engaged with himself that none of them even noticed me as I walked past their undulating tableau. I turned into the huge walled cemetery that shares the hilltop with the castle and wandered among the tombs of the dead who at least always provide peaceful company. Many of the graves were decorated with bright flowers though almost all of these were artificial.

☙

Valladolid sits in a great valley, possibly volcanic, "scooped by some mighty convulsion out of the plain ground of Castile," Borrow tells us, though the dramatic setting has been somewhat diminished since his day by the inevitable and remorseless growth of urban sprawl which creeps up every little valley away from the city and eats into even the most awesome surroundings. The modern city, which now has a population of a third of a million people, is on the pilgrim way to Santiago.

At the tourist office I inquired about the two inns at which Borrow had stayed—the Posada de las Diligencias, which he said looked magnificent but provided awful service, and the Trojan Horse, to which he moved and found more congenial. The tourist office had not heard of either. On the other hand, the English School where Borrow had been well received did still exist although it had been combined with the Scottish School. The main church or cathedral of grey stone remains unfinished. Borrow tells us that "it was intended to be a building of vast size, but the means of the founders were insufficient to carry out their plan."[2] It still only has one of its proposed two towers but is grand enough all the same.

I got lost in the centre of the city as I searched for the English School so sought directions. There were lots of people hurrying past to choose from as it was midday, but a kind of inborn perversity led me to select a middle-aged woman whose robust physique, big bosom and severe features would generally earn her the description of "forbidding".

"Por favor, Señora..." I began, but with a sweeping gesture she said, "I do not speak to strangers."

"But madam, I am lost."

"Señor, I repeat, I do not speak to strangers."

"But I am not a stranger, I am only lost."

"What do you mean, not a stranger! I have never seen you before."

"That does not make me a stranger, madam."

"Then what, may I ask, are you?"

"I am an Englishman."

"You are English?" She invested her voice with astonishment: "The English are all by the seaside." This was an appropriate rendering of her contempt for a people who only went through her country to sunbathe on the Costa Brava or Costa del Sol. She looked at me with new interest: "You are English, you say?"

"That is so Madam and I seek your help."

She stood like a battleship temporarily becalmed but getting up fresh power: "How may I be of assistance?" she asked, the earlier suspicion in her voice now tempered with a softer note of helpful inquiry. I gave her the address of the English School.

"The English School!"

She had not heard of it, so I enlightened her: "It was established in the reign of your King Philip II, in 1590," I said and added, for good measure: "We used to come here for other reasons in those days, not just the sea."

And then she smiled and gave me precise directions.

The English and Scottish Colleges were founded in 1590 and 1790 respectively. Borrow visited both but now they have been merged. He described the picture gallery, small church and library of the English School, which is enclosed behind high stone walls and in his time appeared to be more flourishing than its Scottish rival. A massive door opened into a porch but a second set of doors was firmly closed. I rang the bell but there was no response, no sound at all from within. I rang again. I tried the great knocker but though the sound reverberated in the porch its echoes did not draw forth a priest or scholar to assist me. I found a second bell at the side by a little grille marked Pedro Fernández whom I thought might be the duty porter or priest and rang this too. I spent ten minutes alternately ringing the two bells or banging with the great knocker but the school remained mute, though whether they were all away on vacation or at prayers or meditations I was never to know.

I then found the little Escueva river which was no more than a wretched stream though Borrow claimed that it flowed through a beautiful public walk; there was, it is true, a public walk of sorts but high- rise flats to either side had largely destroyed whatever may once have been exclusive or attractive about it.

That evening, after walking through the splendid Campo Grande park and idling my time sitting at a wayside café in the Plaza Mayor,

I set out to find an interesting place in which to dine. I examined several restaurants but none came up to my requirements, for I was in a finicky mood. Then, just off the main square, I glanced through an archway into a courtyard that was open to the sky with tables set out for refreshment and was startled to see a large, brilliantly coloured representation of a horse painted on the wall opposite the entrance: El Caballo de Troya, the Trojan Horse. A balcony round the upper floor looked down on the courtyard just as Borrow describes it. A restaurant occupied one side of the courtyard while steps at the back led down into a large room with a long bar running the length of the rear wall. About twenty dried hams of varying sizes hung behind the bar. This must once have been the stable and travellers would have ridden their horses through the courtyard and straight down into it. I took a stool at the bar and ordered a glass of wine; then I asked my waiter whether the establishment had formerly been an inn. He was a surly man, that waiter, and merely shrugged and replied: "How should I know?" His was an oddly discourteous rebuff so perhaps he had had a bad day. Other guests arrived, since the Trojan Horse was a fashionable eating place, and I ordered a second glass of wine and asked my waiter again. The quickening pace of business seemed to have taken the rough edge from him as this time he replied far more civilly and said that he would ask one of the other waiters who had been there longer. He beckoned a colleague to whom I repeated my question: "Of course, Señor, it was a famous *posada* for four hundred years."

Later, when I dined in the restaurant I found the same waiter looking after me and during a lull in activity, he came over with the head waiter, who was also interested. They told me it had been an inn since the sixteenth century and that the bar, as I had surmised, had been the stables. It had always been an inn, they told me, until about forty years earlier although they argued with each other as to the exact date when it had stopped being used as a *posada*; for a time it had been an elegant shop, they said, and now it was a restaurant, the best in Valladolid.

"How did the Señor know that it had been an inn?" they wanted to know. By then I was enjoying an excellent meal and vintage Rioja and did not feel up to Borrow and his Bibles so I told them that an ancestor of mine had stayed there in the 1830s and that I had spent the day searching all over Valladolid for the Trojan Horse and had been on the point of giving up in despair when I found it. They were delighted.

26

Palencia, León
and Astorga

The wines of Dueñas—Palencia—the Cid again—strange
rooms—the cathedral of León—Astorga—Antoni Gaudí—a
pilgrim—the Maragatos

THE next leg of my travels I covered by train: Dueñas, Palencia,
León and then Astorga, which would put me on the pilgrim path
to Santiago de Compostela. Borrow often speaks of a short league,
which is understandable though the expression is more difficult
to comprehend when it becomes a question of numbers: thus
he describes Dueñas as being six short leagues from Valladolid.
Was it five and a half full leagues or just an easy journey? Dueñas
is a dramatic place on high ground with a steep conical mountain
crowned by a ruined castle. It is the centre of a wine-producing region
where caves scooped out of the hillsides were used to store the wine.
Here Borrow fell in with a group of soldiers who wanted to take his
horse; they turned out to be gypsies.

Palencia is a charming little city, but though it has an ancient
history its early period is obscure; in the twelfth century it became
the seat of the Castilian kings and in 1208 King Alfonso IX founded
a university there although this was soon removed to Salamanca.
Its most important feature is its Gothic cathedral, which is a
repository of many pictures and other objects of art. Borrow claimed,
mistakenly, that it housed a collection of Murillos. It does, however,

have a number of paintings but most of these, though grand, were so dark that it was difficult to make out their subject matter, especially as the cathedral was also maintained in a state of permanent gloom.

Spain's hero, the Cid, married Ximena here in 1074 although that was before the present cathedral was built. It is a matter of constant amazement that the truth about those who have been elevated to the status of heroes is always ignored. The Cid spent half his life fighting as a soldier of fortune on the side of the Saracens and the other half on the side of the Christians so that he earned the contemptuous description from the Arab chronicler Abu Bassam of "a Galicion dog, without honour or loyalty or faith."[1] That no doubt accurate description did not prevent the Cid's elevation.

By this time on my travels I had become something of a connoisseur of churches and cathedrals, of which Spain has an abundant supply, and though I never entered these monuments in pursuit of religious solace, I did enjoy them as places of relaxation— when they were not in service—for as a rule they are peaceful. Though not one of the most splendid of Spain's cathedrals, that of Palencia does possess a grandeur of the second rank which gives it a more intimate character. Palencia is an elongated, narrow city, hemmed in on either side between the River Carrión, which forms its south-western boundary and the railway which runs parallel to the river to the north.

More wheat country lies between Palencia and León, the latter being an altogether grander city of wide imposing streets whose principal attractions are its cathedral and extensive remnants of walls. Its name is a corruption of the Latin *legio*, or legion, and in its time it fell to the Goths and then the Moors before it became the capital of the kingdom of Asturias and León in the tenth century. Much of its medieval importance arose from its position on the pilgrim route to Santiago de Compostela. From this point onwards the pilgrim route became of increasing historical and actual importance to the places through which it passes and both their prosperity and political influence had come to depend upon the role a city played in relation to Santiago.

Just as I was becoming a connoisseur of churches and cathedrals so also was I becoming something of a self-appointed arbiter in the matter of inns and boarding house rooms and that which I secured in León was one of the most eccentric in which I stayed. León was one of the places where I spent a weary hour searching for accommodation and I must have been turned away from at least six places that were full before I discovered that strange first-floor *fonda*. The establishment was part of a large former merchant's house and was now in a state of genteel dilapidation and galloping decay. It was arranged in two wings, one to either side of the entrance, the corridors had creaking floorboards which, no doubt, assisted the landlady to keep a check on the movements of her guests while its furniture was so cheap and old that I was in constant fear that anything I touched would fall apart. My room was immensely high-ceilinged and had a balcony onto a busy street below; one of the cabinets for clothes was crammed with old newspapers, another had become a repository for children's sports equipment, while my bed, when I sat on it, sank gracefully to the floor although when later I used it for sleep turned out to be remarkably comfortable.

The old city of León with its recurrent walls and alleyways is a pleasure to roam through while its glory is the cathedral. This possesses twin though non-identical spires and an imposing façade but its greatest attraction consists of its stained-glass windows, perhaps the finest such collection of any cathedral in Europe; its two huge rose windows alone make a visit to León worthwhile. Strangely, Borrow makes no mention of the windows and, indeed, is somewhat dismissive of León generally: "There is nothing remarkable in Leon which is an old gloomy town, with the exception of its cathedral, in many respects a counterpart of the church of Palencia, exhibiting the same light and elegant architecture, but, unlike its beautiful sister, unadorned with splendid paintings."[2] A footnote by Murray, his publishers, however, claims that, "The west front and the painted glass windows in the aisles are of unrivalled beauty." Certainly of the two cathedrals, I would place León well above Palencia for aesthetic attraction.

I took the bus to Astorga and after walking hundreds of kilometres in Spain without encountering a solitary walker now began to see energetic walkers with their staves, for I was finally on the pilgrim way to Santiago. An English couple in their early thirties sat in the seats ahead of me in the bus; they got off at an inn halfway between León and Astorga and since both carried packs and walking sticks I assumed they, too, intended to join the pilgrims. By this time I was becoming distinctly nervous because, for me, walking should be a solitary business although my route now gave every indication of turning into some kind of pilgrim superhighway.

The ancient city of Astorga lies in the foothills of the massive Telleno mountain and occupies a strategic eminence that guards the road. The old Roman city of Asturica Augusta was described as magnificent by Pliny but later fell into decay only to revive as a station on the pilgrim road to Santiago when it also became a centre of pilgrimage in its own right. It has some splendid (restored) Roman walls, an indifferent cathedral and the extraordinary Bishop's Palace, now a museum, designed by Antoni Gaudí. First, however, I was obliged to search for a room; all the inns in the centre of town were full and I had to walk out on the road to Bembibre for about a kilometre before I found accommodation and even then I was only just in time to secure the last free room. Astorga was simply brimming with pilgrims, old and young, though mainly young. In the tourist office I obtained maps of the pilgrim way and was told about campsites and hostels and the places where the pilgrims had to report if they were to get full marks for their efforts; the two helpful girls in the office also told me how the pilgrims, unless they had booked ahead, set off earlier and earlier each day to make sure they could obtain a bed space at the next stopping place. It sounded rather grim, like some form of relay race, and I was not at all sure that I wanted to be on the pilgrim way for any length of time.

The Catalan architect Antoni Gaudí produced an extraordinary style of his own, much of it characterised by the way he used colour and texture; he spent most of his life and did most of his work in or near Barcelona so that his Episcopal Palace at Astorga represents a geographic departure. It was designed and constructed between

1887 and 1893 but could as easily have been built as a museum, which it had now become, than as the bishop's palace which was the original intention. The grounds in front of it are open to the public and overlook part of the town below as the museum rises above massive ancient city walls. Pilgrims were everywhere and hucksters playing flutes had taken over the museum porch. The basement was given over to Astorga's Roman history since the city is rich in Roman remains; the next two floors were devoted to the "Museum of the Ways to Santiago de Compostela" and contained endless pilgrim relics. The top floor, refreshingly, exhibited the contemporary art of León.

❧

It was at Astorga that I began to wonder just what the pilgrims got out of their pilgrimages. It is extraordinary how much and how often people choose to flaunt and proclaim themselves. In that part of the museum devoted to the pilgrim way was a young American woman, hardly out of her teens, of robust physique and dressed in shorts that

did not suit her; she possessed an open though basically vacant face which was now filled with the seriousness of being both young and devout. She carried a hefty pilgrim staff, a necessary accoutrement of all these earnest young walkers. At each step she took through the museum this young woman tapped her staff fiercely on the stone floor to remind all the lesser mortals around her that she was A PILGRIM.

Astorga is in the middle of Maragatos country and Borrow, who prided himself on his understanding of ethnic differences, is nonetheless somewhat vague as to their origins. He describes the Maragatos as Moorish Goths and suggests they were Goths who had originally sided with the Moors when the latter invaded Spain and had, as a result, become isolated by the surrounding people among whom they lived. He says they are slow and plain of speech, employing coarse thick pronunciation like German or English peasants attempting to express themselves in the language of the Peninsula. On the subject of their religion, Borrow found "their hearts gross, and their ears dull of hearing, and their eyes closed," a passage perhaps intended for the Bible Society. Yet one of these gross Maragatos offers to take Borrow's chest of Bibles to Lugo for him— at an exorbitant price—and when this offer is turned down the man instead purchases two of Borrow's New Testaments, not however with the intention of reading them himself but because he believes he can sell them at a higher price than the one Borrow demanded. Whatever else they may have been, they were enterprising. "So much for the Maragatos," Borrow concludes.[3]

In his *History of Iberian Civilization*, Oliveira Martins has a different explanation for these people and claims that they were Berbers who remained behind after the Christian conquest of the region; he suggests that the Christians, in their hatred of the Berbers, designated the region they inhabited as Malacoutia, hence the name Maragatos and even in 1930, a hundred years after Borrow was there, when he was writing his history, Martins says they still formed a separate group in the population of León: "They remain Berbers, shave their heads except for a tuft of hair at the back, speak a language which is not genuinely Castilian, with a harsh, trailing pronunciation, and are for the most part muleteers, that is to say nomads."[4]

27

The Pilgrim Way

Friendly advice—the place of apples—a vast slate quarry—a tunnel—the valley of Bembibre

I NOW set out on the road to Galicia following the centuries-old pilgrim way to Santiago. Bembibre was forty-two kilometres distant, so I faced a long day's walk. I rose early as usual and by seven had paid my bill and taken a large coffee in the bar but others were already ahead of me. The bar was crowded with young pilgrims though several older ones appeared in the role of guides, mentors or organisers—I was not certain which; in the hallway they had piled their rucksacks. The group left in a body just before I did so I feared they would be competing with me for walking space. When I stepped outside the inn I found, to my considerable astonishment, that they were loading their rucksacks into a van. Then they set off unburdened, many tapping their freshly acquired staves on the ground in a self-conscious manner as they accustomed themselves to these unfamiliar aids to walking. I alone departed from that inn with a pack on my back, a fact that gave me a justified sense of superiority. I took the road to Bembibre while the pilgrims rapidly disappeared up a back path to seek the authentic pilgrim way, which was off the main road, so my walk, or so I believed, would be as solitary as ever.

I had just completed the first kilometre and was settling into my stride when there came towards me on a bicycle one of those large comfortable friendly women who spend their lives helping other people, whether asked to do so or not. She wobbled to a stop as she beamed a greeting:

"Buenas Dias, peligro?"

"Si, si" I nodded, "soy peligro."

She was an organiser, I could tell even before she began to give me instructions. "But you are on the wrong road, Señor, this is not the pilgrim's way."

"It is my way," I replied firmly, "I am going to Bembibre."

"But are you not going to Santiago like all the others?"

"Yes, I am going to Santiago as well, but not like all the others. I take a tortuous path." This Jesuitical comment of mine was not well received.

Slightly flustered but determined to do her good deed for the day she became stern: "But the path is back there," and she pointed behind me. "You are going the wrong way."

"Señora, Bembibre lies ahead of me," and I pointed behind her but she only shook her head with irritation.

"The pilgrim way lies over there," she repeated, now spacing her words slowly in case the foreigner was not understanding properly, "and you must take it in order to be a proper pilgrim."

"I know," I replied, "but I want to go this way. I saw where all the other pilgrims went," I added mendaciously, "and besides, I am not a proper pilgrim."

She ignored this odd statement of mine, perhaps she did not understand what I meant, and continued: "But you do not understand: a *peligro* has to go along the path."

"But I am a different sort of *peligro*, I am walking all the way to Cape Finisterre," I exaggerated for I have always found that a little exaggeration does wonders for an argument. Exasperated and angry with me because her intended help had been rebuffed she let out a long sighing "oooh" and shrugged a dismissal as she heaved herself back onto her bicycle and continued on her way. She did not deign to answer my "Gracias, Señora", which made me feel I had been mean not to surrender to her good intentions.

The road rose steadily into the hills, the views improved dramatically and a sharp freshness gave to the air a nectar-like quality so that I wanted to breathe in huge gulps. The occasional large dog barked at me from a distance and one huge brute followed me for at least a kilometre, keeping parallel along the hillside. I reached

Manzanal del Puerto at the top of the pass in under four hours of steady climbing; it was at a height of 1,225 metres and 19 kilometres from Astorga, so I was maintaining a good pace. There was a pull-in café for truckers where I relaxed for half an hour over a beer. Borrow records how he refreshed himself at Manzanal (the place of apples), "a village consisting of wretched huts, and exhibiting every sign of poverty and misery."[1] There did not appear to be much more there a century and a half later though the poverty may have lessened.

Now the road rolled with the hills although a great modern highway has been cut round the shoulder at the top of the valley, which stretched out of sight on the other side of the pass. Borrow took a disastrous short cut at this point, descending to the valley bottom where he became enmeshed in a bog and was obliged to seek the highway on the hillside again. There he says: "We now began to descend the valley by a broad and excellent carretera or carriage-road, which was cut out of the steep side of the mountain on our right." Although the modern road followed the same route the scenery must have changed out of recognition and it is worth following Borrow a little further.

> *On our left was the gorge… The road was tortuous, and at every turn the scene became more picturesque. The gorge gradually widened, and the brook at its bottom increased in volume and sound; but it was soon far beneath us, pursuing its headlong course till it reached level ground, here it flowed in the midst of a beautiful but confined prairie. There was something sylvan and savage in the mountains on the farther side, clad from foot to pinnacle with trees, so closely growing that the eye was unable to obtain a glimpse of the hillsides, which were uneven with ravines and gulleys, the haunts of the wolf, the wild boar, and the corso, or mountain stag.*[2]

This splendid description of wilderness no longer holds, for half the bottom of the valley has been turned into a vast slate quarry, and as I walked along the hillside high above the valley floor the drone of great trucks came up to me from below where they strained in slow motion, huge latter-day prehistoric monsters with their loads. The sylvan savagery that impressed Borrow has been replaced by the modern savagery of industrial exploitation. The far hillside, too, had lost much of its covering of trees though fresh plantations now grow where the quarrying operations have ceased. Slate must have been mined in a small way in Borrow's time, as he describes a wretched village in the valley: "The huts were built of slate stones, of which the neighbouring hills seemed to be principally composed, and roofed with the same, but not in the neat tidy manner of English houses, for the slates were of all sizes and seemed to be flung on in confusion."3

Once, when I was lecturing, someone asked me what happens to all the holes that man makes in the earth as he quarries and beavers away for the minerals by which he sets such store. That valley bottom, being ruthlessly carved away for its slate, reminded me of other holes in the earth that I have visited in various parts of the world where copper or bauxite or coal has been gouged out of the ground to leave a wasteland of devastation behind. As a rule, through history, we have done nothing about the holes we make; although now, in an increasingly ecology-conscious age, we sometimes make an effort to cover them up or fill them in.

By midday the temperature had risen to the high eighties to make this day's walk both memorable and taxing. At Torre del Bierzo I was obliged to pass through a short tunnel of two hundred metres which was forbidden to pedestrians although there was no alternative route; the prohibition made sense as there was no walkway and the great trucks plying between Madrid and La Coruña all but filled the tunnel. The road continued to wind along the mountainside although it was steadily descending at the same time and while the distant views were magnificent before they were lost in a blue heat haze, the nearer hillsides were scarred by the slate mining. I saw the occasional labourer in the small fields below me but they were not singing at their toil. Borrow, an incurable romantic, describes the side of this great gorge as dotted with little yellow fields of barley and says: "We saw a hamlet and church down in the prairie below, whilst merry songs ascended to our ears from where the mowers were toiling with their scythes."4 Anyone who has attempted to scythe a field of barley on a steep hillside in eighty degrees of heat is unlikely to have much breath left over for merry songs.

Then the road entered another tunnel. This one was 1,100 metres long and a notice warned: No Pedestrians. I cannot imagine what I or any other pedestrian was supposed to do at that point: turn back and find a way down into the valley below, although I had not seen any side road for some distance; climb the almost vertical mountain through which the tunnel had been bored; or wait at the entrance to the tunnel to hitch a lift? Perhaps "authority" simply did not expect anyone to choose to be a pedestrian at all. I walked through the tunnel. There was no side path for pedestrians, the tunnel was black and sooty, and for over half the distance I could not see the exit at the other end. Traffic roared through that tunnel to create a deafening crescendo of noise as each truck approached me from either direction while the oncoming headlights blinded me. For safety, to ensure that I did not stray into the path of an oncoming truck, I put my left hand out against the tunnel wall. The tunnel turned into the most awful kilometre I have ever walked. By then I had already covered about thirty-five kilometres and was tired and one foot had developed a blister. I wanted to rest but instead hurried at top speed all 1,100 metres, hugging the wall, sometimes stumbling over mounds of hard-packed dust piled against the tunnel wall—part of a cleaning-up operation that had been abandoned—with dust in my eyes and the endless roar of traffic in my ears, for all the trucks in Spain seemed to have converged on the tunnel to coincide with my passage. That tunnel became my idea of a walk in hell and when finally I emerged into the brilliant sunshine at the other end to meet a wall of heat it was sheer heaven.

I came to a roadside resting place with space for half a dozen cars and sat wearily under the shade of a tiny tree; the only other shaded area was occupied by a Spanish family whose car was parked nearby. They looked at me with a kind of astonishment. I think my face was streaked with sweat and dirt from the tunnel's dust, and the man came over to greet me and then asked me where I came from.

"Astorga!" He was astounded. He and his family, he told me, came from Córdoba and were on their way to La Coruña for their annual holiday. He was even more amazed when I told him I was on my way to Cape Finisterre and expected to walk much of the way.

"You are not young to be walking," he said.

"I can manage," I replied and he had the grace to look abashed, but still shaking his head in disbelief he said, "I must tell my wife" and returned to his family. He reminded me of disasters and made me feel like one. Whenever you tell someone that a disaster has occurred, a death for example, he or she will say: "I must go and tell my wife" or husband or someone—it does not really matter whom—as long as it is possible to speak about the event. Disaster is an infallible promoter of communication and can make even the most taciturn suddenly loquacious.

The last six kilometres into Bembibre, happily, were downhill all the way. Borrow was eulogistic about Bembibre's valley:

> *Perhaps the whole world might be searched in vain for a spot whose natural charms could rival those of this plain or valley of Bembibre, as it is called, with its wall of mighty mountains, its spreading chestnut trees, and its groves of oaks and willows, which clothe the banks of its stream, tributary to the Minho.*[5]

In the distance as I descended the valley I could see a great chimney belching forth smoke, so times had changed. A bridge on the outskirts of Bembibre crossed high above a lovely sparkling stream, which chuckled in the sun and then I found an inn, the Tio Pepe, and resolved to go no further. I had covered forty-two kilometres.

28

Knights Templar

Bembibre—like Switzerland—Ponferrada—the Knights Templar—competition on the Pilgrim Way—Cacebelos—Villafranca

BEMBIBRE was a considerable place of old winding streets, grey with slate from the quarries in the valley, which I had descended the day before. It is situated to the south of the El Vierzo district, a region that was little known in Borrow's time and is probably still one of the lesser-known parts of Spain today. The region has been described as the Switzerland of León and there were certain resemblances in both the houses and small hills to lowland Switzerland. Bembibre lies in the centre of a wine-producing area and, in his retreat to La Coruña, General Moore, whose timely death did more for a mediocre reputation than anything he achieved while alive, is reputed to have lost more of his men here through intoxication, as they drank the wines of the valley, than he did in fighting the French. Borrow lauded the beauty of the valley but dismissed Bembibre itself as "a village of mud and slate, and which possessed little to attract attention."

The road to Ponferrada which I now followed passes through a broad valley that is totally surrounded by mountains, and when I reached the top of a long hill I was able the more easily to appreciate why the region had been compared with Switzerland as I gazed down on the little alpine-style villages nestling beside their individual hills.

The iron bridge across the Sill river at Ponferrada which gives the town its name was constructed in the eleventh century for the benefit of pilgrims on their way to Santiago, while the ruins of a great castle of the Knights Templar dominate the town; it was built in the twelfth century when the protection of the Pilgrim Way was entrusted to their safe-keeping. The town, which is situated at the confluence of the Sill and Boeza rivers, is also "protected" by the miraculous image of the Virgin that, reputedly, was found in a nearby oak tree.

℃⊅

The story of the Knights Templar illustrates perfectly that strange doom attraction which sometimes compels human beings to seek oblivion in disaster like intelligent lemmings who know where their path is leading them but cannot under any circumstances draw back from the void that lies before them. Like so many religious orders whose beginnings lay in devout simplicity the Templars ended in the arrogance of power and corruption, feared, almost begging to be destroyed, and the destruction was duly visited upon them.

The Knights Templar were a religious-military order, first established at Jerusalem with the object of safeguarding pilgrims on their way to the Holy Land. The order was created in 1118 by a group of men who promised to devote themselves to the service of God and to live in perpetual chastity, obedience and poverty. Their first residence, which was close to the Temple, was given to them by Baldwin II, King of Jerusalem, and at first they were known as "poor soldiers of the Temple". Later they came to be called Templars or Knights Templar. Theirs was the classic beginning for such an order, and in an age of pilgrims whose many "ways" had to be guarded the order flourished to become immensely rich and powerful while its knights became increasingly arrogant and luxurious, inevitably attracting the enmity that led to their downfall. They also became extremely secretive and have been seen as the ancestors of the Freemasons. The result was predictable, and fear of their power as well as greed to lay hands on their wealth led Philip IV of France, "Philip the Fair", to bring about their destruction. In 1312 Philip persuaded the Pope, Clement V, to consent to their suppression; they were accused of heresy and immorality and their grand master was burned at the stake. Their wealth was seized by the greedy and ever-needy monarchs of France and England and, for example, provided

Isabella of France with her dowry when she became the bride of England's Edward II. The trials of the Templars were conducted in strict secrecy and accompanied by the use of torture so that all the required evidence of heresy, idolatry and moral corruption was duly obtained. Priests in the north of England, to their great credit when the inquisitors demanded the use of torture, replied that the practice was unknown in England and asked whether torturers should be imported from abroad. Suppressions of this nature are always shameful yet all too frequently those who are suppressed have brought the disaster upon themselves, for arrogance also breeds its own insensitivity.

∾

When I set off the next morning I discovered that the pilgrim way was marked with various cabalistic signs; in any case, there were pilgrims everywhere, both walkers and cyclists, so that periodically I found myself looking back over my shoulder to see who was sneaking up on me. The cyclists, as elsewhere in my walking, would be upon me without warning, while the hearty variety of walker also liked to overtake silently to stride by on padded feet. There was a certain unChristian competitiveness about all these pilgrims; in part they were like motorists whose instinct was to overtake the vehicle ahead of them; but also, no doubt, they had in mind that night's accommodation and their chances of obtaining a place for the night should too many other pilgrims get ahead of them. Once or twice during that day when long vistas opened up I felt like a participant in a cross-country run, with pilgrims ahead of me as far as the distant horizon and pilgrims behind me, including those I myself had caught up and passed, and sometimes pilgrims by the wayside resting or taking refreshment.

Cacebelos was the halfway point for my day's walk. Borrow contrived to arrive at Cacebelos in the middle of the night, as he did in a good many other places, was refused accommodation at its two *posadas* and so had to find his way out of the town in the dark and back onto the road to Villafranca. "We found it no easy matter to

quit the town, for we were bewildered amongst its labyrinths, and could not find the outlet."[1] Eventually, for a peseta, he found a guide who led him to the bridge, which, he was told, led to the Villafranca road. I could sympathise with his dilemma, for even in broad daylight Cacebelos proved a jigsaw of little streets, which threatened to lose me, and I doubt it had changed much over a century and a half.

Villafranca was an easy walk from Cacebelos and I took my time despite the competition so that, as I made my leisurely way up a long hill, three elderly men came puffing past to cause me momentary irritation until I saw that they were unencumbered with backpacks. Villafranca lies in a basin or steep saucer surrounded by mountains, and the old part of the town is of medieval splendour. Although most of the pilgrims made for special camping sites I did not even attempt to find cheap accommodation but made my way straight to an elegant parador where I enjoyed a room of luxury. I sat for a while on my balcony to inhale sharp, fresh mountain air which came straight down from the hills.

Borrow reached Villafranca in the dark and became lost as earlier in the night he had been lost in Cacebelos though he did eventually find a place to sleep. In the sunlight of the following day, with his servant Antonio, he inspected the town before hurrying on to Galicia.

> *I walked forth into the market-place, which was crowded with people. I looked up and could see the peaks of tall black mountains peeping over the tops of the houses. The town lay in a deep hollow, and appeared to be surrounded by hills on almost every side. "Quel pays barbare!" said Antonio, who now joined me; "the farther we go, my master, the wilder everything looks. I am half afraid to venture into Galicia; they tell me that to get to it we must clamber up those hills; the horses will founder."[2]*

Villafranca had great charm. Its curiously turreted castle, twisting, picturesque streets and medieval buildings are a joy to wander through; the pillars in its huge church are so vast that it would require four men with arms outstretched, fingertip to fingertip, to encircle one of them.

29

The Pass of Pedrafita: Into Galicia

The pass of Fuencebadon—a steady stream of pilgrims—I take the high road—Borrow's accuracy—I rejoin the Pilgrim Way—the silent people of Ruitelan—the gateway to Galicia

IT was to be a wonderful day of walking though more than usually tiring, for the road rose steadily all the way to reach the Pass of Pedrafita, the gateway to Galicia. Modern roads may unite distant provinces but they also divide in two the land through which they pass, and the elegant high bridges that carry Spain's highways hundreds of metres above great gorges have this effect upon the countryside. Drivers of the heavy trucks or of private cars taking foreign holidaymakers to the south coast or Spaniards to the north may glance at the unfolding scenery from these great bridges, the wayside villages that the old road was once obliged to negotiate, but now they do so as though they are looking at a foreign land. I spent the day passing, being passed and re-passing pilgrims while, every so often during that morning, the lush green of the trees in the deep valley was sharply and colourfully broken by wayside stalls piled with bright ripe cherries, red and yellow and gleaming in the sunlight, to invite endless indulgence.

The journey from Villafranca begins through the "far-famed pass of Fuencebadon". Borrow says of this stretch of highway: "It is impossible to describe this pass of the circumjacent region, which contains some of the most extraordinary scenery in all Spain." But he does describe it superbly:

> *The traveller who ascends it follows for nearly a league the course of the torrent, whose banks are in some places precipitous, and in others slope down to the waters, and are covered with lofty trees, oaks, poplars, and chestnuts. Small villages are at first continually seen, with low walls, and roofs formed of immense slates, the eaves nearly touching the ground; these hamlets, however, gradually become less frequent as the path grows more steep and narrow, until they finally cease at a short distance before the spot is attained where the rivulet is abandoned, and is no more seen, thought its tributaries may yet be heard in many a gully, or descried in tiny rills dashing down the steeps. Everything here is wild, strange and beautiful: the hill up which winds the path towers above on the right, whilst on the farther side of a profound ravine rises an immense mountain, to whose extreme altitudes the eye is scarcely able to attain.*[1]

Borrow became enveloped in mist at the top of the pass, the Bretima as he was told by his servant Antonio, but I walked in blazing sun throughout the day.

I departed early that morning to find my way through the twisting streets of the town and out onto the old road, as the new highway which passed close to the Parador entered one of the great tunnels to pass through the mountain which rose immediately to the north of Villafranca. Pilgrims by the score were emerging from the nearby campsites to take the road which enters a deep valley almost before it leaves the last house of Villafranca, and it was cold in the shadows for as yet the early morning sun only touched the tops of the hills sheer above. At a turn in the road just before the spur of a hill cuts off the view it is possible to look back at Villafranca, whose squat twin-turreted castle rose black and grim above the little town.

There are castles all along the pilgrim way and some, though not all, were built like that at Ponferrada, to guard the route. But whatever their original purpose, each castle, over many centuries, must have witnessed these passing pilgrims. The clothes have changed, the speech has altered and the levels of devotion have fluctuated according to the prevailing piety of the different ages, but the pilgrims still make the journey to Santiago de Compostela.

I found myself wondering how many of the pilgrims I saw—mainly young and clearly enjoying themselves as they competed in speed and fitness along the way—were motivated by faith as opposed merely to taking an active and enjoyable holiday.

The road runs alongside a rushing stream, deep in a tree-covered gorge, whose torrential progress made itself heard rising up through the cover of the trees, sometimes roaring and sinister, sometimes gurgling and playful, much as Borrow described it. The sharp coolness of early morning gave a bite to the air so that the pilgrims in their pairs or groups—almost never alone—were frisky and playful: occasionally their voices came clear from a distance, wafted echoing along the funnel of the gorge. During those early hours I passed and was sometimes passed by others—though I have to say not often, as I walk at a cracking pace—and I found myself getting drawn into the competitiveness of the road so that I begrudged even a short stop to eat cherries and have a drink of water since, as I did so, three young men whom I had seen earlier came striding past, grinning at the sight of me because it meant that they had outpaced one more competing pilgrim.

I came to a fork in the road: the highway rose sharply, carved into the mountainside, while the old road followed the bottom of the valley twisting and turning out of sight among the small fields and little villages before it, too, would rise to the head of the pass. Perversely, I took the upper road although a kindly intentioned pilgrim shouted after me that I was on the wrong road but I ignored him—pride before a fall!

I rose very sharply and before long could look down from a great height upon the Lilliputian figures of pilgrims in their bright-coloured anoraks as they wove their way in pairs or groups, strung out along the old road in the valley below me. But I was alone again, clear of competing pilgrims, except for passing traffic and a group of toiling cyclists who came up silently behind me, only announcing their approach at the last moment with the odd squeak of wheels, when their leader came abreast of me. I greeted them but they had little breath to spare for pleasantries and merely grunted back a minimal response.

Across the valley, rising sheer, was a great mountain—the one whose "extreme altitude the eye was scarcely able to attain"—and on one of its spurs to dominate the narrow gorge below stood the ruins of an old monastery. Now this raises an interesting point about the accuracy of *The Bible in Spain*. On his passage from Bembibre to Villafranca, Borrow describes just such a place:

> *Halfway up the mountain, over whose foot we were wending, jutted forth a black frightful crag, which at an immense altitude, overhung the road, and seemed to threaten destruction. It resembled one of those ledges of the rocky mountains in the picture of the Deluge.*[2]

Impressed by this dramatic description, I had searched in vain for such a sight on the previous day's walk. Now I had found a ruin on a crag that exactly fitted his description but in the wrong place, and I suspect that in writing his book four years after he made the journey Borrow had confused in his account the place where this dramatic scene occurred. It was not something he did often. Now, however, I was in trouble myself.

The highway on which I was walking was then some 150 metres above the old road that wound its way through the valley below; it was about to cross one of the spectacular bridges which carry such highways over gorges and immediately beyond the bridge it entered a tunnel. On consulting my map I saw that this was about a kilometre in length and I decided that I did not wish to repeat the misery of the tunnel walk I had experienced on the road to Bembibre. Once across the bridge, however, I could see no way down to the valley road below, so I decided to descend the steep hillside and rejoin the pilgrim path that I had so scornfully rejected earlier. As Borrow says, "The most singular feature of this pass are the hanging fields or meadows which cover its sides." And this is what I could see now stretching steeply below me to the valley floor, a series of small fields with at least one crazy looking farmhouse clinging to a ledge. The village below, half under the high bridge, was Ruitelan.

So I began my descent, first through an almost sheer cover of bushes whose branches I had to grasp to prevent myself losing control before I came to the first "hanging field". At one point I came through a hedge and slithered down a bank to a sitting position on a little footpath to find myself staring into the face of one of the enormous guard or shepherd dogs for which the region is famous. By accident rather than design I had assumed the posture recommended by Borrow for facing down such brutes. We stared at each other for a long moment and then the dog padded gently on its way, though whether this had anything to do with the fact that I had by chance got my eyes on a level with his I had no means of knowing. I crossed the path to continue my descent down the next field and through more rough, bush-covered ground to come out onto the road. There was not a pilgrim in sight, and all those little figures I had watched from above were now somewhere ahead of me. I walked for about a kilometre into Ruitelan.

✧

Many years before, when I was a child, I remember being deeply impressed by a play on the radio when it was called the wireless. The story concerned a man lost in a strange village in the dark, and every time he met someone and asked directions he found with mounting horror that each person he addressed was faceless. At last, in terror, he fled along a dark road into the countryside and ran into the huge figure of a policeman. Sobbing out of control, he buried his head in the policeman's chest while the latter, in time-honoured British fashion, said: "Now then, Sir, what's all this?" Gradually as he got control of himself the man explained about the faceless people in the village while the policeman kept interrupting to say, "Come, come, now, Sir." But the man persisted with his tale until the policeman appeared to believe him for he said: "Are the faces of the people in the village anything like mine?" And the man looked up at the policeman's face for the first time to see only a blank and ran screaming into the night.

I was reminded of this strange nightmare play by the people of Ruitelan. They were not faceless, but they did seem to be without speech. Perhaps it was the effect of the great bridge which now carried the highway some 150 metres above the gorge in which the village lay. Not so many years earlier, before the bridge was constructed, all the traffic must have passed through the village; now none did so, and though some of the villagers no doubt welcomed the change others may well have felt that modern life, the excitement of constant traffic, had passed them by.

Ruitelan was the last village before the pass which marked the end of old Castile and the beginning of Galicia, and Borrow claimed that though the people in these remote villages spoke Castilian it was of a coarse and unpolished variety. I wanted to test this assertion if only by persuading people to speak to me although my limited knowledge of Spanish as well as my total lack of philological expertise would probably mean that I should be as ignorant after hearing their speech as I certainly was before doing so.

I met a solitary woman as I entered the village and greeted her. She ignored me. A little further into the village I came upon a group standing in the middle of the road but though I wished them good day they said nothing in return, staring instead at the trees beyond me. I met another solitary woman and she did acknowledge my greeting but not, alas, with speech; she merely gave an inclination of the head and a most slight one at that. Then an old woman came towards me with a tiny child clasping her hand and her, too, I greeted, but the only effect of this salutation was to make the little girl burst into tears and turn her face into the old woman's skirt so as to blot out the sight of me altogether while the woman gathered the frightened child to her and stared stonily ahead. Then a tiny, ancient old man whose astonishingly bowed legs came close to making a perfect circle, tottered towards me, tapping his stick at each faltering step. He appeared to be three-quarters blind and was closely followed by a magnificent brown, long-haired Alsatian, more like a wolf than a dog, which I assumed to be the ancient one's guardian. I do not think he even heard my greeting. By this time I had reached the far side of the village and the road at once rose sharply into a narrowing gorge thick with trees. The brown dog now padded back past me to fall in beside a stolid man who was plodding up the hill ahead of me. I came level with this plodding man who was careful to look straight to his front; nonetheless, I produced yet another greeting although by now

I hardly expected a reply. All he managed was a guttural mumble of quite indistinguishable meaning.

I was at a loss to explain so universal an uninterest even in courtesy. Perhaps, now that the bridge carrying the new highway had left the village isolated once more, the passage of endless pilgrims all through the summer was seen as an unwanted invasion, an attempt by an outside world the villagers did not wish to know to intrude upon their age-old remote privacy. At this thought I began to wonder just what had happened to all the pilgrims, and it was only after I had risen considerably higher up what had become a wild and lovely tree-covered road that I glimpsed far below me once more a field bright with anoraks. There must have been a campsite or resting place for pilgrims there and I, after all, was ahead of them again. The main highway was still far above me, cut through the sheer hillside, and once when I rounded a spur to wind along a side gorge another of the spectacular road bridges carried it sixty metres above me to disappear again into the mountainside. Finally, two kilometres ahead, I saw a cluster of buildings at the top of the pass.

The Puerto de Pedrafita do Cebreiro at a height of 1,099 metres marked the pass across the great Cordillera Cantábrica and the entrance to Galicia. The small village consisted of little more than the inn, a cluster of houses and a few shops filled with trinkets and other oddments to sell to pilgrims and tourists. Half the shops displayed Santiago cakes with the cross of St James on them.

Pedrafita marked the end of the pilgrim way for me since, from there, I intended to take the road to Lugo and La Coruña, while the pilgrims would head for Sarria. I found a remote place to sit and examined the view from the pass into Galicia, which was magnificent, but a cold bite in the air reminded me how high I was and I returned to the inn.

30

The Road to Lugo

A long descent—beautiful Nogais—William Tell and whisky—wolves—the walls of Lugo—the Roman baths

I SET off the next morning from the Pass of Pedrafita in sharp intoxicating mountain air and soon began the long descent down the northern side of the great mass of the mountain barrier that separates Galicia from León and Old Castile towards the little village of Nogais in the valley below. The sun played hide and seek with fast-moving white clouds while the hills ahead of me stretched into an endless distance even as I descended into a deep valley that cut back to the pass as though a giant ploughshare had gouged out a single great furrow in the mountainside. The road twisted and turned in and out of side gorges, and I crossed one of these on a bridge so high that I felt dizzy even without looking over the side. The clear atmosphere threw the outlines of the hills into sharp relief, and for beauty of outline and grandeur of perspective that valley descent must offer one of the finest prospects in all Europe.

Nogais lay at the bottom of the valley eighteen kilometres from the pass and I reached it after three hours on the road, having maintained an exact six kilometres an hour although it had been downhill all the way. Borrow, as so often with him, arrived at Nogales, as he called it, just before sunset and he describes it in glowing terms:

> A hamlet situate in a narrow valley at the foot of the mountain, in traversing which we had spent the day. Nothing could be more picturesque than the appearance of this spot: steep hills, thickly clad with groves and forests of chestnuts, surrounded it on every side; the village itself was almost embowered in trees, and close beside it ran a purling brook.[1]

At the village Borrow joined a large group travelling with the grand post from Madrid to La Coruña, for the road was infested with bandits, and so he departed in the middle of the night. Nogais was recognisably as Borrow describes it, attractive in brilliant sunshine, with a lovely stream running through. But now the modern highway bypasses the village, and a cluster of new buildings—an hotel, an inn and a garage—cater for travellers as Nogais has been developed as a holiday centre. I sat for a while on the verandah of the inn, the village in a slight hollow before me, the green part-forested hills rising sharply behind.

From Nogais the road rose as steadily as it had descended for the first part of the day and the views were equally spectacular. I passed a Spanish family who had set out their food on a roadside table for a picnic and the children clapped me as I strode by. The road was cut high along one side of the valley and deep below in thick forest an isolated watchtower stood like a sentinel on a knoll that rose from the depths of the gorge. I think it was Roman. Then the road swept round a curve along the top of a great escarpment with Galicia spreading out into the distance before me while the main highway disappeared into another of the road tunnels. This time, however, the old road swung off round the side of the hill through which the highway had been tunnelled and I followed this in an immediate sharp descent into a valley thick with trees. The road was deserted although it must have been the highway until a few years before. The lushness of the vegetation under the trees and the sudden silence created by the absence of any traffic was filled instead with the sound of birds to make that stretch of road quite magical. Then I rounded a corner to see, high above me, another of the great road bridges which came abruptly out of the mountainside where the tunnel ended. The bridge spanned the deep valley in which I was walking for the best part of a kilometre and at its centre must have been over a hundred metres above me. Grotesquely, like some prehistoric monster, a giant truck now crossed the slender bridge, its square awkward shape in startling contrast to the idyllic greenery through which I walked far below.

Still descending I rounded another corner where stood a dilapidated half-timbered house with a dozen steps leading up to a high verandah. Two enormous dogs lay on the roadside in front of it: one came to its feet and padded towards me, the other which was even larger, only raised a languid head. The one that approached first circled me sniffing carefully and then fell in beside me. An elderly, crippled woman was standing on the verandah, supporting herself on two crutches, no doubt alerted to my approach by her dogs as passing walkers must have been the rare exception rather than the rule. I called a greeting to her and she replied warmly and the dogs were satisfied though I remained wary of the large one loping along at my side. It saw me fifty metres down the hill before returning to its station in front of the house.

After reaching the bottom of the gorge the road rose again through the small, slate-roofed, dilapidated village of Cruzul. A forge was at work and though no one was in evidence I sensed other work in progress behind the façade of the old street. I came to a little village store and went in to seek refreshment. The dark interior was like a film set: a counter ran down one side of the store in front of which stood two rickety, lopsided high stools; the end of the shop was a piled jumble of goods, a mountain that had accumulated without any semblance of order so that the extraction of any one item threatened to bring down the whole pyramid. An old man sat behind the bar, his hat pulled down square over his head, his eyes glued to that indispensable aid and comfort of modern living, the television set. But, astonishingly, the shelves behind him were stacked to the ceiling with one of the

finest selections of whiskies I have ever seen while a separate cabinet boasted a wide variety of Havana cigars ranging from small through medium to giant size. The old man turned his unwilling attention to me and I asked for a beer. He was totally deaf and my request made no impression whatever. I tried again, pointed at some bottles—but wanted to make sure it was cold—and then to my relief he called to the door at the back end of the bar and a woman in her sixties, I judged her to be his daughter, now appeared to serve me. She produced a cold beer and I took my place on one of the stools just as another customer entered the shop. He looked in astonishment, first at me and then at my pack, which I had propped against the only bit of free wall space I could find, and we exchanged greetings before he also had a beer and settled himself on the other stool. Then the four of us, the woman standing behind the old man, solemnly watched the television which was showing *William Tell, the Saga*.

I asked about Becerrea, which was my destination, and they told me it was only a short distance up the hill out of the village and back onto the main highway. They watched me curiously as I donned my pack to depart but were too polite to ask where I came from or where I was going. From Becerrea I decided to take the bus to Lugo; I had to wait for this in a café and while drinking a coffee I examined the enormous head of a wolf that stared out at me from the wall, its great fangs displayed in a ferocious snarl. There are still wolves to be found in parts of Spain and this one, I was told, had been killed some years back in the neighbouring mountains.

From Becerrea the road to Lugo passes through low, rolling hills, gentler than the mountains from which I had emerged, not unlike the border country between England and Wales. In Lugo I found a *pensión* just outside the city walls. One of the few gates through the walls was near my inn, so I entered the old city and found its main square with the cathedral at the lower end.

Borrow reached Lugo in a state of exhaustion and fever and put up at a large *posada* outside the wall of the town "built upon a steep bank and commanding an extensive view of the country towards the east,"[2] a description which fitted my *pensión* as to situation though it was certainly not a *posada*. Borrow sold thirty Testaments in Lugo, all that he had with him, though only after recovering from two days in bed with fever. He dismissed the cathedral as a small, mean building and though it could be described in such terms when compared with other, grander Spanish cathedrals, nonetheless had somewhat more character than he allowed. Curiously, though he says Lugo has many Roman remains in the vicinity, he only gives its walls a cursory, passing mention. These, in fact, are the glory of Lugo and entirely encircle the old city; they date from Roman times, are about four metres thick and run for two kilometres with a sentry walk all the way round to provide Lugo's citizens with a perfect parade. I took a slow promenade round the walls, examining the city spread out below me as I did so, or staring over the plains of Galicia, and then made my way to the square by the cathedral.

At least Borrow was complimentary about this square, which he described as "a light cheerful place, not surrounded by those heavy cumbrous buildings with which the Spaniards both in ancient and modern times have encircled their plazas."[3] Lugo had a mere six thousand inhabitants when Borrow visited it and he dismissed the city as of little importance though wrongly describing it as the former Roman capital of Spain. Its modern growth followed the coming of the railways, which enabled it to supply the mass markets of Madrid and Barcelona with the agricultural produce of the region, and today it has a population of more than 70,000 people. The square, under its lush thick mantle of trees, was alive with evening promenaders, youths with their girlfriends, old men and old women enjoying their day's gossip, families walking small children.

I looked down from my window the next morning upon the encircling walls where joggers were taking their early exercise while beyond the city in the distance the plain was streaked with light mists that the rising sun had yet to drive away. I visited the covered market which at eight o'clock was in full swing, crowded with shoppers, and displaying a rich variety of fruit, vegetables, meat, fish and cheeses, the smells and the colours vying with each other to attain an equal impact upon the senses. In a tiny corner bar I had coffee and freshly fried *churros* dipped in sugar for about half the price I would pay anywhere else. Drunken porters, their night's work over, leant solemnly against the little bar taking brandy with their morning coffee, or just taking brandy, while two pretty teenage girls worked non-stop behind the bar to serve the stream of customers. The square which had just been washed down for the day sparkled in the morning sunlight and inside the cathedral, dark and heavy with age, the confessional boxes stood ready, all down one side, for their quota of daily penitents.

Just outside the city, on the banks of the Mino, warm springs flow into the river. The Romans constructed baths here but these were ruins in Borrow's time although he describes how they were crowded with the sick hoping to benefit from the healing power of the springs.

> *One evening I visited the baths, accompanied by my friend the bookseller. They had been built over warm springs which flow into the river. Notwithstanding their ruinous condition, they were crowded with sick, hoping to derive benefit from the waters, which are still famed for their sanative power. These patients exhibited a strange spectacle as, wrapped in flannel gowns much resembling shrouds, they lay immersed in the tepid waters amongst disjointed stones and overhung with steam and reek.*[4]

The baths have now been incorporated into an hotel; the receptionist gave me permission to view them, but all I saw were the modern equivalent of Borrow's patients: an assortment of elderly men and women swathed in towelling robes, parading slowly up and down, their wrinkled ancient faces glistening with sweat from the heat of the thermal chambers.

31

A Foreign Strand

The gardens of San Carlos—Sir John Moore—his
misfortunes and defeat—bandits—the Tower of Hercules—
La Coruña and the English connection—a blind lottery girl

THE gardens of San Carlos in the old quarter of La Coruña are on
a high promontory overlooking the sea. It is a former battery about
eighty metres square, and trees that were young in Borrow's time have
now grown to maturity to provide deep and welcome shade in high
summer. In the centre of these little gardens stands the white marble
tomb of General Moore, built as Borrow tells us "by the chivalrous
French, in commemoration of the fall of their heroic antagonist."
The original inscription simply said: "John Moore, leader of the
English armies, slain in battle, 1809." It is a most peaceful and
beautiful place and there I watched three elderly Spanish ladies settle
themselves on one of the seats facing the tomb, one raising an elegant
little parasol, quite unnecessarily under the shade of the trees, while
they made themselves comfortable as a preliminary to the conduct of
their afternoon gossip.

A number of myths have gathered round the name of Sir John
Moore. Borrow, who praises the elegance of his simple tomb, which
was beautifully looked after by the Spaniards, says Moore achieved
immortality unexpectedly and without seeking it:

> *Yes, there lies the hero, almost within sight of the glorious hill where he*
> *turned upon his pursuers like a lion at bay and terminated his career.*
> *Many acquire immortality without seeking it, and die before its first ray*
> *has gilded their name; of these was Moore. The harassed general, flying*
> *through Castile with his dispirited troops before a fierce and terrible*

enemy, little dreamed that he was on the point of attaining that for which many a better, greater, though certainly not braver man, had sighed in vain.[1]

Although controversy surrounded Moore's decision to retreat north through Spain to La Coruña, his death in battle raised him to semi-mythical status as hero to be celebrated in one of the best known poems in the English language:

Not a drum was heard, not a funeral note,
As his corse to the rampart we hurried;
Not a soldier discharged his farewell shot
O'er the grave where our hero we buried.

The evacuation of the remnant of Moore's army from La Coruña with Soult's superior forces just outside the city was the Peninsular War's equivalent to Dunkirk. The British, who have a special talent for a particular kind of myth-making, always manage to elevate their losers into winners of heroic stature. In *The Bible in Spain* Borrow speaks feelingly of Moore: "His very misfortunes were the means which secured him immortal fame; his disastrous route, bloody death, and finally his tomb on a foreign strand, far from kin and friends."[2] But writing twenty years later in *Wild Wales*, Borrow quotes a man who had served under Moore and swore that he had been shot by his own soldiers.[3]

As he lay dying Moore expressed the hope that he would be justified for his actions in Spain, but whatever the subsequent historical judgements the immediate impact was that Britain had sustained a military disaster. Moore had always been a stickler for discipline and extremely particular over regulations regarding dress, and the breakdown of discipline during the retreat to La Coruña has made that slow progression northwards of his dispirited army an epic of bad leadership. Moore, according to one of his critics,[4] signally failed to cooperate with his Spanish allies, while according to another historian he

despaired of rescuing Madrid when he saw how little reliance could be placed on Spanish assistance. His opinion was already formed that the task which had been laid on his shoulders was utterly hopeless, that the

Spaniards were spiritless, that Portugal was indefensible, that there was nothing for it but withdrawal.[5]

It was time for Wellington to take over and prove that Moore's judgement had been at fault. There was much controversy at the time of Moore's retreat and death as to his tactics, and he was blamed for not standing firm against the French while, after his death, he provided a convenient scapegoat for what at the time appeared a typically disastrous military foray.

Borrow's route into Galicia and then on to La Coruña, which I had followed more or less exactly, was also that taken by Moore's retreating army: Astorga, Villafranca, Bembibre, where many of his troops were lost to the wines of the region, Cacebelos, Nogales (Nogais), Lugo, Betanzos and La Coruña. Galicia may be poor but it is a green land. Borrow, who set out from Lugo with the post for protection against bandits, became bored halfway to La Coruña and pushed on alone, except for his servant Antonio who proved his salvation, for as he rode along two bandits appeared and aimed their carbines at him but then fled when they heard Antonio's horse coming along in the rear. This occurred at the bridge of Castellanos, and only a short distance before he reached it Borrow had passed three "ghastly heads stuck on poles," banditti who had been executed about two months earlier. As I passed this once desolate region I was greeted, alas, only by civilisation. La Coruña is surrounded by a circle of high hills and now has a population of about a quarter of a million.

One of the most extraordinary monuments in La Coruña is the Tower of Hercules, the only Roman lighthouse that is still functioning. I sat on the green grass that slopes down from the lighthouse to the cliffs and watched the grey sea as the Atlantic mist rolled in towards the shore.

Then I explored the town. I have always been attracted by seaports and La Coruña, apart from a long history with both Roman and Moorish connections, has played a particular role in Anglo-Spanish relations. John of Gaunt, Duke of Lancaster, landed here in 1386 to pursue his claim to the throne of Castile; the Spanish Armada first took refuge from storms and then finally set sail from La Coruña on its fateful journey to conquer England in 1588, and the port was partially sacked by Drake the following year; and Moore made his last stand here. The old part of the city is charming, while the crowded modern part has been developed as a seaside resort and I was amused on taking an early morning walk along the seafront which was as yet empty of its massed ranks of bathers and sun worshippers to see tractors, trailing special rakes, driving along the golden sands to smooth them over for a new day's swarm of visitors. It was an aspect of tourist concern I had not encountered before.

Borrow stayed at a *posada* in the Calle Real, which is now a pedestrian walkway and La Coruña's most fashionable street. I took a table outside a café and sat for an hour at midday over a glass of wine while I watched a blind girl selling lottery tickets on the other side of the street. Unlike most lottery vendors she did not shout to advertise her wares and when not dealing with a customer sat quite still, her head tilted to catch the sunlight; most of the narrow street was in shade but her spot was so placed as to capture a shaft of sunlight that blazed down between the buildings of a narrow alleyway across on my side of the street. At first I did not realise that she was blind and though she worked hard to catch the sun her skin seemed possessed of a quality that resisted all colour for it was quite pale, as though she spent her entire life indoors. She was obliged to alter her pose whenever a customer approached her but would then reposition her head at its angle towards the sun and I sketched her in this position. Her face, always set and staring sightlessly at the sun, was smooth and young but in my sketch it came out harrowed, the eternal blackness of her life revealing itself through the smooth exterior.

32

The Unlikely Saint

*The legend of St James—the destruction of Santiago—a
city of pilgrims—midday mass—Borrow in two minds—the
censers—a gigantic fair—the Alameda—Vigo—a history
lesson—British sea power and Vigo*

IT is historically highly unlikely that St James or James the Great,
who with John was known as one of the "Sons of Thunder", ever
set foot in Spain, yet his shrine at Santiago de Compostela is second
only to Jerusalem as a place of pilgrimage for Christians. The claim
that James preached the Gospel in Spain before his martyrdom first
surfaces in the seventh century. This was followed by the second
legend that his relics were taken to Santiago, via El Padrón, in the
ninth century, although neither legend is any longer believed, at
any rate not outside Spain. For some reason that is not clear one of
the alleged hands of St James escaped from the rest of his relics in
Santiago to find a resting place in the abbey of Reading in Berkshire.
The legend of St James grew to such proportions during the tenth
to sixteenth centuries that Santiago became the principal centre of
pilgrimage in Western Europe over this period, more especially, no
doubt, because Jerusalem was in the hands of the Saracens for most
of these centuries.

One result of the legend was the building of monasteries along
the route to provide hospitality for the pilgrims, while the journey to
Santiago became so popular that images of the saint were decorated
with the pilgrim hat and scallop shield that are associated with
Compostela. Another result of the growth of the St James cult was
to link Galicia—then seen by Europeans as the end of the earth—to

the rest of Europe by the route from Santiago across the Pyrenees, into France and Christian Europe to the north, at a time when most of Spain was in the hands of the Moors, so that the endless stream of pilgrims provided this remote corner of Spain with a sense of solidarity with a wider Christian world.

El Mansour (Abu Amir al-Mansour), the ruler of the Umayyid Caliphate in Spain from 978 to 1002, wanted to humiliate the Christians in those parts of Spain that he did not control, and in 997 he used the pretext that his vassal, King Bermudo II of Galicia, had refused tribute as an excuse to invade Galicia with his army and destroy Santiago. His invasion was referred to in Moorish accounts as the "Campaign of San Yacoub"; on his way to Santiago El Mansour burned the sanctuary of St James at El Padrón and then arrived before the walls of Santiago whose population had already fled. El Mansour's army pillaged everything it could carry away and totally laid waste this greatest centre of Christian pilgrimage so that not a trace of the church was left. The destruction of Santiago was a major catastrophe for Christian Europe, which trembled beyond the Pyrenees in fear that El Mansour would come north, though he never did.

ↅ

When Borrow came to Santiago eight centuries after this cataclysmic event he claimed that its glory as a place of pilgrimage was rapidly passing away, but though this may have appeared to be the case in the troubled 1830s a reversal of fortune has clearly taken place since. Santiago is surrounded by green hills, and almost everything about it is connected with the legends of St James, while relics of the saint, El Mansour's depredations notwithstanding, are still, it is claimed, housed in the cathedral.

Unversed in matters relating to saints and ignorant as to their dates, I came to Santiago on 15 July—only ten days before the Saint's Feast, which falls on 25 July—so that my visit coincided with the rapidly approaching climax of the Holy Year when all devout pilgrims would like to be in Santiago, and I found the city overflowing. I came to it by bus from La Coruña and as I walked from the bus station on the outskirts of the city towards the centre I became part of a steady stream of pilgrims all making for the great cathedral. Some had come by bus and others, no doubt, had their own means of transport but most of them, as far as I could judge, were walking into Santiago from the various pilgrim ways that converge on the city, which was packed solid either with pilgrims or sightseers who had decided to take in Santiago on their travels.

The cathedral faces a great plaza, and its baroque eighteenth-century façade is unique; twin sets of steps lead up to the massive doors, which are set high above the level of the square, and these were crowded with slow-moving, shuffling people. Even for devout pilgrims and enthusiastic sightseers this shuffle into the cathedral appeared excessive, but then my ignorance in matters religious was once more to blame because, fortuitously, I had arrived in time for the midday mass, which the other shufflers no doubt knew about in advance. So I had to queue to get into the cathedral and noticed that as the line of pilgrims ahead of me entered the great doors they traced with their fingers the cross of St James that was indented into the stonework beside the door.

The cathedral was packed: every seat in the nave and the transepts

had long been taken and the people were standing ten deep in the aisles while others had climbed onto the projecting stonework of the great pillars in order to obtain a view. I could just see the high altar by standing on tiptoe and peering between the heads of those in front of me rather as I remember doing in packed cinemas as a child when I tried to get a better view—or any view at all—between the heads of much larger adults in the rows in front of me. A slow moving queue, four abreast, shuffled a step at a time round behind the altar to view the relics or treasures of St James.

A priest, meanwhile, was conducting community hymn-singing while the enormous congregation waited for the service to begin. He had a lovely voice and would first instruct and encourage the people sitting in the nave and they would sing a verse in response to his efforts; then he would turn to those in the transept to one side of him and repeat the exercise, followed by those on the other side. When the three groups had each received instruction and sung a practice verse he would make them sing together. But though his was a feat of charismatic and expert singing leadership which earned my admiration, I could not help regarding him as a sort of senior Scoutmaster controlling a gigantic campfire singsong, the climax of a two-week jamboree.

By chance I found myself outside the door of the robing room which was open, so I was able to watch the Cardinal Archbishop and his acolytes as they assumed their final accoutrements and the mitre was placed on the Cardinal Archbishop's head and a quite small man with rubicund face and undistinguished physique was transformed by mitre and cope and gold and red into a figure of significance. Then, to great excitement and craning and turning of heads, the Cardinal's procession proceeded up the aisle and the service began.

Borrow, the complexities of whose religious beliefs intrigued me more and more as I followed him round Spain, first paints a wonderful picture of the cathedral which he describes as

> *a majestic venerable pile, in every respect calculated to excite awe and admiration; indeed, it is almost impossible to walk its long dusk aisles, and hear the solemn music and the noble chanting, and inhale the incense of the mighty censers, which are at times swung so high by machinery as to smite the vaulted roof, whilst gigantic tapers glitter here and there amongst the gloom, from the shrine of many a saint, before which the worshippers are kneeling, breathing forth their prayers and petitions for help, love, and mercy, and entertain a doubt that we are treading the floor of a house where God delighteth to dwell.*[1]

But having bestowed this encomium of awed delight upon the cathedral, Borrow remembered that he was a Protestant and that

Santiago de Compostela belonged to the Pope and all his works and so, perhaps mindful of the Rev. Brandram and the other devout members of the Bible Society back in London, he continues in a very different, classic Borrow vein: "Yet the Lord is distant from that house; He hears not, He sees not, or if He do, it is with anger. What availeth that solemn music, that noble chanting, that incense of sweet savour...?"

I became claustrophobic: with the sheer numbers, with the induced religiosity and, also, in inverse proportion as ritual attempted to replace logical thought, yet such feelings were all cast aside by the mighty sweep of the great censer whose vast arc extending from the vault of the high roof almost to the floor of the huge cathedral holds all who view it in awe. As I watched this great urn leaving its trail of incense in the air to fill the cathedral with its sweet scent I imagined one of the huge Manchegan bulls standing at bay, stolid and formidable, in the aisle at the exact spot where the censer achieves the lowest point of its trajectory, the bull confident in its enormous strength, willing to face this new flying enemy, but the censer at the full extent of its irresistible swing cracks open the head of the huge beast like an eggshell to continue its upward swing leaving the now lifeless hulk of the black monster limply dead, a sacrifice on the cold flagstones, as though it had just been killed in the arena.

Leaving the saint's festivities inside the cathedral, I came out to a different variety of festival altogether. In the great square before the cathedral as well as throughout the winding narrow streets that surround this magnificent pile the beggars and hucksters were out in force—money jobbers, and petty dealers, hawkers and tricksters, flute players and other performers were all set to make a profit from the pilgrims and sightseers as no doubt such sleight-of-hand merchants had done since medieval times. Groups of pilgrims were being instructed, tourists were being shepherded by their minders, a quartet of Peruvian Indians played exquisite flute music so that the centre of Santiago had been turned into a gigantic fair. The pilgrims who had made their way to Santiago this year, young and old, devout and curious, holidaymakers or professional beggars, were a replica of those who had done the same thing across the ages. The general mood was that of a holiday, and though many of the pilgrims were, I am sure, believers, many more were on vacation and had decided that the pilgrim way provided as fine a break from their normal lives as anything else.

Borrow found an excellent ally for the distribution of his Testaments in the person of a bookseller:

> *At Saint James I met with a kind and cordial coadjutor in my biblical labours in the bookseller of the place, Rey Romero, a man of about sixty. This excellent individual, who was both wealthy and respected, took up the matter with an enthusiasm which doubtless emanated from on high, losing no opportunity of recommending my book...*[2]

Later, when alone in the Alameda on a moonlight night, Borrow encounters the extraordinary character of Benedict Mol, who makes periodic appearances through the pages of *The Bible in Spain*. Benedict Mol, so Borrow claims, was a Swiss, once a soldier in the Walloon guards whose father had been the hangman of Lucerne. He was now searching for treasure in Santiago. He is one of the odder characters of the many who appear in the course of Borrow's strange narrative.[3]

I went for a walk in the Alameda; this is a beautiful formal park, one of whose ends overlooks the surrounding hills from a high point of the city. The park was virtually free of pilgrims almost all of whom remained hustling and bustling in the centre of the city although I did come across a young pilgrim couple who were so much in love that St James and all his works were for the time being forgotten. They were sitting astride a bench facing one another as they ate their sandwiches, munching their ways towards one another's lips, their packs and staves on the ground beside them, their eyes fixed forever on the future that only love can supply.

I returned to the cathedral in the afternoon to find it practically deserted so that I was able to admire its great arches and the extraordinary machinery on high which is used to swing the giant censers. Then I wandered the narrow streets, many of them oddly deserted once away from the magnetic attractions of the great plaza before the cathedral. I had not even considered trying to stay in Santiago but set off by bus for Vigo.

୧୬

The approach to Vigo is dramatic, its bay one of the largest and most beautiful in Europe; along the steep hills that surround the bay much modern development has taken place as the city has been expanded to form part of a new Spanish Riviera. As Borrow describes it, "The town occupies the lower part of a lofty hill, which, as it ascends, becomes extremely steep and precipitous, and the top of which is crowned with a strong fort or castle. It is a small compact place, surrounded with low walls; the streets are narrow, steep, and winding, and in the middle of the two is a small square."[4]

Since then, however, the town has crept up the hillsides and developed into a substantial city. The wide inlet of the bay was covered by an extraordinary pattern of flat barges, moored in place and none in use. Vigo stretches steeply upwards immediately from the bay and is a thriving busy port, the largest fishing port in Spain, and a major industrial town as well as tourist resort and naval station with a population now in excess of a quarter of a million.

In the old part of the city I came to a sudden opening between buildings and there, spread out below me, was the bay while up a steep eminence behind me were the remains of the old fort. I asked a man with a face like Franco where to find the cathedral.

"The con-cathedral," he replied pedantically.

"Why con?" I inquired.

"You have heard of Tui?" he asked.

"Yes, I have heard of Tui though, alas, it is not on my itinerary," I replied.

"Tui is our provincial capital and so, of course, it had the cathedral. Vigo used to be very small and so did not merit a cathedral. But today, as you can see," and he gestured at the thronged street in which we were standing, "we have grown enormously and are now much bigger than Tui, so it was felt that we should have a cathedral too. You understand?"

"Yes, I understand, and so your church became a con-cathedral with Tui."

"Exactly."

He congratulated me for grasping so readily the explanation he had offered; it was a form of double congratulation—to me for understanding and to himself for the precision of his exposition. He must, I think, have been a schoolmaster for he had spoken throughout with a slowness and clarity that were unmistakable in their pedantic intent to ensure that I should understand every word, which I did.

I pointed to the remains of the fort above us and he treated me to another small history lesson. Then he pointed to a large stone that formed part of the parapet by which we were standing, to indicate a bunch of grapes and a fragment of vine that had been carved into the stonework: "The sign of our city, our province," he said proudly and then, courteously, he excused himself as I had engaged him in historical explanation for some twenty minutes. We shook hands and went our separate ways and when I found the con-cathedral I understood his careful explanation for it was little more than a large and quite undistinguished church.

Vigo Bay has featured prominently, from time to time, in the history of British sea power and Anglo-Spanish relations. The bay, as Borrow says, "is oblong, running far into the land, and so capacious that a thousand sail of the line might ride in it uncrowded."[5] Vigo was twice captured by Drake in 1585 and 1589. In 1702, at the beginning of the War of Spanish Succession, an expedition under Sir George Rooke was sent to capture Cádiz or perhaps Gibraltar, but Rooke's attack upon Cádiz was a fiasco and he refused to contemplate an assault upon Gibraltar instead. Having heard that a Spanish treasure fleet had slipped into Vigo Bay, he set sail northwards. Rooke took Vigo Bay by surprise, destroyed the escort warships and then burnt or sunk the treasure fleet though not before taking treasure to the value of one million pounds sterling. As it happened, little credit for the action could be given to Rooke himself since he was incapacitated throughout the action by a severe attack of gout. The capture of plate led to the naming of Vigo Street in London.

33

To the End of the Earth

El Padrón—Borrow's strange guide—friendly Galicians—
Noia—a Spanish Miss Flite—hórreos—Muros in holiday
mood—a savage coast—the Spanish-American connection—
women gathering the harvest—Cee

ACCORDING to legend, El Padrón, the town of the patron saint, is
the principal place where St James stayed while in Galicia. Its history
goes back to Roman times and it is, or was, a small port at the head of
an arm of the sea. Most of old Padrón lies between the main Vigo to
Santiago road and the Ulla river and consists of tiny twisting streets
and little squares. A magnificent avenue or promenade lined with
huge thick sycamore trees with seats beneath them fronts the river.
It was a popular place and in the early evening each of its bench seats
was occupied by its own group of elderly ladies enjoying their daily
exchange of news. A bridge over the river led to the road to Noia and
Cape Finisterre, which I would take the next day. This part of the
small town could not have changed much since Borrow had passed
through it; on the other side of the main road, opposite my inn, a
botanical garden of elegant symmetry contained trees and shrubs
from half the corners of the world—Mexico, China, the Himalayas,
the Canaries, and other exotic places—each plant with its own plaque
recording place of origin and date of acquisition, while two giant
sequoias dominated the centre of the garden which also boasted a
number of secluded corners suitable for trysting lovers. A marble bust
celebrated a certain Dr D. Ernesto Gende who had been responsible
for its creation in the late nineteenth century. For a change that

226

evening I ate rough in a tiny bar with fixed planks for seats and a limited menu of red wine and tortillas.

I was now ready for my walk to Cape Finisterre. Borrow sent his servant and horses on to Santiago and hired a guide to take him to the Cape though the guide, like others he hired, turned out to be a near useless halfwit. First, the man who had provided him with a horse and promised to act as his guide, brings with him a "strange-looking figure of the biped species" and, after leading Borrow a short distance from Padrón, says that he himself must return but that this strange fellow will lead him: "As for the man, no tengo usted cuidado, he is the best guide in Galicia, speaks English and French, and will bear you pleasant company." When the man, who has already cheated him, demands more money, Borrow in fury rides him down, and the guide, "far from offering any assistance to his principal, no sooner saw the jaca in motion than he ran on by its side, without word or comment, further than striking himself lustily on the thigh with his right palm."[1] Thereafter, the odd behaviour of Borrow's guide increases.

Borrow did not try to justify his trip to Cape Finisterre in terms of his Bible distributing activities—he only had one Testament with him at the time—but was determined to satisfy an urge to visit what in those days must have been a wild place: Cape the End of the Earth from the Latin *Finis terrae*, one of the most distinctive landmarks of all Europe.

Borrow claimed that the Galicians were surly and unfriendly but that was the last thing I found. By eleven the next day I was walking across the Sierra de Brabanza which forms the backbone of the peninsula that lies to the north of Padrón. My winding road missed the villages of this remote region though I sometimes saw them off to the side. Once, just after taking refreshment in a wayside bar alive with newly spawned kittens, I met an old farmer driving half a dozen cows across the road: he squinted at me from under the peak of his cap, then transferred his gaze to my pack before greeting me with a high-pitched cackle of delight to tell me I would become much hotter before I reached Noia. He proved only too right, for though I had set off in the cool of an early morning mist the day became exceptionally warm. Other farm labourers whom I met on the road were equally friendly in their greetings but possibly this had something to do with my rarity value for, unlike the pilgrim way, I doubt that many solitary hikers came along this particular road. I descended from the Sierra de Brabanza through a mixture of high forest of eucalyptus trees and open farmland with occasional glimpses of the sea at the bottom of the steep valley ahead of me. It was a Saturday and when I came to a bar on the outskirts of the little village of Portobravo I found half the workers of the place stopping off for a drink to celebrate the end of their week.

Noia was crowded with Spanish holidaymakers, for the season was now well under way. The town, an untidy yet pretty place, sits at the end of an arm of the sea and though sufficiently unremarkable to escape the attention of guidebooks possesses a charm of its own. I took a drink at one of a number of tables outside a bar to become spectator at an embarrassing spectacle as an aggressive, alcoholic woman approached to demand cigarettes from the other drinkers. None smoked or were prepared to offer her a cigarette so she began to curse them. She took the spare seat at a table already occupied by an elderly inoffensive couple and her vilification forced them to get up and leave. Others turned their backs upon her, so she focused her attention upon me.

"Cigarillos!" she shouted as I stared at the park on the other side of the road.

"Cigarillos!" she repeated several decibels higher.

"No entiendo, soy extranjero," I replied with suitable mendacity. She began again, this time with a long stream of abuse. I haltingly replied: "I am foreigner, sorry, no understand, no speak the Spanish."

A waiter had now appeared in the doorway where, however, he merely stood pondering action, reluctant to intervene as I had noticed to be the case with waiters elsewhere in Spain. They appeared either to be more tolerant of such misbehaviour than English waiters in comparable situations or less ready to have a confrontation with an awkward customer. Now, however, my drunken interlocutor heaved herself to her feet with more oaths and departed up the road shouting. The waiter came to my table, shrugged and smiled, relieved that he had not been obliged to take action: "We have to put up with them sometimes," he said. "The Señor did not mind?"

From Noia to Cape Finisterre was a remarkably beautiful stretch of road, much of it deserted with comparatively little traffic. Borrow cut across the hills with his strange guide who runs away from him and then, when Borrow finds him again, pretends to be someone else. I, however, kept to the coast road, switchbacking up and down headlands, and for most of the time I was in sight of the sea. Sometimes it rained and dull heavy Atlantic clouds made the landscape gloomy and threatening, but otherwise the sun played games from behind light white clouds as these raced inland over the barrier of mountains. It was a walk of impressions and oddly attractive vignettes. In one village I sought refuge from the rain in a roadside bus shelter while eating a mid-morning snack and was reminded that it was a Sunday as the good ladies of the community came past me, umbrellas battling against a rainy breeze, on their way to church. One little old lady, dressed all in black, was carefully ignored by the others; she was possessed of a certain contained raffishness of manner as though she merely awaited a suitable opportunity to give it full rein while her sombre black clothes were enhanced with strange additions, wisps of garment that fulfilled no obvious purpose although they fluttered from her shoulders and waist in the breeze, invitingly ready to be seized by mischievous children. She wore an enormous wide-brimmed black hat which served her as an umbrella and from whose curled up brim little spouts and cascades of water shot out in front of her every time she nodded her head. She waved at me and when I returned her salutation from across the road her whole face lit up with pleasure. She had the appearance of a Spanish Miss Flite on her way to Chancery.

Later, when the rain had stopped though the day remained overcast, I came to the brow of a gentle hill to be met by a band oompahing its way up the long reverse incline: the band was composed solely of men; they wore uniform white shirts and thin black ties and black trousers, the Spanish equivalent of the Salvation Army on their way to a church parade.

It was on this walk that I first saw the curious little barn-like structures or *hórreos*, the ancient wooden or stone granaries built close to houses, like little chapels, for the storage of the harvest grain. They are oblong in shape and raised five or so feet above the ground on stout posts or stilts so as to protect the crop from rats, while the slatted sides allow a breeze to keep down humidity. Their steep gabled roofs, often covered with bright tiles and ornamented at the ends with elaborately carved curlicues, had much in common with the Dayak mausoleums to be found along the banks of rivers in Borneo. They are peculiar to Galicia and the Asturian coast.

Muros was crowded with Spanish holidaymakers whose festive mood was much increased by the garish and noisy funfair on the small harbour mole. All along the front people sat at tables outside the many cafés or wandered along the parade in the semi-aimless fashion of those with time on their hands and nothing to do with it. The town rose sharply behind the seafront, and as I was exploring it I passed two women who were conversing in the unmistakable accents of the English shires, one mentioning High Wycombe. In a little square back on the seafront I sketched five old ladies sitting on a bench, the last of whom—nearest to where I sat—was a little dwarf, her small legs dangling like a child's above the ground. She would bend forwards to peer along the line of the other ladies whenever she wished to make a contribution to the conversation. My sketch was not much good though I enjoyed doing it. At another table, closer to mine, a group of teenage children were drinking Coca-Cola and idling away their time as only teenagers can; one of the girls came ostensibly to ask a question, but in reality to see what I was sketching. Her eyes widened in delight at my grotesque effort though it did make her turn sharply to look at the bench of old ladies; then she returned to have a giggle with her friends.

There was no one about the next morning as I walked out of Muros along the front except for workmen dismantling the funfair ready to move on to the next seaside resort on its itinerary and a few fishermen laying out their nets on the shingle. Of this coastline, Borrow says:

> *There is an air of stern and savage grandeur in everything around,*
> *which strongly captivates the imagination. This savage coast is the first*
> *glimpse of Spain which the voyager from the north catches, or he who has*
> *ploughed his way across the wide Atlantic... From what land but that*
> *before me could have proceeded those portentous beings who astounded*
> *the Old World and filled the New with horror and blood. Alva and*
> *Philip, Cortez and Pizarro—stern colossal spectres looming through*
> *the gloom of bygone years, like yonder granite mountains through the*
> *haze, upon the eye of the mariner. Yes, yonder is indeed Spain; flinty,*
> *indomitable Spain; land emblematic of its sons!* [2]

I rose round a steep point to the little resort of San Francisco whose name reminded me of the enduring Spanish-American connection. If one examines a map of the United States half the names of its largest state, Texas, are Spanish as they are in intervening states—New Mexico, Arizona or Nevada—before California, the most Spanish as well as the richest state of all. There is beauty in the Spanish names: San Diego de Alcalá, San Luis Obispo, Santa Rosa, Pueblo, Amarillo, San Angelo, San Carlos, Santa Cruz, Los Angeles and San Francisco itself; and apart from the saint names the map is everywhere strewn with Spanish geographic terms—*rio* and *mesa* and *sierra*.

After rounding the point of San Francisco I began to walk due north and across a calm blue sea I could distinguish the hazy grey outline of Cape Finisterre on the horizon, pointing like a finger out into the Atlantic. On my right the mountain rose, rounded and old like the Highlands of Scotland, at first sharply green with occasional stunted trees, later to become more rugged with increasingly frequent outcrops of rocks.

The harvest was being gathered along this stretch of coast, the work all done by women; often they were bent double as they gathered the stooks of maize and most were middle-aged or elderly with tough sunburnt, seamed brown faces. They wore dark voluminous dresses that spread elegantly from the waist, even in the fields, and black headscarves that were drawn tight over their skulls and then knotted at the back so that the ends hung down like twin pigtails, and over these they placed wide-brimmed straw hats.

At the end of a very long day's walk I topped an immense headland to look down upon the bay of Corcubión though it was still some miles distant. I stopped for a final refreshment in a little bar whose only other guests were two swaggering policemen sporting the inevitable large revolvers at their hips. My hostess brought me a bowl of cherries, compliments of the house to a weary traveller. I was accompanied on my final kilometre by a reeling drunk who appeared from nowhere and tried, happily in vain, to keep pace with me before he collapsed into a ditch hissing out an untuneful song through wine-soaked lips. I then entered the southern end of Cee which looked more attuned to decaying industry than to tourism; it was a drab place with a battered messy waterfront, black from coaling operations, though its shops sold all the cheap gaudy toys of the seaside resort—balls and buckets and spades. Across the bay was the much prettier little town of Corcubión.

34

At the End of the Earth

Interest in pilgrims—Finisterre—the Cape—Borrow helped by his guide—the sea at its most beautiful—Borrow arrested as a Carlist—the Alcalde of Corcuvion—a perfect interlude

WHEN eventually I came to sit on the great promontory of Cape Finisterre and stare out across an endless blue sea I could only reflect on timelessness and mortality. The sea in its changing moods goes on forever yet, as Conrad tells us, has "no compassion, no faith, no law, no memory", while we mortals merely fiddle our way through life thinking we are important before we return to the dust from which we are supposed to have come.

Over my coffee that morning—as far as I could judge I was the inn's sole customer—my hostess asked me where I had already travelled in Spain and whether I had seen many pilgrims on the road to Santiago. She was certainly not the first person to ask me about pilgrims; others had made similar inquiries when they discovered I was walking. They became excited at the prospect of lots of pilgrims which, I think, they saw as a compliment to Spain; but more than that the ingrained Catholicism of the Spanish people, even if they themselves were not churchgoers or believers, saw the huge number of pilgrims as a source of pride: they were coming to Spain to seek the comfort of an icon, a saint who could give them absolution—Spanish absolution—a reminder that Catholic Spain had long regarded itself as the principal guardian of the faith in Europe. The Catholic Christian belief is as integral a part of Spanish custom as is Muslim belief in Islamic countries.

I made a late start that morning since the walk to Finisterre was a mere fourteen kilometres. Corcubión was far more attractive than Cee and was busy with what, for Spain, was a great deal of early morning activity when I passed through it at about ten o'clock. But steady rain deprived the town of the sparkling brightness which had winked at me across the bay the evening before. Once through Corcubión I rose sharply into the hills which formed the promontory of Cape Finisterre. When Borrow reached Corcubión he had to make inquiries about Finisterre, for then there was no road to it, and he was obliged to walk along "a beach of dazzling white sand" rather than along the top of the promontory. Moreover, so strange did his desire to visit the Cape appear to the local people, that he was followed and later arrested as a Carlist spy, a comic, near tragic adventure that provided him with a suitably dramatic sequence in *The Bible in Spain*.

The road I followed was an easy one, up and down through forest, until I came to the edge of a great cliff overlooking a sheltered cove far below where yellow sands sparkled between the green trees which reached right up the cliff side from base to summit. The village of Finisterre with its little harbour lay another five kilometres round the bay. Borrow describes Finisterre as a village of about one hundred houses where he sought in vain for an inn at which he might stable his horse, but he found no inn while the people were suspicious and hostile. Today, Finisterre has half a dozen inns and a good many restaurants while its harbour is crowded with small boats, and the remoteness of Borrow's time has been replaced by the accessibility of the holiday trail. Yet there are still places in the world where visitors are a rarity and where there is hostility to the stranger because he is a stranger although that must now be a rapidly vanishing state of human animation.

Borrow stopped to examine a small dismantled fort facing the bay: "and, whilst engaged in this examination, it more than once occurred to me that we were ourselves the objects of scrutiny and investigation; indeed, I caught a glimpse of more than one countenance peering upon us through the holes and chasms of the walls."[1] The remoteness, which the people in Borrow's time undoubtedly felt, has disappeared;

no one shows the slightest interest in the wanderings of a visitor for he no longer represents anything out of the ordinary.

The extremity of Cape Finisterre lies three and a half kilometres from the little town and the road rises all the way. There is a tiny Norman church halfway up the hill out of Finisterre with a wonderfully carved door and this was gleaming in the early afternoon sun for, after the rain of the morning, the day had turned into one of the most beautiful I could recall: the sky was blue and cloudless, the sea millpond calm, and the distant mountains across the bay beneath which I had walked the previous day rose green-grey to their sharp serrated rock-ridged outlines. Borrow, having approached the Cape along the beach, had then to ascend sheer cliffs from the sea and became exhausted with the climb, so much so that his strange, semi-dwarf guide who appeared entirely unaffected by the effort, was obliged to help him.

To my guide, however, the ascent appeared to be neither toilsome nor difficult. The heat of the day for him had no terrors, no moisture was wrung from his tanned countenance; he drew not one short breath; and hopped upon the stones and rocks with all the provoking agility of a mountain goat. Before we had accomplished one-half of the ascent, I felt myself quite exhausted. I reeled and staggered. "Cheer up, master mine; be of good cheer, and have no care," said the guide. "Yonder I see a wall of stones; lie down beneath it in the shade." He put his long and strong arm round my waist, and, though his stature compared with mine was that of a dwarf, he supported me as if I had been a child...[2]

It was odd that Borrow, who was of large physique, immensely strong and renowned for his walking prowess, should have collapsed in this way although he had suffered from fever at Lugo.

There was a small lighthouse at the extremity of the Cape before it fell away hundreds of metres to the ocean below; there was also a parking space for sightseers, a few small stalls selling trinkets and a refreshment bar. I made my way as far down the end of the promontory as I could, away from other less adventurous visitors, and then sat to contemplate. There were no ships on the horizon, only two tiny boats far below: one a fishing boat chugging out to sea, the other a pleasure craft. The brilliant sun in a cloudless sky

made everything glitter so that Cape Finisterre looked beautiful and inviting and just the place for a siren to attract the unwary onto the rocks. Borrow reported similar weather and no vessels at sea:

> *Of all the ten thousand barks which annually plough those seas in sight of that old cape, not one was to be descried. It was a blue shiny waste, broken by no object save the black head of a spermaceti whale... On all sides there was grandeur and sublimity. After gazing from the summit of the cape for nearly an hour we descended.*[3]

Despite the blue loveliness of the scene I should have preferred a storm to make the Cape wild and dangerous as its reputation demands, for then, truly, it would have lived up to its name—Cape the End of the Earth. I was loath to leave. The Cape has a magic all its own, and just as the Pillars of Hercules guarded the gateway to the unknown for the ancients so Cape Finisterre, remote and wild, a place of legend, was the end of the earth for medieval Spain.

When Borrow returned to Finisterre from the Cape he was arrested on suspicion of being the pretender Don Carlos himself and the episode provides a dramatic chapter in his story: he is sent to Corcubión where he is examined by the *alcalde*, who acquits him of the absurd charges against him and befriends him. The *alcalde* talks of "the grand Baintham" whom Borrow recognises as Jeremy Bentham! Then he provides Borrow with an excellent meal before he takes leave of his rescuer: "'I return to Saint James to-morrow,' I replied, 'and I sincerely hope that some occasion will occur which will enable me as to acquaint the world with the hospitality which I have experienced from so accomplished a scholar as the Alcalde of Corcuvion.'"4

I got back to Finisterre where no one was remotely interested in my doings and watched a catch of herrings being offloaded in the little harbour. I had seen the Cape at its most alluring, though hardly its most daunting. That hauntingly lovely afternoon at the extremity of Cape Finisterre facing the great Atlantic provided an unforgettable interlude in my travels round Spain.

35

Germans, Statistics and Trees

Stereotype Germans—Spain's economy—the naval dockyards at Ferrol—a conversation in a café—the trees of the Alameda—I enrage a patriotic Ferrolese—elm trees

THERE is a British stereotype of the typical German that is the product of two world wars though it goes back considerably further in time. Some stereotypes are crude and brutal, the result of wartime hatred and the exaggerations of propaganda, and often they tell as much about their originators as ever they do about their targets, so that malice and envy are inextricably intertwined. The Second World War signalled the end of the British Empire as well as the inexorable decline of Britain from her top-rank position as a world power and subconsciously the British have blamed the Germans ever since. Today, it is politically quite incorrect to construct stereotypes of other peoples but, of course, we do it all the time. The British think of the Germans as didactic, hard-working, without humour but always attempting to make heavy, laboured jokes that are not funny (unlike British humour), earnest, intense, arrogant, self-important, physically heavy (sausage-eating), easy to laugh at because they take themselves so seriously, and much else besides. They have also been responsible for the German "miracle" whereby they made Germany the most powerful economy of Europe, something the British both envied and admired.

These stereotypes were brought to my notice when I left Cape Finisterre for La Coruña. I had idled the first part of the morning away in the little harbour watching the fishing boats bring home their overnight catches before taking the mid-morning bus to La Coruña; from there I intended to continue by bus on to Ferrol ready for my walk along the north coast. At the bus stop I met a young German on his way to climb in the Picos de Europa. We sat together in the bus and discussed Spain. Like many serious young Germans he was full of information, which he was only too anxious and happy to impart, but what he had not bargained for was the fact that I, too, am full of information.

He had noticed that the hotels and inns were only half full even though it was nearly the height of the tourist season. "Galicia has the highest rate of unemployment in Spain and the average for the country is 22 per cent." "Indeed?" "Oh yes," and he produced figures for the other provinces which, if less daunting than those for Galicia, were daunting enough. My friend was now set. He wriggled himself into a more comfortable position from which to assault me with facts—I was sitting in the window seat—and then dealt with the tourist industry. "They are not doing very well," he said. I suggested that if the tourists did not come, perhaps that was due to the other countries of Europe also being in the economic doldrums. "They have increased their take from tourism steadily over the last five years," I added, "and earn from it nearly double what Germany does." "Ah, but we do other things," he replied, though I do not think he was altogether pleased at the way the conversation was moving, and from tourism he passed, with just a suspicion of haste, to the European Union. "Naturally they are pleased to be in the European Community, because they get great benefits from it." He gave me figures. He reminded me of a schoolmaster who used the same tone when speaking of the ancient Gauls being brought under the yoke of Rome: as a people who had to be disciplined. "But are we not all supposed to get great benefits from membership of the EU? Isn't that the point of it?" I asked. "Yes, it is good for us all, but Spain is receiving large convergence funds," and he gave me more figures.

Our bus passed what looked like a small slag heap, in the process of being "greened", though of what it was composed I could not tell. The sight of it led to another lecture on Spain's mineral production, which was not very substantial, I gathered, a matter of iron ore, zinc and lead. Then to my considerable pleasure he passed on to agriculture and Spain's wheat production. "Spain is the fourth producer of wheat in Europe after France, Britain and Italy," he told me. "What of Turkey and Ukraine?" I asked a little unfairly but he dismissed them as not properly part of Europe. "They might be soon, if we expand as planned," I said, "but in any case you are not correct." "What other countries produce more wheat than Spain?" "Poland and Romania." I do not think they had entered at all into his calculations.

It was a long ride and when we turned into the big bus station at La Coruña I felt sufficiently equipped with statistics to conduct a lecture on Spain's economy. My German friend intended to stay in La Coruña, so we took leave of one another and I proceeded at once to Ferrol.

In Ferrol I made my way to the Plaza de España from which a number of straight, long narrow streets lead towards the centre of the old town and the Plaza de Armas, which boasts a statue of Franco, for the town is his birthplace. There is a degree of symmetry about the street plan which is lacking in most Spanish towns; Ferrol dates from the eighteenth century when a succession of three kings took an interest in it to turn the fishing village at the head of a secure inlet into Spain's greatest naval arsenal and dockyards. These dockyards are separated from the town by stupendous walls though from higher up, for Ferrol rises sharply, it is possible to look down and over the walls into the dockyards beyond them. There were only two or three naval vessels in the docks, destroyers by their lines, and a great deal of unoccupied space. In describing Ferrol Borrow, in one of those changes of mood by which he constantly surprises his readers, exhibited a deep sympathy for Spain's past greatness, which was in marked variance to his sometimes obtrusive English nationalism. He laments Spain's decline: "Sadness came upon me as soon as I entered this place. Grass was growing in the streets, and misery and distress stared me in the face on every side. Ferrol is the grand naval arsenal of Spain, and has shared in the ruin of the once splendid Spanish navy."[2] He found that half the inhabitants of Ferrol begged their bread. The present population of the town, at 90,000, is ten times what it was in Borrow's day although there were few signs of overt prosperity.

When I came to have supper that evening I chose a small restaurant in the Plaza de España where my host, after gesturing towards his empty tables, bewailed the state of the economy only to be astonished at my apparently inexhaustible grasp of his country's affairs as I happily unloaded upon him the wealth of statistics which I had learnt from my German companion of the morning's bus ride. In between our bouts of gloomy conversation and our mutual conclusion that perhaps membership of the European Union was not the answer to every problem my host would wander to the entrance where he peered round the big square in hopeful expectation of customers who, however, never materialised; or, he examined the live lobsters as they attempted to claw their way up the sides of a big glass container of water in his window.

It is depressing to visit a city whose size and pretensions have outrun its present performance, which was my general impression of Ferrol. The giant naval dockyards were almost empty and the long straight streets of shops appeared to lack the most important essential of a thriving city: that is, people actually shopping. At the main gates into the naval dockyards a notice announced *Armada*, and while watching a guard examine the passes of all who entered I reflected upon that one word; in many respects it sums up, however unjustly, four centuries of Anglo-Spanish history, for the British love key words which, one way or another, us or them, announce disasters: Hastings, Armada, Waterloo, Dunkirk.

In *The Bible in Spain* Borrow often mentions trees which he is careful to specify and in Ferrol he describes the elms: "The alameda is planted with nearly a thousand elms of which almost all are magnificent trees, and the poor Ferrolese, with the genuine spirit of localism so prevalent in Spain, boast that their own town contains a better public walk than Madrid."[3]

I walked the length of the alameda and visited Queen Sofia's Park but though I found trees of every description—ash, sycamore, fig and silver birch as well as palms to remind me that the north of Spain is as far south as the Mediterranean coast of France—I did not find a single elm. I took to examining trees, reaching up to pull down leaves to see if they possessed elm-like characteristics and I became so absorbed in this preoccupation that more than once I found that I myself was the object of surprised attention.

It is often curious how people react to strangers. I went to take a photograph of a large dilapidated building that was isolated on an island between two roads, empty of tenants, forlorn, and ready for demolition. The structure was not especially old, but its advanced state of decay appealed to my aesthetic sense. As I positioned myself to ensure that I captured the entire structure I became conscious of an onlooker hovering just behind me. When I had taken the photograph I turned to greet him since he was so clearly absorbed in my doings. He was a small, dapper man with a bald dome of a head and hooked Franco-nose. He responded to my greeting with an eloquent shrug, part disdain and part another emotion that was closer to anger and then, pointing at the dilapidated object of my photography, asked abruptly: "Why do you photograph that ruin?" The vehemence of his question was almost shocking. "And why not? I am interested in old dilapidated buildings." But with a curiously wooden gesture he appeared to sweep aside the building, which hardly deserved such attention, and retorted: "Ferrol has grand things to offer, the docks for example; it is a fine city. You do not need to take pictures of something like that."

He was, I suppose, one of the Ferrolese to whom Borrow alluded, possessed of that "genuine spirit of localism so prevalent in Spain" and now, quite beside himself with anger which was only part assumed, he first pointed in the direction of the alameda and one of the very few churches that I had seen anywhere in Ferrol before stumping angrily away.

I had a further hour to pass before my bus, so settled at a table for coffee in a pretty little square and began to read my current Spanish book but my mind strayed from Spanish vocabulary and I began instead to study a double row of large old trees just beyond the roadside tables where I was sitting. The under-side of the leaves was silver-white and though there were not many of them they were, indubitably, elms.

36

The Spectacular Cantabrian Shore

A dramatic coastline—Borrow's guides—Martin of Rivadeo—Viveiro—a dead man—Atlantic mists—old Ribadeo—Asturias—sleight of hand—"Oyee"—Navia

THE north coast of Spain is wonderfully dramatic. Viveiro, Foz, Ribadeo, Navia, Luarca, the Bellotas form fixed points on a spectacular road that follows the line of the Cantabrian shore, sometimes in sight of the ocean, sometimes climbing over great headlands where mountain

spurs fall into the sea. Rivers cut deep gorges through the land and only enter the Bay of Biscay after hollowing out exciting coves, which are hemmed in on all sides by sheer cliffs, where small ports are hidden from view until the last moment when a traveller up on the bluff chances upon them from above.

There was no coast road in Borrow's day, and he makes much of the drama of his journey from Ferrol to Oviedo. As seemed his practice, he hired an assortment of generally useless or cheating guides only one of whom, Martin of Rivadeo, turned out to be both worthwhile and good company. "Many is the wetting you will get, my masters, before you reach Oviedo," he is told, and indeed he spent much of his time travelling along the summit of a line of hills or up and down steep ravines through thick forest in heavy rain to arrive at towns or tiny dirty villages in the middle of the night. On one occasion his servant Antonio, who often appears to take command for Borrow, inspects two or three dirty hovels which they came to in the middle of the night only to tell his master: "We cannot stay here, mon maitre, without being devoured by vermin; we had better be amongst the hills than in this place. There is neither fire nor light in these cabins, and the rain is streaming through the roofs."[1]

Their guide, however, refuses to budge so they hire someone else to lead them to Viveiro. The two guides then converse together in Gallegan, discussing what might be in Borrow's baggage, but again his servant Antonio who understands the dialect warns them that his master knows their possible thieving intentions and tells them only to speak in Castilian. They reach Viveiro in the middle of the night. At Rivadeo their guide steals part of the harness but is caught by Antonio and his dishonesty is revealed to the local people, but when they ask him whether he is not ashamed to have attempted to rob two innocent strangers he replies in a rage: "'Strangers!' roared the fellow, who was by this time foaming with rage, 'innocent strangers, carracho! they know more of Spain and Galicia, too, than the whole of us.'"[2] It was a dramatic situation made for Borrow and he makes the most of it as he does of the whole journey along the coast.

Then he hires Martin of Rivadeo, a jolly fellow who tells stories and accompanies him for the next stretch of his journey. He is one of the most interesting characters to appear in The Bible in Spain and sings the intriguing stanza:

A handless man a letter did write,
A dumb dictated it word for word;
The person who read it had lost his sight,
And deaf was he who listened and heard.[3]

In a letter to the Bible Society, Borrow describes this part of his journey: "This journey was a terrible one; during the greatest part of it we had to toil up and down mountain gorges and ravines, to force our way through bushes and thickets, and to wade rivulets and torrents swollen by the rain, which descended continually."[4]

When Borrow had originally proposed his journey to the north of Spain, the Bible Society in London reacted cautiously and the Rev. Brandram asked the pertinent question: "Can the people in these wilds read?" But on his trip to the north of Spain Borrow was not only self-dramatising but also putting the adventure of the wild travel before its object, which was the distribution of Testaments.

Borrow, who admittedly reached Viveiro in the middle of the night, did it less than justice: "Presently we beheld before us the walls of Viveiro, upon which the moon was shedding its sickly lustre. We entered by a lofty and seemingly ruinous archway," while the next morning, he tells us, he viewed the town, "which consists of little more than one long street, on the side of a steep mountain thickly clad with forest and fruit trees."[5]

This meagre description hardly conveys the little town's dramatic situation to one side of a spectacular arm of the sea which cuts a deep gorge into the hills that rise behind the town and crowd down to the coast. There is a Charles V gateway, no doubt restored since Borrow's time, though hardly a lofty one, for it would only just have permitted a mounted man to enter through it. An hour's slow wander was sufficient to circle the old town and examine its walls and grim-looking monastery, the Grotto of Lourdes or the shops. Present-day Viveiro, unlike the town Borrow describes, was crowded with holidaymakers from nearby beaches and resorts.

I walked out of a silent Viveiro early the next morning, down the town's one long street, past the monastery, through the main square where the sun caught the crumbling façade of the deserted buildings and out the Charles V gateway onto the road to Foz. The pale bright morning sun cast sharp shadows to turn the yellow-grey stonework of the old town to burnished gold. The first life I encountered was in a covered market on the edge of town where I purchased cherries for my walk. From Viveiro to Oviedo took me a week of walking and the weather varied by the day between hot sun and scudding clouds, overcast, wind and rain and sometimes an Atlantic mist lying just offshore of a morning or, more coldly menacing, rolling inland at the close of day.

ॐ

I saw a dead man through a window. At least he had every appearance of great deadness about him. I had completed a long stretch of road, it was well past midday and I was both hungry and thirsty, when I came to a huge crumbling old *posada*; it stood solitary at the roadside, unattended by outbuildings or any sign of life, not even a dog. Once, long ago, it might have been built as a private mansion, but now it was come down in life and only a battered sign of peeling paint announced its function as a *posada*. I tried the front door but it was locked. I walked round the sides but could not gain entry or rouse anyone and finally, though only after wiping a thick layer of dust and grime from a pane, peered through a window into what must have been the bar. And there, sprawled in a huge chair, gripping its arms with bony-knuckled hands for reassurance, his legs stretched halfway across the floor to the bar, was an immense old man; his head was thrown back, his mouth was open, his great beaked nose pointed at the ceiling, and there was no sign of life in him at all. I knocked again, loud and sharp, but to no avail so I left him to the peace of his crumbling mansion.

ॐ

Foz sits on the mouth of a great estuary where the Masma comes down to the sea. It is a fishing port and holiday resort for Spaniards; the modern town sits on the bluff, the fishing port lies sharply below and there I sat at a little bar to watch an Atlantic mist build itself up high about a mile offshore and then advance slowly yet inexorably upon the land until the waterfront became chilly and damp and grey.

In the last century Ribadeo (spelt Rivadeo by Borrow) was an important trading port. It was here that Borrow, who had already had much to put up with from his worthless guides, hires Martin of Rivadeo; or, rather, Martin insists upon accompanying him as far as Gijón:

> *"You must now hire my mare and me as far as Gijon, from whence there is a conveyance to Oviedo. To tell you the truth, I am by no means sorry that the guides are absent, for I am pleased with your company, as I make no doubt you are with mine. I will now go and write a letter to my wife at Rivadeo, informing her that she must not expect to see me back for several days."* [6]

Today Ribadeo is a regional centre, while its old port has been turned into a marina for holidaymakers. The town sits on the western bank of the Eo, which forms a wide estuary at this point; the two banks are connected by one of the high, elegant, dizzy-making bridges in which Spain excels and the river separates Galicia from Asturias and is here about a mile wide. The town has many magnificent old buildings, testimony to a great commercial past, and a handsome square adorned with thick-leaved horse chestnut trees. The main town sits on the top of a cliff, while stepped streets descend sharply from behind the eastern façade of the square to the harbour below. Old mansions, with three storeys facing the town, had added an extra basement storey on the side towards the estuary so as to take up the slack of the steep hillside that falls sharply away from them to the harbour below, but now many of these grand looking houses have become dilapidated and, if not deserted, had about them a battened down appearance as though even in high summer they anticipated a grim cold winter.

I crossed the high bridge over the Eo early in the morning to pass from Galicia into Asturias and made myself dizzy as I leant over the parapet to take a photograph of Ribadeo as it peered out of a grey mist on its cliff edge. My first encounter in Asturias was with a cemetery: it stood alone, walled, its small area filled with gravestones and monuments, on a knoll above the road, gloomy and content with its dead. A big jolly fat man came cycling past me on the other side of the road and shouted that I was going the wrong way for Compostela! Later, having completed his business, he came cycling back towards me, this time to favour me with a great white-toothed grin. In a small bar where I took coffee my host asked me whether I liked Asturias, not Spain, and when I admitted that I had only entered his province earlier that morning he first laughed at his own provincialism but then insisted that it would prove better, "friendlier than Galicia."

In another little bar much later that morning I watched idly as an old man sat on a high stool at the bar to talk without cease to the company at large; the company consisted of me—and I could not understand a word of his thick accent—and an old bent woman who alternately mopped the floor and served behind the bar. Later we were joined by a young mother with a troublesome child in tow. My bill came to 300 pesetas and since I had no change I handed the stooped woman a 1,000-peseta note. She went to her till and fumbled with coins and I knew instinctively that she was up to something in the roguery line. Sure enough, she counted into my palm two 100-peseta coins and then, with a flickering sleight of hand reminiscent of a more interesting youth than her present employment mopping floors, first she took back one of the 100-peseta coins into her other hand to add it to four more 100-peseta pieces which she handed to me saying, "and here are the other 500 pesetas." It had been beautifully done and the dexterity of her thin bony fingers at their dubious work was more than compensation for being swindled out of 100 pesetas.

Only in Asturias did I come across that curious mixed response to information, which combined the expression "Oyee" with shaking the hand from a limp wrist as though the speaker, by mistake, had picked up something too hot to handle. A young waiter eyed my pack and asked whether I had been to Compostela and whether I was walking

and when I told him "yes" he responded with a long drawn out "Oyee" and shook his hand from a limp wrist as though he had picked up a burning iron. Others responded in similar fashion when I answered their questions about my walking as I made my way along the Asturian coast so that I found myself telling stories with the sole purpose of eliciting this double reaction from my listeners.

Navia is a dramatic little town on the mouth of a deep firth with a high viaduct carrying the railway overhead and a small harbour facing the wide estuary and distant breakers of the open sea. It is ringed in the background by the Sierra de Burón mountains. In a tiny *pensión* bar I secured the only available seat directly under the television set which was fixed high up the wall and so was able to sketch a couple who sat holding hands, totally mesmerised by whatever images were appearing above my head. He was spare of frame with a long, pale, bearded "El Greco" face; his wife was dumpy and shapeless with a pudding-like face and mobile indeterminate features.

37

Cracking the Bellotas

Thirty kilometres a day—Luarca in its hollow—the round ocean—cracking the Bellotas—the Casa Fernando—a comedy of sensibility—Novellana—the Cabo Vidio

WHEN I had covered most of the distance between Navia and Luarca I stopped at a roadside bar for a glass of wine where I was served by a plump, friendly, gently inquisitive woman.

"The Señor is walking?" she inquired.

"Yes, I am walking along the coast—to Santander."

"Oyee!" and she shook her hand from a limp wrist. "And how many kilometres do you walk in a day?"

"About thirty—sometimes more, sometimes less."

"Oyee!" and she repeated what by then had become my favourite intimation of approval as she worked, once more, upon her hand.

"And where do you come from now?"

"Navia."

"Ah, that is nineteen kilometres back along the coast; and where will you stay tonight?" There was a sly geniality about her open friendly face and she hoped, and I knew, that she had trapped me.

"Luarca," I replied.

"But Señor, that is only another two kilometres," and she looked at me as one looks at a child that has been caught out in a lie.

"I agree. Today is a short day for me. I wish to visit Luarca which," and I spiced my answer with an appeal to regional patriotism, "I believe is especially interesting. And besides," I felt constrained to add in my defence, "I wish to give my feet a rest for they have been overworked."

And there was a sudden puckering at the corner of her eyes and her fat face beamed in a smile, but when she said "Oyee" for the third time and shook her hand from a limp wrist once more some of the energy had gone out of the operation as though, this time round, she would prefer not to part company with her hand.

Luarca lies in a deep hollow carved into the high cliffs and there is no sign of any town until the traveller is right on top of it. Borrow describes its situation as most singular: "It stands in a deep hollow, whose sides are so precipitous that it is impossible to descry the town until you stand just above it. At the northern extremity of this hollow is a small harbour, the sea entering by a narrow cleft."[1]

The road drops and winds its way down through steep rocks and into the little town and fishing harbour which is hemmed in on three sides by the cliffs and on the fourth by the sea. Here the Rio Negro, which is crossed and re-crossed seven times through the town by bridges that are all in sight of each other, looks far too small and inoffensive a stream to have cut so formidable a gorge down to the ocean. Borrow found a large comfortable *posada* in the middle of Luarca, so I inquired in the tourist office whether any of the existing inns had been in business a century and a half ago. The woman I asked was astonished by my question but prompt in her answer: "The *cocina*," she said and came to the door of her office to point it out to me. It was a low-lying building on one side of the main square which actually gave the appearance of not having been altered in a century and a half, but when I inquired they were full so I settled instead for a *pensión* in a back street.

I climbed to the headland, which forms the eastern side of Luarca's hollow, and the holidaymakers on the beach below steadily diminished in size to become colourful dots to illustrate a holiday brochure, while the noise of powered water skis rose sharp in the clear air as four young men zigzagged across the still waters of the sheltered bay to create a bewildering pattern of bubbling surf streaks. Luarca's white-painted houses, framed by the green-topped cliffs of their hollow, sparkled in the sunlight. A small lighthouse, a church and a cemetery occupied the headland and from it I could see the undulating line of cliffs, every whit as white as those which Dover boasts, whose line I would follow the next day; now they stretched as far as the eye could see until they faded into a hazy blue distance. Only a few people had made the climb to the headland which was a little oasis of peace; these few included a couple who looked so ancient that they must have spent half the day toiling to the cliff top where they now occupied a bench against the wall of the church for all the world as though it was theirs and they its permanent and sole owners. The day was cloudless, the sea stretched blue and still to the far horizon where the ocean curved against the sky in perfect justification of Tennyson's description:

And the round ocean and the living air.

The next day, which I associated with old crones and acorns, proved to be my longest and hardest walk as I "cracked the *bellotas*." I left a near silent town early in the morning and rose at once up a great hill to the cliff top and all day long my road wound up and down the promontories and in and out of defiles. Sometimes I was in sight of the distant blue sea, far below me at the extremities of the gorges that cut through the cliffs; at others I walked inland up the side of the great defiles towards the mountains until the gorge narrowed and I executed a vee turn across a bridge with a mountain stream tumbling and roaring far beneath me. Shortly after ten I came down to Carnero in its lovely valley; when Borrow reached this point he had to be ferried across the river and the ferryman told him that the stream was famous in all Asturias for its trout. Now the river is crossed by a bridge but, though I rested on its bank before tackling the *bellotas*, I saw no trout.

A road branches inland from Carnero for Oviedo, while the coast road continues along the cliff tops to Avilés and Gijón. There were no such roads when Borrow made the trip and, in keeping with the drama he so loved, his guide demanded of an old crone whether they were on the correct way for Gijón and Oviedo.

"For Gijón and Oviedo!" replied the crone, "many is the weary step you will have to make before you reach Gijón and Oviedo. You must first of all crack the *bellotas*: you are just below them."[2]

The *bellotas* (acorns) is the name given to seven great hills that come down to the coast in ridges or spurs from the mountains which rise steeply beyond the road and they are separated from one another by deep defiles or gorges to make this one of the most rugged and spectacular coast roads in all Spain. Borrow describes a long day on horseback during which he and his guide went up and down the hills from defile to defile through thick forest and across rushing streams. And though there is now a fine road, this follows much the same course and gave me my toughest day's walking in Spain. I met no old crone in Carnero though there were some ruined buildings just across the bridge over the trout-less stream where such a person might have been expected to sit. From Carnero the road at once rose steeply and I now began a walk of spectacular beauty with high forbidding hills crowding the road to one side into which the great gorges that separated the *bellotas* poked their way like inquisitive fingers. These defiles were thickly wooded with great trees, while their streams dropped into the dense foliage of the great gorge below to disappear on their way to the sea. A village on a bluff might appear through the trees, no more than a kilometre distant, as I thought, but then I would be swallowed once more in another gorge and only come to it much later. The middle gorge among the *bellotas* was the most impressive of all with the mountain rising almost sheer from its head.

Once, on an open bluff where the forest had fallen below me, I came round the corner of an isolated house whose side jutted onto the road; a man and woman stood talking and smiled a greeting which I returned just as a huge black dog leaped out at me but luckily only to the end of its chain where it choked in rage. It was so close, however, that I was forced to step out into the middle of the road and was nearly killed by an oncoming car which had just rounded the corner ahead. The couple, who were now holding their dog, laughed at this little drama and I joined them in their laughter to show there was no ill-feeling. Later, as I toiled up the steepest hill of the day with a great mountain rising sheer behind me a long line of vehicles came toiling slowly up the road in the wake of a grinding truck and their drivers looked in astonishment at the solitary walker, pack on back, though one grinned at me from his open window and shouted "hero."

The railway appeared and disappeared: at Carnero it had been carried on an immensely high viaduct and periodically thereafter it put in a fresh appearance, sometimes above me as it was transported between two tunnels through the hillside on another picturesque viaduct at the head of a gorge, and sometimes below me when I caught sight of it snaking through the forest between two black tunnel mouths. The toil of this walk was rewarded by sudden stunning views of the sea, which stretched still and blue below me beyond distant coves at the end of plunging green valleys. This stretch of coast certainly earns its name as the Costa Verde. Eventually, in the heat of the day, I came up a hill onto an open area of fields and saw a cluster of buildings that lay on the outskirts of the village of Ballota where I sought refreshment in the Casa Fernando.

The Casa Fernando turned out to be as inviting as it looked. After quaffing a beer *à la* Borrow, for I was very thirsty, I managed to find a little table by the window in the crowded dining room where I enjoyed one of the best meals I ate anywhere in Spain; I began with Pote Asturiana and finished with a soft blue cheese that was so strong it hardly required the accompanying wine to set it off, and while relaxing over this meal I watched a little comedy. Too much sensibility can defeat its purpose and sometimes the mere exercise of this essentially sophisticated human quality exposes the objects of its concern to greater ridicule than if no attempt has been made to overlook what it is impossible to miss. I became intrigued by a particular display of Spanish politeness in which, it seemed, the entire population of that dining room played a part. A couple had been shown to the next table to mine just as I began my meal. The man was heavy-built, in his fifties, wearing thick horn-rimmed glasses and exhibiting all the more obvious signs of being a successful businessman. His companion, in her twenties, was an archetypal dumb blonde, the softness of whose face would be accentuated into pudginess before many more years had passed; now, however, she was enjoying the full splendour of both face and figure. Their relationship was not just obvious but cried out for attention. I do not think the lover of this paramour was a man of much sensitivity yet even he became aware of the extraordinary delicacy exhibited by the diners around him, none of whom ever—or so it seemed—even thought to glance in the direction of his table despite its central position which, perhaps, had been chosen deliberately by a waiter with a sharp appreciation of his own for the comedy to come.

The man was a dedicated gastronome and concentrated upon the dishes before him yet, whenever he did look up from his food, even he must have been struck, as I think in the end he was, by the way in which all those around him always had their attention fixed firmly in other directions. His companion, on the other hand, had not come to eat, though this is not to suggest that she did not enjoy her food, but to be observed and her forehead became increasingly puckered with a kind of vague query—nothing too pronounced, for that was beyond her range—because whenever she looked round, which it was her nature to do frequently in search of the admiration she had come to expect as her due, she also failed to catch anyone's eye and this was an eventuality for which she was quite unfitted to cope.

From the Casa Fernando I had another eight kilometres to walk to the village of Novellana where I intended to stay; I set off on what I imagined would be a relatively easy end to my day, for the hills appeared to have receded and I thought the *bellotas* were behind me. I was wrong. There was a short stretch of easy walking to begin with but then, once again, I found myself toiling round another of the great defiles. The temperature had risen and the sun now blazed down on my hatless head. I came to Novellana at six o'clock and stopped at a bar for a drink and sat on its verandah facing the distant sea. Then I went to the bar to inquire the whereabouts of the inn.

"There is no inn, Señor," the woman behind the bar assured me.

"But it is listed," I replied.

"Yes, but it has been closed all summer for refurbishing."

"Where else can I stay in Novellana?" but I knew the answer before she replied.

Meanwhile, a thin, seedy man of nondescript appearance who had been standing up to the bar had drifted closer, attracted by a conversation which promised him a vicarious thrill, however, slight, at my expense. He was the sort of man to be found propping up bars the world over whose principal occupation is to involve himself in other people's affairs. Now he nodded vigorously in support of the hostess: "There is nowhere else in Novellana," he said with an air of satisfaction and the woman and the man and I laughed though the pleasure was theirs rather than mine.

"Where, then, is the nearest inn?" I asked. Ascertaining my direction, they replied in unison: "Soto de Luina." After another consultation and some doubtful shrugging of shoulders they told me it was seven or eight kilometres further along the road.

"I have already come thirty-four kilometres," I said and we all laughed again.

I had two more of the great defiles to walk before reaching Soto de Luina and the sun became even hotter and I felt my forehead burning but at last, after a walk of forty-two kilometres, I came to an attractive little hotel, the Cabo Vidio; from my room I looked down a rolling valley past green woods to the sea glistening in the evening sunlight.

38

Travellers' Fantasies

*Advice on bus times—historic Oviedo—Borrow and the
ten gentlemen of Oviedo—travellers' tales—the solitary
traveller—truth and fiction mixed—knowledge of
languages—travel as escape—gilding the lily*

SOTO de Luina to Soto del Barco was a mere twenty-two kilometres,
an easy morning's walk, although the road was dramatic enough. I
passed the village of Muros where Borrow stayed in a large rambling
posada to dry out after being soaked by never ending rain: "It was just
one of those inns which romance writers are so fond of introducing
in their descriptions, especially when the scene of adventure lies in
Spain. The host was a talkative Asturian."[1]

At Soto del Barco I sat for an hour over wine and cheese before
taking the bus along a main highway to Oviedo. I asked about bus
times at the bar only to find myself the recipient of much conflicting
advice from three old men who usurped the intended response of the
barman: the bus had just gone; no, it would go in ten minutes; it
always went at two-fifteen; there were no buses today; two o'clock.
In the end I settled for two o'clock and left the old men arguing
furiously with one another about a bus schedule, which presumably
had operated for years outside the bar they so lovingly patronised.
The bus came at two thirty precisely.

Oviedo, with a population of about 190,000, was the largest town
I had been in since Ferrol and had the appearance of a prosperous
city; its original prosperity was based upon the development of nearby
coalfields during the nineteenth century. The city was founded
by Fruela I in the eighth century, so lacks the Roman ingredient

common to most of Spain's older cities. It became the capital of Asturias in 810 and was never conquered by the Moors, also enjoying an uninterrupted Christian history from its foundation. The old city clusters round the cathedral, which houses the pantheon of eleven Asturian kings, and is a maze of narrow streets, alleyways and ancient mansions that are in elegant contrast to the modern city which has expanded all round it.

ᨓ

Borrow stayed at an old *posada*, the former palace of the counts of Santa Cruz, but I was unable to find this. It was at Oviedo that Borrow claimed to have experienced one of the more bizarre encounters of his entire journeys through Spain although a little reasoned reflection would suggest that the whole episode was a figment of his lively imagination. He recounts the following remarkable episode:

> *It was past ten, and the rain was descending in torrents, I was writing, but suddenly ceased on hearing numerous footsteps ascending the creaking stairs which led to my apartment. The door was flung open, and in walked nine men of tall stature, marshalled by a little hunchbacked personage. They were all muffled in the long cloaks of Spain, but I instantly knew by their demeanour that they were caballeros, or gentlemen. They placed themselves in a rank before the table where I was sitting. Suddenly and simultaneously they all flung back their cloaks, and I perceived that every one bore a book in his hand; a book which I knew*

full well.

After a pause, which I was unable to break, for I sat lost in astonishment, and almost conceived myself to be visited by apparitions, the hunchback, advancing somewhat before the rest, said in soft silvery tones, "Señor Cavalier, was it you who brought this book to Asturias?" I now supposed that they were the civil authorities of the place come to take me into custody, and, rising from my seat, I exclaimed, "It certainly was I, and it is my glory to have done so. The book is the New Testament of God: I wish it was in my power to bring a million." "I heartily wish so too," said the little personage with a sigh. "Be under no apprehension, Sir Cavalier; these gentlemen are my friends. We have just purchased these books in the shop where you placed them for sale, and have taken the liberty of calling on you, in order to return you our thanks for the treasure you have brought us. I hope you can furnish us with the Old Testament also."2

As Borrow explains, he had only sent his last remaining forty Testaments to a bookseller willing to distribute them that same evening, so the appearance in his *posada* a few hours later of this remarkable contingent of nine tall men marshalled by their dwarf would have been truly astonishing, had it ever occurred. One would not have been surprised had the nine men, having thrown back their cloaks, then burst into a chorus *à la* Gilbert and Sullivan—"We are Oviedo's true believers"—while the hunchback conducted. After half an hour in which Borrow and the dwarf converse, the latter says "Good night, sir", wraps his cloak around him and walks out; the nine, who had stood the whole time without saying a word, all repeat "Good night, sir" and wrap their cloaks round themselves and also depart.

The story is a mixture of farce and burlesque: Borrow having fun at the expense of the Bible Society while also conveying an important message—that he was having an impact; Borrow at bay, for to begin with he thought they had come to arrest him and defies them by saying that it was his glory to have brought the Testaments to Oviedo; Borrow the Caballero, who despite his aversion to "gentility nonsense" at once recognises that they are all gentlemen; or Borrow simply improving less dramatic material for the sake of effect. Perhaps one small man and one large man came to see him after dark, because they did not wish the authorities to learn of their visiting him at all and, to make a tale worthy of his already exciting travels, he reduced the small man to a dwarf and multiplied the large man into nine tall, silent men in cloaks.

Critics of Borrow suggest he did not have a lot of imagination (that, for example, he was not capable of writing a novel) and could only write of what actually happened to him. This may be partly true but he undoubtedly had an enormous talent for embellishment. One of the great advantages—and joys—of being a solitary traveller is that no one can gainsay you. From Marco Polo to Baron Munchausen "travellers' tales", whether true or false, have been exaggerated and whether exaggerated or not have raised eyebrows: the first European explorers to report a snow-covered mountain on the equator in Africa (Kilimanjaro) were not believed back in Europe. Borrow, of course, was not merely reporting a journey; he also needed to convince the Bible Society in London that he was successfully spreading their version of the Gospel in Catholic Spain, though whether the good clerics of Earl Street believed in the ten gentlemen of Oviedo is another matter entirely although they certainly regarded this particular agent of theirs as one of the most extraordinary people ever to have been employed by the Society.

The solitary traveller, almost by definition, is a fantasist: when alone and bored he can indulge his own fantasies as he travels. In the land through which he passes he can make up stories about himself back in his own country; and at home he can represent himself as having endured or passed through all sorts of adventures which may or may not be true. He can embellish an incident in his own mind into what could have happened and after a while he himself may well believe that it really did happen as invention becomes reality and takes over. After all, who is to know? Above all, he can enhance the adventures through which he passes to add flavour to what otherwise might be a less than stirring account for, as Walter Pater asks: "Don't you know that these roads are infested by robbers?"

There is an art in putting together a number of different incidents to make a single whole or taking the physiognomies and characteristics of half-a-dozen people and weaving them into a suitably compelling though unlikely figure of menace or humour. Students of *Lavengro* or *The Romany Rye* have suggested—and indeed assumed—that Borrow fused people and incidents to make a more dramatic account. And if he did that in his autobiographical books he certainly did it in *The Bible in Spain*. A traveller likes to see himself as a sort of knight errant on the road; he travels in hope of adventure, and if no real adventures occur then one or two need to be invented and the solitary traveller, with care and an eye to credibility, has opportunities to indulge his fantasies and turn them into realities. And what more appropriate country than Spain in which to do this, for in Don Quixote, the Knight of La Mancha, Cervantes provided us with the greatest fantasist of all.

Certain literary devices can be used to enhance the effect of travel, and from time to time Borrow, for example, says, "I pass over this period since little happened," which makes his readers all the more eager to believe the next fantasy he recounts. Perhaps the more discerning readers of travel books are able to separate fact from fiction although that is likely to be far more difficult than reason would suggest, for the art of the travel writer is to weave the two together until the one acts as a cement for the other and the two components of his art are indivisible.

The greatest aid to any traveller is command of language and in this respect Borrow enjoyed an immense advantage, for he spoke many languages sufficiently well to create doubts as to his own nationality. There is an interesting account of him by Lieutenant-Colonel E. Napier, then stationed at Gibraltar, who describes meeting Borrow in Seville in 1839:

> *I approached him with a "Bonjour, monsieur, quel triste temps!" (for it was pouring with rain). "Yes, sir," replied he in the purest Parisian accent; "and it is very unusual weather here at this time of the year." "Does 'monsieur' intend to be any time at Seville?" asked I. He replied in the affirmative. We were soon on a friendly footing, and from his varied information I was both amused and instructed. Still I became more than ever in the dark as to his nationality; I found he could speak English as fluently as French. I tried him on the Italian track; again he was*

perfectly at home. He had a Greek servant to whom he gave his orders in Romaic.

He conversed in good Castilian with "mine host", exchanged a German salutation with an Austrian Baron, at the time an inmate of the fonda; and on mentioning to him my morning visit to Triana, which led to some remarks on the gypsies, and the probable place from whence they derived their origin, he expressed his belief that it was from Moultan, and said that, even to this day, they retained many Moultanese and Hindoostanee expressions such as "panee" (water), "buree panee" (the sea), etc. He was rather startled when I replied "in Hindee", but was delighted on finding I was an Indian, and entered freely, and with depth and acuteness, on the affairs of the East, most of which part of the world he had visited.[3]

What is interesting about this passage is its double revelation: Napier's description of Borrow demonstrating the full glory of his multilingual capacity and the narrator's care to make plain the diversity of his own experience and knowledge of languages, while each of them, no doubt with probing care, attempts to attain a position of "one-upmanship" in relation to the other.

We are not all Borrows with so many languages at the tips of our tongues, but even the smattering of a language can go a long way provided it is supported with determination, a dictionary, a readiness to be extrovert and make a fool of oneself, and snatches of other tongues that can also be brought into service. Travel is a particular form of escapism: it is to see new and interesting places, of course, but it is a mental as well as physical escape that equips the imagination with new parameters and scope and takes the form of a personal statement: "I wish to escape the confining world that I have left into a quite different world of my own." How much of this world is a figment of the imagination and how much is true the reader must determine for himself. Such an approach to travel was a powerful motive for Borrow. Solitary travel allows for the creation of a personal make-believe world and, as one critic of Borrow asks: "The perennial question with Borrow is 'by how much?'"[4]

Gilding the lily is not solely a writer's art nor is the practice just confined to travel writing although travel writers certainly tend to suggest they have battled against greater odds than they probably encountered in reality. Perhaps the travel writer's rule of thumb can be stated as follows: a mundane event becomes a happening; a happening develops into an adventure, while a mishap becomes a danger and all adventures are turned into highlights.

39

Rain and Cider, The Old Men of Colunga

From the Picos de Europa—Gijón—rain—Spaniards never drink tea—Villaviciosa—the Casa de Pedro—an incident of Spanish history—a glass of white wine—putting a head on the new cider—Colunga's bar of old men—establishing my nationality

MY final stretch of walking was to be along the north coast from Gijón to Santander: Villaviciosa, Colunga, Ribadesella, Llanes, San Vicente and Santillana del Mar, with a backdrop of high mountains for much of the way. The walls of the reception hall of my *pensión* in Oviedo were covered with enlarged photographs of rocky mountains, climbing country that looked familiar, like Glencoe. I asked about them when I paid my bill and the landlady's plain, rather careworn face came alive with pleasurable animation.

"That is where I come from," she told me, "those mountains there," and she pointed at a deep valley scene. "I lived there as a child." They formed part of the Picos de Europa, inland from Ribadesella, which I would pass through in a few days time. She looked at my pack and asked me whether I had been walking and if I liked mountains and at my affirmative response to both her questions she became positively friendly. "Where had I walked?" she wanted to know, so I rehearsed for her my by now familiar litany to make her shake her wrist in the Asturian fashion and give me a friendly parting "oyee."

I spent a day in Gijón, the old part of which occupies the point of the Santa Catalina headland in the centre of a great bay. To the west of the headland lies the old port, to the east a long beach so that Gijón combines the role of industrial city and port with that of holiday resort. The port has a long, disturbed history—Romans, Goths, Moors—and for a time acted as the capital of Asturias; it was frequently attacked by corsairs during the sixteenth and seventeenth centuries, while in 1588 the remnants of the Armada took refuge there. Gijón was much damaged during the civil war but has since expanded to become a city of more than a quarter of a million people. My day there was a gloomy one; rain fell intermittently, which at least aided my exploration of the bars in the old town since I was frequently obliged to seek shelter. These bars in the fishermen's quarter had a style all their own though tourism, no doubt, will persuade them to become fixed in a readily saleable mould of quaintness, which will be a pity.

I left Gijón at seven in the morning for what I thought would be a comfortable walk of thirty kilometres to Villaviciosa but I had reckoned without the rain. There is a certain art to getting wet. At first outer coverings protect you and provide a sense of false security. Then the drips find their way down your neck, your trousers cling to the calves and even a good anorak has its limitations until finally, as the rain breaks through all defences and you know you are going to end up thoroughly soaked despite protective clothing, you let the rain have its way. By the time I reached the top of a long winding hill down which rivulets of water had cascaded to meet me I was completely soaked and shivering with cold, so the sight of a wayside bar gave me considerable pleasure. My pack was dripping and I knew the contents would be wet inside, little rivulets of water ran down my anorak, my hair was plastered to my skull and water dripped from my trousers so steadily that I had not been at my table for five minutes before pools of water had materialised round my feet. They looked at me, the assembled company, with expressions that were both inquiring and yet polite, as though I were a sort of curiosity, but otherwise they offered no comments. And yet there was an eloquence in their silence: if I had to be so foolish as to walk in such weather that, after all, was my affair.

The road wound still higher and for a time both the clouds and the rain were below me, half obscuring the distant sea; then I passed through a great wood where wind as well as rain became my enemies as sudden gusts of stormy wind made the branches of the tall trees creak and shook the leaves above me, so that I received a double ration of water, both raindrops and leafdrops.

I came to an old wayside *fonda* where for a change, on a whim, I asked for tea. Perhaps, before doing so, I ought to have remembered Borrow's instructions to Mrs Clarke to bring with her to Seville "tea things and urn (for the Spaniards never drink tea)." The woman behind the bar looked at me blankly.

"The Señor wants coffee?" she asked after a pause.

"Tea," I replied.

Her blank expression increased: "Tea! What is tea?" I was cold and wet and I knew she was being awkward for some reason best known to herself. Perhaps she didn't like the English! After further repetitions I said "TEA" yet again, loudly, and banged the bar in a rage. There was a boy sitting up to the bar on a high stool and he suddenly grinned at me and then said to the woman: "Tea." "Oh, tea," she said and went to prepare it. Now each of us—myself, the woman, the boy—had pronounced tea (*te*) in exactly the same way, for it is, after all, a short word that does not permit of infinite variations in pronunciation, so her obtuseness made me wonder. But the boy gave me a sly glance, as much as to say "you have to watch her," and the pot of tea then appeared. I sat by the wall next to the door and watched the other customers, realising later that the boy was the woman's son.

The first break in the weather came at midday when the rain ceased and patches of blue sky appeared between the clouds as these moved steadily inland from the bay. I came round the shoulder of a great hill to see the best vista of my walk when, as frequently happens after heavy rain, the landscape is sharply defined in a sort of dull exactitude that does not depend upon sunlight. I was now about eight kilometres from Villaviciosa and began the long descent of a dramatic valley. Big dogs on their chains outside farmhouses made their usual friendly leaps at me as I passed and I often speculated about the chains which secured these beasts and what would happen and what I should do if one broke when the furious guardian reached the end of it and was jerked to a halt. The chains, I liked to think, had all been forged of Toledo steel.

Borrow was dismissive of Villaviciosa:

> *Late in the afternoon we reached Villa Viciosa, a small dirty town,*
> *at the distance of eight leagues from Oviedo: it stands beside a creek*
> *which communicates with the Bay of Biscay. It is sometimes called La*
> *Capital de las Avellanas, or the Capital of the Filberts, from the immense*
> *quantity of the fruit which is grown in the neighbourhood.*[1]

Borrow found great difficulty in obtaining a handful of the nuts for dessert in his inn, as, he was told, they were all exported to England. I saw no sign of them.

It began to rain once more as I reached the outskirts of Villaviciosa and when I looked down into a wide stream as I crossed a bridge into the town I saw its waters were teeming with trout; indeed, they were so plentiful that I thought it would be possible to stretch a hand into the water and tickle a fish onto the bank like a good poacher. I had learnt to tickle trout in my teens and thought of the sensation I might cause if I walked into the reception of an inn, trout in hand, and requested them to cook it for my supper. I obtained a room in the Casa de Pedro. It was a strange old, jumbled building, arranged in a series of levels as though it had been added to periodically with haphazard indifference over the years to create a children's "hide-and-seek" delight. After drying out I descended to the bar behind which stood Pedro himself, massive and impassive, a huge man with a rubbery face that could take on a dozen different characters; he had something of the likeness of the Hollywood actor Sidney Greenstreet, and when he moved to serve a customer it was with a studied slow motion as though he had missed his real metier in life as a film villain. I sat there for half the afternoon while it rained without cease.

An extraordinary incident of Spanish history occurred at Villaviciosa when the future Emperor, Charles V, landed at the little port with his Flemish courtiers in 1517, ready to take possession of his new dominion of Spain. The town went to great lengths to welcome Charles but a mistake had been made, for he was really supposed to have gone to Santander. The new monarch was not amused.

At about six that evening, when the rain had finally ceased, I set out to explore Villaviciosa which Borrow had dismissed so easily as "a small dirty town". I found it an attractive place of narrow streets and alleyways, old mansions and bars. Villaviciosa is in the centre of the cider-brewing region and the year's new brew was everywhere on offer; but I was not expecting cider and, indeed, had never associated the drink with Spain, my narrow parochialism only ever assigning cider to Devon. As a consequence of this personal obtuseness I became increasingly surprised at the sight of waiters in several bars I passed serving what I took to be wine in the oddest of fashions, for just about everyone appeared to have a bottle of rich golden wine on the table in front of him. At the top end of an inclined square with the town hall in its centre I came to a large crowded bar: all the outside tables were occupied while inside the number of people standing at the bar was more reminiscent of an English pub than most of the Spanish establishments I had come to know. Everyone appeared to have a bottle of the rich golden wine in front of him and everyone was drinking from a pint tumbler while waiters constantly circulated to pour for their customers and still I did not realise what I was witnessing. At the bar I asked a small, rotund tough-looking character for a glass of white wine.

"White wine?" he said, "Well, I suppose you can have white wine." Then he shouted down the bar: "The Señor wants white wine."

It was, of course, a cider bar and the new brew was being tasted. I watched fascinated. Each customer purchased his own bottle of cider, which had to be uncorked, and was provided with a tumbler in which to drink it. A waiter would hold the tumbler at the full extent of his left arm directly down in front of him, the tumbler tilted at an angle, while he raised the bottle of cider as far as he could reach above his head with his right arm to tip it so that a stream of golden liquid cascaded down in front of him to strike the tilted lip of the glass. They never poured more than about an inch or an inch and a half of cider into the tumbler at a time since the object was to obtain a maximum head. The customer then drained as much as he wanted or could manage, for it was very strong, before dashing the remainder onto the floor. The waiters circulated constantly and when they saw a guest with an empty glass they picked up both this and his bottle of cider to pour another libation. There was a dramatic art to this pouring and the waiters were nonchalantly expert at it. The floor was stone and the waiters wore Wellingtons.

I watched this extraordinary, almost Rabelaisian, scene for about an hour, for it was a large bar and there were many variations of style among both waiters and drinkers, while nursing my indifferent white wine. Then I called my burly little barman for an explanation and he told me why they poured the cider in this dramatic fashion. I do not like cider but I ordered a bottle and he came to perform for me, my *faux pas* in asking for white wine now forgiven.

One waiter in particular attracted my attention. He was an exceptionally tall young man with an extraordinary thin El Greco face and jet black hair; his arms, longer than average, matched his frame. With a glass held in his left hand almost level with his knees and a bottle in his right hand stretched halfway to the ceiling, exactly above his head, he would commence pouring. He never looked up at his bottle and every time he performed I was convinced the cider would strike his forehead or miss the lip of the tumbler below but it never did, the jet of cider passing within an inch of his forelock and striking the exact centre of the lip of the tumbler which he held. And all the time he performed he stared straight before him, maintaining a fixed expression of bored indifference that never varied. Plates of crabs claws were served with the cider and there was much cracking of shells with pincers and loud talk while the more experienced or extrovert of the drinkers, those standing at the bar, would dash the remnants of cider from the bottom of their glasses onto the stone floor with a dramatic flick of the wrists after each drink in a knowing demonstration of connoisseurship. For the first time in my life I took positive pleasure in drinking cider.

I found a small nondescript bar halfway up the steep hill into Colunga whose interior consisted of a single square room with a bar running the length of one side; it was clearly not a place patronised by holidaymakers. Two old men sat at a table with their backs to the window while a third man sat facing them. Two more old men sat at a bench behind another table facing the bar across the room. And a sixth old man, the oldest of them all, sat behind a table facing the door. At my entrance conversation ceased. I took off my pack which clunked on the floor and the third man at the table by the window got to his feet—he was perhaps ten years younger than any of the others—and walked behind the bar. I asked for a glass of wine, which I took to a small vacant table by the wall facing the window, next to the oldest man in the room. Although they were not tall men dressed in cloaks, nor perhaps even *caballeros*, they were certainly all old and had reached that phase of life in which contemplation is liable to replace action. They were also all very curious. I leant my walking stick, the elegant cane I had purchased in Lisbon, against my table. There was a walking stick hooked onto the back of a chair by the oldest man who, meanwhile, was looking at mine with interest. He "asked" with a sudden animation of his face whether he might inspect mine and I handed it to him. The elegance of my cane was matched by its strength, it was one of the finest walking sticks I have ever possessed, and the old man handled it like a treasure, carefully inspecting its markings and clearly coveting it as well.

The others watched this inspection, then one of the men by the window asked: "Alemán?" No, I was not German. They paused to consider this. The second man asked: "Francés?" No, I was not French. A further pause ensued while they digested this double failure to identify my nationality. The two men with their backs to the window murmured in consultation and then the first one asked: "Italiano?" though there was a shade of doubt in his voice. No, I was not Italian. They had probed gently, as far as courtesy permitted, and it was now incumbent upon me to enlighten them. "I am English," I said. "Ah, English," and they nodded at one another as though they had really suspected this all the time. The oldest old man beside me had, meanwhile, finished inspecting my cane which he restored to me but the men at the window clearly wished to inspect it as well so, despite the hurried shaking of their heads in disavowal for they did not wish to interrupt my refreshment, I took it across the room, presenting it to them crook first like a sword of honour. It looked like a Spanish cane, they thought, but no I told them, it came from Lisbon. "Ah yes, a peninsular cane," and they were satisfied. So I took it back and the first old man had another look at it.

These formalities completed, we each returned to our own affairs: the two men by the window resumed their conversation and were rejoined by the host, for no one else had entered the establishment, and one of the men on the other side of the room resumed reading his newspaper which he had laid down while my nationality was being established, and the other man slowly heaved himself to his feet and announced that he had business to attend to at which the others nodded a comprehension that implied he was always expected to go about a particular errand at this time of day while the oldest man of all, next to me, resumed his contemplation of infinity.

40

At Home on Holiday with the Spanish

*Mountains and sea—Sunday morning church—a room
with a family—a one-way conversation—the Spanish on
holiday—Je suis française*

THE last stretch of coast that I walked was deep in Spanish holiday country. The ridge of the Mir del Fito mountains rose sharply from the coast to a height of twelve hundred metres to provide a perfect backdrop as I approached Ribadesella: sometimes I was in sight of the sea, at others it disappeared behind sand dunes or small hills. Once, as I passed through a village, I heard a roaring noise somewhat like a train, a sound that was both familiar and strange at the same time, and only when I came in sight of the sea again did I realise its source as I saw the waves breaking on a great stretch of golden beach below me. It was a beautiful coast. At one point the road rose quite sharply into the hills and then I might catch glimpses of the blue-green sea, beyond a spur, stretching to the horizon, or turn a corner to look down upon a little cove or bay of sparkling yellow sand, while at other times there was no hint that the sea was just over the nearby hills. Everything was green in the golden sunlight.

I took a mid-morning break outside a tiny shop on a hillside and watched a sleepy village come to life as the good people made their way to church, for it was a Sunday. The church was set back on a knoll overlooking the village below and the bell tolled from a white tower thrown into sharp relief by the green hills that rose beyond it. The people stood in groups, talking, greeting friends and gradually disappearing into the church and then, at the last moment when the bell had ceased its call to the little community, some children came hurrying up the path when everyone else had disappeared inside.

Ribadesella lies on an arm of the sea which thrusts deep into a dramatic circle of mountains at its head. Every inn and hotel I approached was full but in the end I was directed to an apartment block where a woman took in holidaymakers. I secured her last room, she told me, surprised that I was English, and since by then it was half past two and I was not a regular Spanish holidaymaker she invited me to join her husband and herself for lunch. It was the first occasion I had shared a meal with a Spanish family in their own home.

"You are English? We have never had anyone from England to stay with us before. How are you travelling…?"

"Walking! And where have you been in Spain until now?" So I rehearsed my travels, which by then were coming towards their end, and they said I had seen more of Spain than they. "And we are Spaniards." They had retired to Ribadesella, they told me, but as "times were hard" took in people during the holiday season. "We want to stay here," the man said, and "forever" hovered on his lips but failed to leave them as he recognised the awful finality of the word. We discussed politics and I asked them about the elections just over. They both shrugged an indifference to their politicians which now appears to be universal throughout Europe.

"They do not make much difference, we voted for the Socialist Workers Party but…" and they shrugged again. Nor did they think membership of the European Union really made much difference to them either, "except for the fishermen," he added in a sly dig at the English—at which I laughed. From their window I watched a tramp steamer nose its way into the small harbour beyond which rose a sharp headland crowned by a lighthouse. My host offered me a brandy or a Marie Brizzard and I chose the latter since I had never drunk it before.

We were about to break up—my host was thinking of his siesta, his wife of the washing up and I wished to explore the town—when one of their lodgers erupted into the room. She was a middle-aged woman, thickset and short of figure but with a magnificent head of noble proportions; her countenance was neither beautiful nor handsome yet it would command instant attention anywhere. She ought to have been on the stage though I had no idea what her profession might be. Individually her features were all wrong: deep brown penetrating eyes, a too wide mouth, high Slavic cheek bones, a stubby almost flattened nose yet in combination on a seamed face they produced an altogether astonishing effect of confident humour, while her general expression suggested that she had long since come to terms with the worst the world could offer and was no longer bothered by its vagaries.

She was talking as she came into the room: "I interrupt, I am sorry, it is only for a moment but I have a query," then she turned to me. "Pardon, Señor," and she turned back to her landlady, "there is a little rattle in my room, a little rattle of the window"—and then at astonishing speed she told a story about the wind which I could not follow but my host and hostess laughed. "Naturally I like it here, I love the sea," and she turned to me, "we Spaniards love the sea, like you English," and then she told another story about a woman taking a seaside holiday which I could only half follow. I begged her to speak more slowly to accommodate my poor Spanish. "But of course, Señor, I speak like a slow train," but she speeded up at once with another story. She had changed some money earlier in the week at the bank but the cashier had been stupid and wasted her time: "Not as they do it in Madrid," and she turned to me: "I am Madrileña, of course," and she smiled with her huge mobile actress's mouth and continued her story which I could only half follow. "But, I interrupt you," and she turned to the door, put her hand on the knob then turned back: "I must just tell you this other little story." And she did so and my host refilled my glass with Marie Brizzard and, in courtesy, offered her a drink which she declined. "Thank you, but no. I do not drink. Not now. I used to drink, of course, and Marie Brizzard," she turned to me, "it is a special Spanish drink, best taken with ice, *naturalmente*, it is the, how do you say in English, epitoom of Spanish drinks." And she beamed before embarking upon another story about drink, too fast for me to follow, and I begged her yet again to go more slowly so she said with careful calculation and incorrectly, "I am, how do you say in English—in the dogcart! We Spaniards," she continued, "we like the wine." She was clearly set for the afternoon.

❧

It was then the first week of August and the town was crowded with holidaymakers, stalls sold garish toys and bright-coloured candy and a miniature open-sided coach drawn by an ancient horse led by an equally ancient top-hatted man in a frock coat took children on a circuit of the town. Every table outside every café was packed with people and I doubt that the holiday atmosphere of the place had changed much in half a century.

A short distance from Llanes are the ruins of what had once been an enormous convent. San Cilorio, Borrow tells us, was one of the largest monastic edifices in all Spain but already in his time it had long been deserted and stood desolate upon a peninsula of the Cantabrian shore. I made a detour from the road through a pretty village to find the remains of this monastery; part of it had been incorporated into a cemetery, while its crumbling walls followed the line of the cliff over the sea. I sat in a tiny bay that faced back along the coastline which I had been following. Higher up the cliff a girl sat reading but after a while she came down towards me and I asked whether she knew anything of the history of the place. "Je ne sais rien," she replied emphatically, "je suis française," and she passed haughtily on her way, Spanish history—and me—equally brusquely dismissed.

Llanes had once been a fortified town and there are some impressive ruins of ramparts and a castle as well as a squat, massive basilica, which took two hundred years to build before it was completed in 1480. Like Ribadesella the town was crowded and when I reached it just about the entire population, or so it seemed, were window-shopping or otherwise wandering on top of one another in the aimless way of holidaymakers who have run out of planned activities. The centre of this busy town, described in a guide book as a quiet resort, was in a permanent state of traffic jams enlivened by the endless shrilling whistle of a policeman on point duty who used it more as an assertion of his authority than for any difference it made to the condition of the busy crossroads he controlled. A non-stop stream of people paraded slowly round the little harbour until they came to the end of its mole and had to turn about; a festival of children's dancing occupied the grounds of the castle and a lively market was another centre of attraction. There was an exhibition of modern Asturian painting in one civic building and an exhibition of photography in another, and everywhere the crowds sought entertainment before feeding time came round once more.

41

The Lone Traveller

*A traveller alone—Borrow the outsider—freedom in
Spain—youthful friends—El Brujo—a Walter Mitty
world—a tinker is free, a married man is not—lonely at the
end*

THE singularity of being a traveller alone is, these days, all the
more striking since the vast majority of travellers move in groups,
like London buses, seeking protection. There is a difference, not
often recognised, between being lonely and being alone: the capacity
and willingness to be alone is an art while loneliness is a condition,
although being alone can also induce a sense of loneliness so that
the condition may feed on the art. The great majority of people
will go to almost any lengths to avoid being on their own and, in
consequence, find great difficulty in understanding anyone who
seeks to be alone by choice. The lone traveller, therefore, is seen as an
eccentric but his—or hers—is an eccentricity which produces its own
rewards, experiences that have a quality of uniqueness because they
are not shared. And while the art of being alone requires a degree of
calculation, the condition of loneliness comes not from being alone
but from the knowledge that there is no other choice.

The single traveller, unfettered by company, is restrained only by
his own intentions. When he does desire converse with other human
beings he can seek it out under a variety of pretexts but is free to
abandon it at will and continue his solitary way. This deliberate
rejection of the group whose togetherness in any case is rarely what
it appears to be from the outside is a prerequisite for creating one's
own world, a world apart that provides its single inhabitant with an

inevitable sense of superiority. One result of this deliberate choice, to be alone, is a growing sense of isolation, so that when people ask how the lone traveller can survive on his own he may well retort that it would be quite impossible to get by in any other company. The lone traveller, therefore, enjoys a sense of self-sufficiency that cannot be enjoyed by those who travel together: they ask, "What shall we do today?" while the lone traveller says, "Today I am going to do this." It is a form of arrogance and, almost by definition, the lone traveller sees himself as special.

જ

George Borrow was a loner. As a young man he identified himself with the "apartness" of the gypsies, and his deep interest in them was derived, not a little, from his perception of them as outsiders, for in many respects Borrow was the archetypal outsider. The two sides of Borrow warred with one another throughout his life: the first side was determined to be the outsider, the lone traveller, the man with a "veiled period" that no one was to know about, and in the first half of his life the outsider triumphed; the second side craved acceptance, wished for worldly fame, wanted the very things he derided as "this gentility nonsense", but by the time he was ready to allow this second nature to triumph his character was already set in the mould of an outsider and he was quite unable to compromise and come in from the cold world he had created round himself with the result that, despite his marriage to the motherly and deeply loving widow, Mrs Clarke, his latter years became increasingly lonely and bitter. When his manic depressions are also taken into account he becomes one of the most intriguing subjects for psychological study in the pantheon of nineteenth-century British writers and, in this respect, he had plenty of competition.

In Spain Borrow was alone in his prime. He could travel as he wished, especially into its wilder parts; he could display to its best effect his mastery of languages; he could consort with gypsies; he could both enjoy and create mysteries; he had a job to do and a job with status that allowed him to indulge his fantasies as a champion of

Protestantism against an all-powerful enemy to be found on all sides in the pervasive presence of the Roman Catholic Church; he was a Caballero and accepted as such wherever he went; and he could seek and take part in adventures. With all these possibilities, what need for company? Yet, as he adventures his way through Spain, Borrow provides an indelible impression of his aloneness. From the evidence of *Lavengro* and *The Romany Rye* as well as accounts of his old age, he never enjoyed, or recaptured, the sense of freedom, of being his own master, able to take on all-comers, as he enjoyed in Spain. This provided the highpoint of his life, and, significantly, his marriage as soon as he had finished with Spain marked the end of the first phase of his life and the beginning of the second which, contrary to what could reasonably have been expected, was often to prove lonely as well as lone and in parts deeply unhappy.

William Taylor of Norwich, the man who perhaps did more than anyone else to launch Borrow as a young man, was himself an outsider; or, at least, by the time Borrow knew him he was old and in the process of becoming an outsider. Apart from Jasper Petulengro (the gypsy Ambrose Smith), only two friends stand out from Borrow's younger days: John Hasfeldt, a young Danish interpreter from the Danish Legation in St Petersburg whose correspondence with Borrow shows a real understanding of his isolated nature; and Francis Arden (Ardrey in *Lavengro*), who was the antithesis of the serious young Borrow in London but with whom the latter appears to have struck up one of the most intimate friendships of his life. They explored London together and, as Borrow explains in *Lavengro*: "He was an Irishman, I an Englishman; he fiery, enthusiastic and open-hearted; I neither fiery, enthusiastic, nor open-hearted; he fond of pleasure and dissipation, I of study and reflection." Ardrey (or Francis Arden) is one of the few individuals that Borrow speaks of in his writing with real warmth and affection.[1]

If travel provided Borrow with the freedom to be both himself and alone, a condition that he so much relished, it was also the freedom of escape; inevitably, therefore, one must ask what he was escaping from. His insufficiency of gentility, for in Spain he never mixed in genteel society? Or from insecurity at home where he had no firm base, no certainty of a career and, until his marriage, no income to support the gentility he so craved and yet affected to despise? He was certainly never going to fit easily into any society, and even in Spain at the height of his powers when he knew so well what he could accomplish he was still escaping.

In January 1836 Borrow "spurred down the hill of Elvas to the plain, eager to arrive in old, chivalrous, romantic Spain," and it was the antiquity and chivalry and, above all, the romance which so appealed to him. Here, for four years, he could give rein to his imagination, indulge his fantasies and fight a giant enemy, for there is more than a little of Don Quixote about Borrow as he tilts at the massive windmill of the Roman Catholic Church. And so successful was he in projecting his extraordinary character—and embroidering it too—that he became known in both Seville and Madrid as *El Brujo*, the wizard, a title that must have compensated him for many setbacks.

Travelling alone whether in the nineteenth century or today, and perhaps especially today, allows the solitary traveller to enter into a Walter Mitty world of his own. Borrow, whose white hair and great height and affected dress each made him stand out as he intended, delighted in doing what others shunned and drawing attention to himself: bleeding a horse to cure it when the Spanish groom had given up, disguising his identity behind the many languages he could speak, as he did in Seville with Colonel Napier, relishing being referred to as *El Brujo* or confounding the gypsies with his knowledge of their language. It is significant, however, that very nearly all the people with whom he makes contact are servants or inferiors or those he can impress with his special skills, while the exceptions, ironically, are Roman Catholic priests; more than once he dismisses the upper or genteel classes while paying almost eulogistic compliments to the Spanish lower orders. As he tells us when he wished to avoid a political discussion in his hotel at Cádiz, "I instantly quitted the house, and sought those parts of the town where the lower classes principally reside." It was not simply that they were the people he was most likely to convert; they were also the people amongst whom he was most at ease, whom he was certain to be able to impress. He has few real friends at his own level but many acquaintances who regard him with awe as someone special—*El Brujo*.

There is in Borrow an almost obsessive need to impress people, and if he cannot then he would prefer to withdraw into himself. And yet, at the same time, he is apparently so self-assured. Some people have always been attracted by the lure of being missionaries, in one sense or another, and there is a strong element of the missionary in Borrow. Yet it is worth speculating whether he ever really believed that he was making converts to Protestantism in Spain: were the Spaniards amongst whom he distributed his Testaments really interested in them, except as momentary novelties, or were they rather attracted by the strange character of Borrow himself, the singer not the song? Given his own extraordinary early life it seems more likely that he went to Spain as a "missionary" for something to do, because the task was there, rather than from any profounder conviction. His life is full of such questions.

It was inevitable that in the end Borrow would fall out with the Bible Society and in the later correspondence of the Secretary, Rev. Brandram, with Borrow this becomes increasingly apparent though there is no obvious cause. But a cause was not really needed and the wonder, rather, is that he worked for them so long: his strangeness and lack of conventionality, his pride and aloofness, his pursuit of gypsies, his unorthodox methods and readiness always to seek out low company, his love of ale, were none of them characteristics likely to endear him for very long to the staid biblical gentlemen of Earl Street. By 1839, after he had been called back to London to explain how he was carrying out his mission in Spain, Borrow must have known that his days with the Society were numbered. And so, with a foresight that was aided by the fortuitous circumstances of Mrs Clarke's own affairs, which required her absence from her estate for a while, Borrow was able to arrange for her to stay with her daughter in Seville during 1839 in the strange secluded house he had rented and also occupied. And there, one must suppose, he wooed and won the widow whom he married in April 1840 after returning to England and severing his connection with the Bible Society. Mrs Clarke, at last, provided him with permanent security: an income—though she always controlled the purse strings—and security of place and position on a minor estate from whence he could make other journeys, as he did, during the ensuing years.

And then, curiously, Borrow falls out with the Spain, that he had so much enjoyed. Richard Ford, who had read *The Bible in Spain* for John Murray, the publisher, and was both a friend and champion to Borrow, asked him in 1845 to write a review of his own *Handbook on Spain*. Borrow owed Ford much, but already a terrible bitterness was setting in and he took the opportunity of the review to launch a bitter personal attack upon Spain: "Accursed land! I hate thee, and far from being a defence, will invariably prove a thorn in thy side." Lockhart refused to publish it in the *Quarterly Review*.[2]

It is difficult to know what made Borrow so bitter—he was then writing *Lavengro* though it would not appear for another five years—but maybe the true explanation lay in his loss of freedom. By marrying Mary Clarke and accepting the security that came with their union he had given up forever that first, most forceful side of his character which had predominated during the earlier part of his life, as the loner, the free man who was not tied down and could roam at will. From this time on he could only roam courtesy of Mary and the Oulton estate and to paraphrase himself: a tinker is free but a married man is not. And nothing really compensated for the loss, more especially as he never achieved the position and gentility he had affected to despise but, instead, remained to the end an odd, outsider figure who was never fully accepted.

The latter part of his life, despite the love and understanding of Mary Clarke, now his wife, became increasingly lonely and bitter: Borrow quarrelled with his friends, made new enemies, suffered from the melancholia and depression that had been with him since he was a young man, became increasingly disappointed and morose and, following the death of his wife, spent long periods in dismal solitude. One of his biographers, Seton Deardon, provides a bleak picture of his end:

> *Borrow had inspired little affection during his life, and there was none to cheer his end. Lonely he had lived, and alone he was to meet the awful solitude of death.*[3]

He was one of the most original, most misunderstood and, in the end, saddest of nineteenth-century literary figures. But if he was misunderstood and ended lonely and alone, he had only his own pride and stubborn perversity to blame though it is always open to question whether anyone, ever, can alter his own nature.

42

Over the Hills to San Vicente

Early morning mist—establishing my nationality again—the bridge of San Vicente—the working-class district—finding a room—part of the community—the dramatic old town—a formidable matron

THE coast road from Llanes to San Vicente is accompanied by the great barrier of the Sierra del Cuerra mountains. These rose sheer on my right hand as I walked in the early morning, and one ridge after another revealed itself as the clouds were thinned and then dispelled by the sun, the intensity of whose rays increased in proportion as the whole range lost its thick morning shroud of heavy white drapery that hung over the precipitous ridges and stretched far down the green hillsides until only thin wisps of mist remained. The massive front of the mountains gave the impression of an impregnable barrier protecting Spain with ridge upon ridge falling in place behind it. I developed a crick in my neck from constantly turning my head to look upwards.

The inn was low-lying, to the side of the road, and it was in sight for some distance along a straight stretch of highway. The woman came to the entrance—to admire the mountains or get a breath of air—and then saw me trudging towards her and remained at her door in expectation: curiosity to examine the solitary traveller at close quarters or possibly no more than a desire to make sure of a customer.

We greeted each other in unison and she swept me inside, and since I had then walked for about two hours I was ready for refreshment. There were no other customers though a youngish man at a corner table, I think her son, was going over the accounts, so she came to my table for conversation. I was, she told me, an unusual customer for most people travelled only by car though she did have groups of cyclists. "What was I doing and where had I been?" By this time on my travels my answer to such questions was almost a litany: Borrow and Bibles and how much I could walk in a day and the places I had visited and the sights I found most interesting and pilgrims and Santiago de Compostela about which the Spanish appeared to have a fixation although it may only have been because it was a Holy Year and more visitors than usual had come. Before I finished her husband had joined us and their son in the corner had abandoned his accounts to take part, too, although I think he was less interested in my journeyings, delivered in my halting Spanish, than in seeking an excuse to take a rest from his figures.

After passing the small town of Unquera, which marks the boundary between Asturias and Cantabria, I rose steadily to a pass over a great headland with a deep valley and then mountains on my right and the sea out of sight over the headland to my left. On a bar at the top of this pass a friendly traveller engaged me in conversation, intrigued by my pack and the realisation that I was both a foreigner and walking. He guessed that I was German and then Scandinavian and then Austrian and then French. He dismissed Italy but seemed reluctant to consider Britain and appeared surprised when he finally discovered that this was where I came from. I had experienced this Spanish difficulty in recognising me as British before and wondered whether, like the lady in Valladolid, he assumed that all Britons only ever passed straight through Spain to the sun coasts of the south to be beside the sea. Establishing my nationality only required a paragraph in our conversation yet his obtuse determination to assign me to almost any country in Europe except my own was, for me, a source of amusement, even pleasure: I like to be mistaken for a German or Scandinavian, even for a Frenchman! And yet this was not always the case and I reflected just how much one's attitudes change, though always, hopefully, for the better. If, when I was a young man, anyone had said to me with a note of inquiry: "You are English?" as though readier to assume that I came from somewhere else, I would have been shocked that my Britishness was not immediately self-evident and replied, "Of course" and done so, moreover, with *hauteur* if not anger. Now, when such doubt is expressed, I am flattered: perhaps they think I am international!

Nationality disposed of, my friendly interlocutor asked me about the rigours of walking in Spain, and when I had told him a few this little round jolly man, whose physique precluded any form of serious walking, exclaimed: "What a marvellous thing to do!" So we had a drink together and I enjoyed my new discovery of Marie Brizzard with ice. Beyond the pass I began the descent into San Vicente while the sea reappeared on my left.

The approach to San Vicente was down a very steep hill and I could see the whole town on its estuary gradually opening up before and below me. The old fortified town, gloomy and black with the remains of a castle and a great church, is perched dramatically on a rocklike hill that oversees the rest of the town spread out below it. Beyond the town is the wide firth crossed by an ancient bridge of many arches to the farther shore where more hills rise abruptly from the waterside. Borrow described San Vicente as

> *a large and dilapidated town, chiefly inhabited by miserable fishermen.*
> *It retains, however, many remarkable relics of former magnificence: the*
> *bridge, which bestrides the broad and deep firth on which stands the*
> *town, has no less than thirty-two arches, and is built of grey granite.*
> *It is very ancient, and in some parts in so ruinous a condition as to be*
> *dangerous.*[1]

Bridges and aqueducts appear often in the pages of Borrow's book and he devotes considerable care to describing them; I found every one that he mentions still in place, some no doubt restored and renovated, others much as he had seen them. Apart from the great aqueduct of Segovia, which I had still to see, the bridge at San Vicente was the last such monument which I saw that Borrow had noticed and described.

I stopped halfway down the hill to count the arches of the bridge, then perhaps a mile distant and starkly etched, arch by arch, in the brilliant sunlight, but only made out twenty-seven rather than the thirty-two recorded by Borrow. Later that evening I re-counted them and found that there were only twenty-seven operative arches, while the last five at the eastern end of the bridge had been blocked in to make a permanent causeway, these no doubt representing that part of the bridge which Borrow described as being in "so ruinous a condition as to be dangerous."

San Vicente had an attractive main square, thick with trees, while the surrounding buildings with their arcaded porticoes provided shelter for an almost continuous line of restaurants whose tables covered the sidewalk. The town is no longer only inhabited by "miserable fishermen" but has been developed for tourism as it combines a fine large beach on the firth with ancient monuments and lovely surrounding countryside, the perfect combination for holidaymakers, and it was even more crowded with visitors than had been Llanes the night before. No hotel, inn, *hospedaje* or *pensión* had any room vacant; I was given private addresses but these too were booked. Eventually I was directed back across the bridge over which I had entered the town—not that of the twenty-seven arches—into the working-class district of new apartment blocks where I was told I might find accommodation.

Once I had turned my back upon the old, picturesque part of town the atmosphere changed abruptly. The first thing I noticed was the absence of noise, of that constant hum arising from close-packed holidaymakers wandering in groups or sitting out at tables on the pavement to take refreshment. Here, instead, people went about their business and, as long as I did not look back across the harbour to the busy centre of tourist activity, I might have been in another town at another time. I walked a short distance along the waterfront and then turned up a steep hill towards very new apartment blocks whose gleaming rough-finished appearance promised a rapid deterioration into shoddiness. This district that housed the poorer people would no doubt have been sought out by Borrow and though, perhaps, physically cleaner and more presentable than such a quarter would have been in his time, yet the flavour of change was unmistakable: there were no tourists in the streets, either Spanish or foreign, for there was nothing here for them to see or do.

I came upon a tiny bar crammed with workmen taking a late afternoon drink and though my entrance was observed it was carefully not noticed, so I ordered a glass of wine and asked the proprietor where I might find a room. He paused between pouring drinks, for I had lighted upon that bar at peak time for satisfying thirst, then shouted for his wife and a slatternly woman holding a baby came out of the rear room. He spoke rapidly to her, she nodded and slouched away, and then turned back to me: "She will find out for you, if you care to wait." So I took my wine outside where I had seen a tiny square garden, surrounded by a high hedge, just large enough to contain four tables and their accompanying chairs.

Half-a-dozen middle-aged women, busy in a comfortable chattering conclave, occupied one corner of the garden which otherwise was empty but they stopped when I entered and several smiled a greeting as I took a seat in the opposite corner. Somehow, though in what manner I could not say, but by a sort of spreading osmosis that always operates in such close, tight-knit communities, those women knew already that I was in search of a room. Another woman came into the garden to join the group but as she settled herself among them one said: "Do not turn your back to the Señor," so she re-arranged her seat and nodded in my direction; it was both a courtesy and an acknowledgement of my status.

I had visions of a lengthy search through the district for someone with a spare room; instead, and of course, they knew whom to approach and who had both the room and the most need for money. A new woman now appeared in the entrance to the little garden where she stood for a moment to appraise me, then she went away only to reappear about five minutes later to call upon me to follow her. Her action prompted the group at the table to turn towards me as one and nod, more or less in unison, as though a pre-arranged drama was being played out to their satisfaction, so I gulped the last of my wine, rose from my table and seized my pack. The woman said, "Everything is arranged for you, Señor," so I turned to say *adios* to the group at the table and though in reality our short acquaintance had been no more than a kind of mutual awareness, they looked at me comfortably as though there was something between us, for now I was no longer quite such a stranger.

I followed my guide along several streets until turning into a new one she said, "There he is," pointing to a young man loitering at the other end, "he will show you the place," and then, as the young man came up to us, she added, "Here is the Señor." I thanked my guide and shook hands with the young man who then led me to a nearby block of flats. He took me up to an apartment on the second floor while explaining, half apologetically and half proudly as though he still doubted his right to be there at all, that the whole block had only been opened two months previously and that they—a term which I think he applied to both his own family and all the other new occupants—were lucky to have secured a place in it. The fixtures were new, the furniture was new and half the apartment looked as though it was kept in a state of permanent newness untouched by either human hand or human use. He showed me into the spare room, which gleamed from recent dusting and polishing and was dominated by an enormous double bed covered with a garish spread. This the young man pulled back to show that there were no sheets, for the bed had yet to be made up.

"My mother will be back later and she will make the bed for you," he spoke with a certain hesitant uncertainty, "if that is all right?" I assured him it was—I do not think he had much experience in the room-letting business—so he showed me the bathroom and gave me a towel. I had already agreed with the woman who had brought me to the young man to pay 3,000 pesetas for the room, so I told him I would pay his mother when I came back after dinner between half past ten and eleven. In answer to my query he told me he worked as a merchant seaman but was then on leave, a euphemism I suspect for being unemployed. I set off to explore San Vicente.

On the waterfront of the harbour I met my guide, who smiled encouragingly at me and we exchanged greetings like old friends. On the dockside nearby a girl of about fourteen was standing at the lower end of a ramp, peering into the water; at the sight of me she called to borrow my walking stick. She wanted to fish up a tin mug lying below in three feet of water and now proceeded to do so not without difficulty, using the crook of my cane for the purpose. By this time I felt myself to be part of the working community of San Vicente.

The old part of the town was a dramatic place with ruined walls facing the river, the remains of a grim keep perched at the end of the promontory and a squat, massive old church with Romanesque doors and Gothic aisles occupying a central position. It was the Church of Our Lady of the Angels, and since saints and angels are an integral part of Spanish history I tried to puzzle out the connection between San Vicente de la Barquera (St Vincent of Boatmen), which was the town's full name, and the seventeenth-century French St Vincent de Paul who, with St Louise de Marillac, had founded the Sisters and Daughters of Charity. The town and its church were older than St Vincent de Paul and his orders, so I concluded that the St Vincent after whom the fishing town had been named was a more obscure saint altogether. A little gallery near the church exhibited modern Cantabrian paintings and a wide parade at the end of the fortified hill allowed visitors to wander up and down and peer over ramparts at the view spread out below: the river, a lake, the town, the wide firth and its many-arched bridge. Steep, narrow lanes fronted by ancient houses, led down to the main square.

When I let myself into the apartment late that evening I heard the sound of television in the sitting room so knocked and entered. The young man and his mother watched television in a state of ensconced boredom: they had nothing else to do and watched the screen at least as much in proclamation of the fact that they possessed a television than because its programme held any interest for them. They were a contrast, that mother and son. The young man was slight of build with sandy-coloured hair, nondescript indeterminate features and watery blue eyes; he would not stand out in any crowd but pass through life unremarked and almost certainly unrewarded as well. His mother, by contrast, exuded strength from her large strong body: she, too, had sandy-coloured hair but there the family resemblance ended as though she had retained all the outstanding family features for herself and only managed to pass onto her son some of her colouring.

Her chin was square and set off by a large dimple that must have been her greatest point of attraction in her youth, her eyes were deep brown, her head massive, its hair drawn back severely, her nose straight and sharply pointed, her bones and frame almost masculine in their structured strength, her hands as big as a man's. The absence of a spouse or any sign of one only served to enhance the forbidding presence of this lone matriarch who had but the one weak son to dominate. Now, from her seat in front of the television, she bent a stern gaze of doubt and suspicion upon me as though I had wormed my way into her household in her absence.

I greeted her and knowing the quickest way if not to her heart at least to a state of mutual understanding took out my wallet and produced three 1,000-peseta notes. She acknowledged my promptitude in the matter of payment with an inclination of the head and told me the bed was made up ready for me. She expressed the hope that I would be comfortable, then asked, "What time will the Señor leave in the morning?" and looked relieved when I said eight o'clock. I bid her good night and turned towards the door, and with a snap of her fingers she told her son: "Show the Señor to his room." The young man leapt startled to his feet, came past me to open the door, stepped across the little hallway to the best bedroom with which I was already acquainted, opened its door and then stood in his nearest approximation to attention for me to pass.

43

The Santillana of Gil Blas

Comillas—Gil Blas country—Richard Ford—the picaresque novel—Santillana del Mar—a tourist attraction—I have walked from Gijón—a cockney dwarf

SAN Vicente to Santillana del Mar was to be my last walk along the north coast and, as if responding to sympathetic magic, my feet began to hurt though more in protest at what they had done already than at the rigours of this particular stretch of coastline. The old road which I followed was thickly lined with trees and switchbacked up and down over the hills, usually just out of sight of the sea. About halfway between San Vicente and Santillana lies the curiously dramatic little town of Comillas where the road twists along the cliff high above the sea, and on a great bluff stands the red-stone Papal University which contrives to look forbidding like a prison rather than attractive like a place of learning. In the afternoon, following a long and pleasant lunch taken at a wayside inn, I had a rest beneath a great tree overlooking a little valley where a family of a man, his wife and three children gathered in the hay and piled it high on a haywain. Periodically, the children's voices were wafted up to me on the afternoon heat haze from a tableau that reflected the unchanging timelessness of peasant occupations.

Borrow extols the countryside round Santillana as beautiful and fertile and, inevitably, refers to it as Gil Blas country from the novel

293

of that name. Richard Ford, Murray's reader who became such a champion of Borrow, told the publisher how much he liked the sincerity and style of *The Bible in Spain* and the effect of incident piling on incident. It reminded him, he said, of *Gil Blas* with a touch of Bunyan, both references that would have been pleasing to Borrow who was to write to Murray one of the few warm appreciations of another person that come from his pen, here of the man who for a time was perhaps his closest friend: "Pray remember me to Ford, who is no humbug and is one of the few beings that I care something about."[1]

Now the picaresque novel was born in Spain and the term was applied to stories of rogues or adventurers and the *picaro*, or picaroon, was a rogue or cheat who lived by his wits: an adventurer. A picaresque novel, told in the first person, recounts the adventures of a lowborn person who moves from place to place, position to position, and possibly from one class to another as he survives and improves his lot. The first such novel, *Lazarillo de Tormes*, tells of a poor boy who works under a succession of hypocritical masters. Other similar novels followed and the genre became very popular and was to be imitated in both England and France. The form reached its apogee in the eighteenth century with Alain-René Lesage's *Gil Blas* or the *Histoire de Gil Blas de Santillane* which, suitably, is set in Spain where the form had originated. It is one of the first realistic novels and is the story of a young valet who progresses from one post to another and outdoes his masters in performance, proving a better quack than the doctor he serves or a better seducer than another of his masters.

The setting for Gil Blas' activities is Santillana del Mar, which had become a fashionable place for the Spanish aristocracy during the fifteenth century when noblemen built fine mansions for themselves in what must then have been no more than a remote seaside village; these still exist and their balconies and coats of arms provide grand façades for the narrow streets of the little town. It is a pretty place and almost every building is of fine stone, most of them several centuries old. The town boasts a Gil Blas *parador*, reputed to be one of the best in Spain. Ford, who was a wealthy dilettante, referred to Borrow as "an extraordinary fellow", "this wild missionary" and a "queer chap", and there is an element of double entendre in his Gil Blas comparison, as possibly there is also a hint of condescension, for not only can Borrow's style be described as in the picaresque tradition but he himself may be seen as a picaresque hero—although he would not have liked to be regarded in such a light since the implication is that he also comes from the lower orders and has about him an element of the rogue on the make. Despite his dismissals of gentility nonsense and the fact that he so consistently sought out the lower classes Borrow would have been deeply offended at any suggestion that he was not a bona fide *caballero*.

Santillana has now become part of the international tourist trail and when I arrived it was very full indeed with many nationalities in evidence as well as Spaniards; for the first time, almost, since I had been in Spain I was more aware of British tourists than of any other nationality. Santillana reminded me of Broadway in the Cotswolds during high summer: it has wonderful old buildings and a long interesting history but has become so aware of its tourist appeal that it has taken on a cloak of artificiality which, inevitably, is accompanied

by endless plastic card signs and money traps. According to Borrow, the population in the 1830s was about 4,000; it is much the same today. The village owes its existence to the relics of St Juliana who was martyred in Asia Minor; these relics became an object of pilgrimage and the Collegiate Church and Cloisters, which began life as a monastery, date from the twelfth century and form a major attraction for visitors.

On my arrival in Santillana I found a café where I took coffee and was served by a big, heavy-built man who contrived to make the production of one cup of coffee into a major operation. He brought the coffee to my table, looking and meaning to look surly, but then happened to glance at my feet. I was still wearing my walking boots rather than the light shoes I normally used in towns for I had yet to find accommodation. He stared at them truculently: "Why do you wear those boots?" he demanded, as though I was insulting Santillana.

"I have been walking."

"Walking: where have you been walking?"

"I have walked from Gijón."

"Gijón!" And at once his truculence left him: "I come from Gijón myself," he said and then, a changed man, he asked about my travels in Spain.

Two parallel streets run through Santillana del Mar to the monastery on its eminence overlooking the town and both are almost entirely fronted by the façades of centuries-old houses. As I stood at the end of one of these streets I watched a little party slowly advancing towards me. It consisted of two men and two women and a child who kept prancing from one side of the narrow street to the other, examining shop fronts or doors, and acting in a most spritely fashion. At first I took little notice as I was positioning myself to take a photograph but as the group came closer I realised that the child was not a child at all but a perfectly formed midget, one more Spanish "dwarf" to add, as I thought, to the roster of Spanish dwarves I had already noted on my travels. His behaviour, however, was increasingly preposterous and other tourists in that crowded street looked at him askance, with obvious irritation or embarrassment. And then, as they came still nearer, I was able to distinguish their speech: they were not Spanish at all but English, cockneys!

I took a long walk round a silent Santillana the next morning when all the visitors were still in bed and was better able to appreciate what a gem of a place it is. The town now lies well inland from the sea and is so beautiful, so carefully arranged—brushed and combed as it were—for tourists that I was immensely relieved when I passed one of the more elegant hotels to see a row of large battered dustbins exuding a stench of rotting food. They contrived to bring me to earth with a sense of ordinary, everyday wellbeing, for behind the elegant façade life was clearly much the same as everywhere else.

44

A Panorama of
Half Spain

*Completing the circle—long days walking—wayside cafés—a
journey of images—Christian and Moorish Spain—north
of Madrid—the English connection—Santander—the
Cordillera Cantabrica—the cathedral of Burgos—the plaza
a centre of life—the police and dry-cleaners—the occupant of
a wheelchair*

FROM Santander which I came to from Santillana I set off due south
to Burgos, Segovia and then back to Madrid, thereby completing
both the great circle of north-western Spain in which I had managed
to keep closely to Borrow's original route as well as my entire itinerary
in which, as far as possible, I had also stuck to the trail followed by
Borrow. But I had not touched upon eastern Spain at all. Drawing
a line from Santander southwards through Burgos and Madrid and
then on to Gibraltar all my travels had been to the west of it. Even
so, I had seen open up before me a wonderful panorama of half the
Iberian Peninsula.

From Lisbon on its seven hills and dramatic Sintra on its rocky
eminences I had crossed the Alemtejo through the fortified towns
of old Portugal to reach Badajoz and the Extremadura. My growing
acquaintance with Spain was to owe more to the long days when I
walked than to anything else I did, for no other approach, perhaps,
can better convey the flavour of a country so well as to arrive in a

town footsore from a day spent walking through its countryside and its villages and then have to seek lodgings and a meal. And this growing feel for Spain owed a great deal to the little wayside café-bars, often scruffy, sometimes offhand, whose owners might be friendly or indifferent, curious or uninterested. They served surprisingly good food and provided me with some of the best conversations I had, despite my poor Spanish, for those of my hosts who did get into conversation with me did so from interest rather than in the manner of their counterparts in towns who were used to entertaining the constant flow of visiting tourists.

It had been a journey of images. The old men expectorating with skilled indifference in the square of Evora as they exchanged the day's news; Pizarro on his huge stallion in the ancient square of high Trujillo staring forever towards distant Peru and its silver, sword in hand for conflict and conversion; or storks gliding to rest on their great untidy nests perched on the convenient corners of church towers. There was Toledo, packed with monuments to 2,000 years of Spanish history or the great defensive walls of Cádiz surrounded by the sparkling sea. Then came the extraordinary mixture of Christian and Moorish Spain, the two threads intertwined through centuries of alternating conflict and fascination with each other that is so important a part of the country's history. These two strands meet in Seville where the great mass of the Christian cathedral and the walled Moorish Alcázar of dazzling tiled halls stand side by side, a perpetual reminder of the dual nature of Spain's past. They meet again in Carmona, which shines white in the sun on its great hill and, above all, in the mosque-cathedral of Córdoba. And everywhere, ruined monuments are a mute reminder of the still more ancient world of Roman Spain. The windmills of La Mancha, and Aranjuez, the "Versailles" of Spain, completed my picture of the southern half of the country.

Differences are often impossible to pinpoint and a subtle change takes over once the traveller is north of Madrid: it affects landscape, towns and their architecture and the character of the people. The climate, too, is different: cooler, more rain, increasingly variable. El Escorial has a unique atmosphere of its own: it consists of Philip II's great palace-monastery—and then the little town—but the order is clear, for the town is the creation of the palace. Beyond Escorial lie old Castile and León: fortified Avila and religiosity, endless yellow wheat fields that stretch to the horizon, golden Salamanca with its pile of medieval buildings created to forward learning and glorify God, ruined Medina del Campo whose past magnificence is all but forgotten and then Valladolid, one of the old capitals of Spain. And there the pilgrim trail takes command, weaving its way through ancient towns and under ruined castles as a new generation of young pilgrims, enthusiastic or just enquiring, wielding their unfamiliar staves like awkward weapons, come to take part in an age-old mystery that has defied the changing centuries in the majestic pile of Compostela.

Periodically the English connection with Spain impinged upon me as it did in La Coruña, where unfortunate General Moore lies at rest, or in Vigo where the British fleet came to claim a victory and a great treasure. When I had completed my long walk from Cape Finisterre, the End of the Earth, along the rugged north coast to Santander, I began, despite inadequate language, to feel just a little that I was at home in Spain.

�

Borrow did not linger in Santander: the fresh batch of Testaments he had ordered from England had not arrived and he was ill with dysentery and needed medical attention which he could only find in Madrid so, despite the civil war that was then raging between Santander and the capital, he set off for Burgos and Madrid.

Santander today is a busy industrial city and port. Much of it was destroyed by the cataclysmic tornado which struck the coast in 1941, and now it has the generally shabby, well-used appearance of a hardworking no-nonsense town. I wandered through a lively flea market and then took lunch in an elegant restaurant where my next table neighbours consisted of a monstrously contrasting couple: the man was of huge girth with an astonishing head like a pear whose big end had been rested upon his shoulders so that no neck was visible, just immense bulging cheeks. His wife was thin and scrawny and saw her mission in life as tending to his needs which were overwhelmingly gastronomic. He consumed his own food and most of hers for she spent the meal handing over to him morsels from her own plate, sometimes forking them direct into his capacious maw of a mouth. I took out my sketchbook to draw his head but neither he nor his wife paid any heed, devoting their joint attention instead to his consumption, and only pausing periodically to call the waiter to take further orders.

Nothing had prepared me for the road from Santander to Burgos: a short distance inland it rises steadily into the mountains to cross the Cordillera Cantábrica along a dramatic highway whose spectacular views only occasionally emerged from the thick mist. Heavy clouds had reduced visibility to a few metres as the bus ground its way up ever-steeper gradients until we reached the top at the Puerto del Escudo just above 1,000 metres. Then we left the clouds behind and descended into a great canyon whose stark cliffs and awesome twisted rock formations lasted for fifty kilometres before we crossed a wide plain and came over the lip of the huge saucer in which Burgos lies.

The ruins of a great castle extend in broken walls and part turrets over a large space at the top of the hill that was once the citadel of Burgos and from this vantage point it is possible to obtain a clear view all round the natural basin or saucer in whose centre the city lies. Most of the land up to the distant rims was yellow with wheat while the city lay crowded below, the twin spires of the cathedral rising high above every other building to point, grey and elegant, to heaven. The sun was shining brilliant after a thunderstorm and the buildings below gleamed and glistened as they reflected its light while steam rose from their wet roofs.

Old Burgos is dominated by the cathedral, which is only surpassed in size and grandeur by those of Seville and Toledo, while its frieze front of stone and open-work spires is unique. Its vast gloomy interior both harbours and invites mystery, something at which the Roman Catholic Church has been adept throughout its history. The city is the starting point for one of the pilgrim trails to Santiago.

Burgos has made many contributions to Spain's history: in the eleventh century it became the capital of Ferdinand I's new Kingdom of Castile, León and Asturias; the area is famous for the exploits of the Cid; when Valladolid usurped its role as capital at the end of the fifteenth century it developed as an artistic and commercial centre instead; and during the civil war of the twentieth century Burgos became the seat of Franco's provisional government.

The evening of my arrival the whole city was darkened by a terrible black thunderstorm yet, when it was over, as though by magic, the sun came out to make the Plaza Mayor gleam as the crowds appeared to take their promenade and gossip with their friends while their children played: a square full of people in a Spanish city on a summer evening turns such a plaza into a centre of colour and hubbub and sheer pleasure.

I wanted to get some clothes cleaned for the final journey home and set out to find a dry-cleaner but, instead, spent an hour in vain search. I asked a policeman who used his radio to headquarters and then directed me to a shop which was closed for its summer holidays. I asked a second policeman who used his radio to headquarters and then directed me to another spot but there was no dry-cleaner in sight. I asked a third policeman who used his radio to headquarters and then directed me to yet another location where again I found nothing. Just what the Burgos police headquarters made of these requests for information about dry-cleaners from widely different parts of the city on behalf of an eccentric Englishman I cannot imagine. .

When I took lunch in the plaza in front of the cathedral I found myself surrounded by Frenchmen. At one table sat two couples, impeccable representatives of the French bourgeoisie, the wives solicitously ensuring that the men got the best morsels as well as the larger portions, the husbands, fat and oleaginous, glistening from eating. A second table was occupied by a different couple entirely: a svelte, beautiful young woman with an elegant male companion twice her age who paid her delicate compliments throughout the meal while they toyed with the most exotic dishes the house could provide. While my attention was engaged by France a family party of Spaniards walked past our tables, one of the men pushing a wheelchair. The occupant of this wheelchair had the legs of a man, a heavy twisted body that rose into distorted, odd-angled shoulders from which protruded a long thin neck on which was perched the head and face of a boy of fourteen, and that terrible monstrosity of a human being was the centre of attention and love from the whole group.

45

Under the Hundred and Seventh Arch of the Aqueduct of Segovia

*Segovia's dramatic setting—Borrow's assistant Lopez—
meeting under the aqueduct—which was the hundred and
seventh arch?—the Alcázar—La Granja, the "Versailles" of
the north—Abades—a yellow landscape—progress—a last
look at the aqueduct—taking leave of George Borrow*

THE setting of Segovia on its great rock, surrounded on three
sides by the gorge of its river, is even more dramatic than that of
Toledo and it must be one of the most spectacularly beautiful cities
in all Europe. Borrow went to Segovia from Madrid to spend time
distributing Testaments in the surrounding villages on the bleak
treeless plain. He had already done the same thing in the villages
round Toledo and while at the village of Villa Seca had stayed with
Juan Lopez, the husband of his landlady in Madrid, who became his
ardent supporter in distributing Testaments.

> *But he who put the labours of us both* [Borrow and his servant Antonio]
> *to shame, was my host, Juan Lopez, whom it had pleased the Lord
> to render favourable to our cause. "Don Jorge," said he, "yo quiero
> engancharme con usted (I wish to enlist with you); I am a liberal, and
> a foe to superstition; I will take the field, and, if necessary, will follow*

you to the end of the world: Viva Inglaterra; viva el Evangelio."
Thus saying, he put a large bundle of testaments into a satchel, and, springing upon the crupper of his grey donkey, he cried, "Arrhe! Burra!" and hastened away.[1]

Lopez was clearly a man after Borrow's heart and Borrow engaged his services again when he went to Segovia.

I had decided to make Segovia the final stop on my journey before returning to Madrid and thence to London. I came to the city from the north: after miles across the undulating plain the road drops over an escarpment to reveal Segovia, rearing up like a ship on the rock which has been isolated by the river in its chasm below. The bus circled the city and though I was amazed at my first glimpse of its astonishing Alcázar (with which I was more than familiar since it adorns the front of Hugo's *Spanish in Three Months*) and was then impressed by the golden mass of the cathedral as it rises from the centre of the city, my only concern was to set eyes on the Roman aqueduct. I glimpsed two of its high arches, briefly, between buildings but lost sight of them at once. Only when I walked into the city from the bus station did I see this extraordinary splendour of Rome in all its magnificence.

I found a small inn just off the main square in front of the cathedral; later, over a leisurely evening drink in the Plaza Mayor, I watched the storks gliding in to their favourite perches on top of the cathedral whose yellow stonework glinted golden in the evening sunlight against a brilliant blue sky. All the restaurants and cafés in the narrow streets that wind away from the square now came to life and I settled upon a friendly place for my supper, which I patronised for the rest of my stay.

Borrow loved the dramatic and went out of his way to create mysteries; by the time he went to Segovia he had been denounced by the priests for distributing Protestant Testaments and so arrived there expecting trouble.

> *After a stay of twenty-four hours at La Granja, we proceeded to Segovia. The day had arrived on which I had appointed to meet Lopez. I repaired to the aqueduct, and sat down beneath the hundred and seventh arch, where I waited the greater part of the day, but he came not, whereupon I rose and went into the city.*[2]

Later, Borrow finds Lopez in the village of Abades.

On the morning after my arrival, which was a Sunday, I set off to examine the aqueduct and, in particular, to determine which was the hundred and seventh arch. Now, counting the arches of an aqueduct is considerably more difficult than it might sound: it is easy enough to count a dozen arches, for example, but then the acute angle from which they have to be observed makes the more distant arches run together so that the enumerator of arches is obliged to walk parallel to the aqueduct to improve the angle, as otherwise an arch may be missed, in which case the counting must be started all over again.

It was a wonderful morning when I set out to determine which arch Borrow had sat under while waiting for his assistant Lopez. Most Segovians were sensibly at home, probably still in bed, and even the ubiquitous tourists were not yet astir, so I had the aqueduct pretty much to myself. I began my count at the point at which it enters the high city where there were four small arches and evidence that another three had been blocked in. Then I descended steep steps to the base of the high arches that carry the aqueduct across the valley; in the centre of this huge span they reach a height of thirty metres above the Plaza del Azoguejo. There are forty-three elegant lower arches and forty-four upper arches which form a second tier until the aqueduct takes a right angle turn; then a further seventy-five single arches gradually diminishing in size until they come to an end in a simple wall which carries the duct from the control tower where the flow of water would be regulated.

This counting of arches absorbed me for a considerable time, not least because I kept pausing to examine the stonework whose huge, irregular-sized blocks were fitted together two thousand years ago and yet have lasted down the ages without benefit of cement to bind them so that today the aqueduct is still in working order.

Having made my count I faced a new problem: which was the hundred and seventh arch? Should I count from the high city outwards, beginning with the tall arches, or should I begin at the control tower end and work inwards? If I counted from the upper city, where the arches are at their tallest, that would bring me across the valley to the right angle turn and then for the distance of a further sixty-four of the remaining seventy-five arches to the twelfth arch from the water control tower which would be number one hundred and seven. That arch was higher than a man and the stone at the base in the form of a buttress proved a perfect seat where Borrow might well have made himself comfortable while he waited for Lopez to appear.

However, if I counted the other way round, then the tallest arch of all, which virtually acts as a gate into the lower part of the city, becomes the hundred and seventh. Borrow does not indicate which way he counted the arches and though the more obvious arch to choose would be the big one that also would have been more public and so more likely to have been under observation while the smaller arch would have been further from the city and away from prying, priestly eyes. Borrow liked

mystery but was also shrewdly cautious when the necessity arose, so it could have been either arch. I sat on the stone buttress under the small arch and was undisturbed by any passer-by for half an hour; and then I stood awestruck under the tallest arch of all. No other monument in Spain gave me so much pleasure.

Then I visited the cathedral which, in contrast to most of those I had seen, was light and airy. It was built in the reign of the Emperor Charles V and is distinguished by its golden stone and the tall tower that acts as a landmark visible from miles away across the plain. The Alcázar is an astonishing multi-turreted affair and must surely be the original blueprint for all Walt Disney castle creations. Standing at the very end of the rock promontory on which Segovia is built, its fifteenth-century towers and turrets are of far more compelling interest than its contents—medieval armour, furnishings and pictures—repeated in half the castles of Spain. Sheer below its walls lies the valley of the Eresma river where half-a-dozen ancient red-roofed churches and monasteries cluster before the road winds its way up the steep escarpment onto the dusty plain that surrounds the city.

La Granja, Madrid's "Versailles of the north", is the royal palace at the foot of the Guadarrama Mountains some eleven kilometres from Segovia. Built by King Philip V, the grandson of Louis XIV, in conscious imitation of Versailles, the palace is a classic example of eighteenth-century elegance, while the gardens and woodlands, less formal and more natural than the original Versailles, are magnificent. Borrow described its desolation as even greater than that of Aranjuez (Madrid's other, southern "Versailles"): nine-tenths of the people, he tells us, had deserted the village, and wild boars from the forests that covered the mountain slopes roamed the streets and palace grounds. Today, of course, it is a tourist attraction. The gardens slope sharply into the woods of great trees that stretch upwards towards the mountain chain which runs behind and above them to a height of 1,800 metres, and even in high summer the atmosphere under the giant trees is pleasantly cool.

Borrow, having waited for two days at Segovia, heard that men were selling books at Abades: "Abades is about three leagues distant from Segovia, and upon receiving this intelligence, I instantly departed for the former place, with three donkeys laden with Testaments."[3]

Borrow made his headquarters in Abades, which lies seventeen kilometres from Segovia in the middle of the bleak plain, while he distributed Testaments in the surrounding countryside and, by constantly moving, hoped to evade the watchful and hostile priests. He reached Abades at night and stayed in the house of a friendly surgeon, but the local priests soon learnt of his presence and tried to put a stop to his anti-Catholic activities.

I took an early morning bus out to Abades, intending to walk back to Segovia, and arrived in the village as the church bell was calling the people to mass. The flat countryside was yellow with the stubble of newly harvested wheat although the land is only deceptively flat, for on closer examination it undulates constantly and irregularly so that hollows swallow up villages or, alternately, a village may appear to be twice as close as it is in reality. The people of Abades eyed me curiously, wondering what could possibly have induced me to stop off in their remote hamlet; I watched as they made their way to the small church and one last woman, hurrying when all the others had disappeared inside the church, received a complacent, knowing nod from another woman who stood in her doorway, and clearly had no intention herself of going to mass, whose expression was only too plain: "Late as usual."

There was a quality of crystal clarity in the morning air, which produced sharp-edged images of red-roofed farmhouses or villages that were far away across the plain and broke the monotony of the endless yellow stubble. As I walked back towards Segovia the Guadarramas, the ancient mountain chain, which formed the great divide of old Spain, rose blue and misty in the distance, stretching as far as the eye could see in either direction. Flocks of sheep had been turned out onto the stubble and these I approached warily, ready for conflict with their guardian dogs. At one flock a huge dog, circling his charges, ignored me with majestic disdain but as I approached a second flock, I was greeted by an ancient shepherd who was then obliged to shout curses as his two smaller dogs raced to attack me. And straight ahead of me the tall tower of Segovia's cathedral reared up in isolation as if it grew out of the yellow fields, for not another vestige of the distant city was visible.

In the next village of Valverde I spent an hour in a little bar and tried to enumerate the changes which had occurred since Borrow came on horseback with his Testaments over a century and a half ago. Tarmac roads and express buses now link the villages, while television in the bars and houses brings news and visions of a world that was unthinkable in his day. In Abades I had seen the branches of two banks, four bars and a new civic centre under construction. Yet, it remained farming country and the life of the community still revolved round the seasons. Borrow with his Testaments must have been a sensation; the stranger of today is a mild curiosity.

The tower of the cathedral appeared and disappeared according to the lie of the land as I walked back towards Segovia, and the temperature climbed into the high eighties. On the old road which approaches the city beneath the Alcázar I stopped for refreshment at a pleasantly dilapidated little bar where I took wine and tapas before I finally arrived beneath the great rock with the Alcázar perched on its precipitous extremity high above me. By the time I had climbed into the city the heat had become intense though it had not reached the hundred degrees Borrow claimed he suffered as he distributed his Testaments among the villages on the plain.

That evening I made a final circuit of the city. From the walls of the Alcázar I looked over that astonishingly bleak countryside over which the late sun produced dazzling, sharp outlines and the road wound its way up the stark hillside onto the plain. Down in the valley below the roofs and walls of the huge sprawling monastery, mellow reds and browns, glowed gently in the soft light where the sun no longer reached. Then I returned once more to inspect the aqueduct and sat for a while under the hundred and seventh arch, the small one, before returning to the centre of the city and my chosen restaurant where, after four days, I was now greeted like an old friend and treated as a favoured customer.

❧

Although a great deal has been written about George Borrow, whose strange life has been probed by a number of biographers, he reveals most of himself in his books even as he also conceals. In *The Bible in Spain* he recounts the most exciting, active and successful period of his whole life yet, even here, he comes across in all his lonely perversity. Having travelled through Spain in his company, his book a constant point of reference, I like to take leave of him in Segovia: defying his enemy, the Catholic Church or, possibly, only its priests, riding through the remote villages where his tall white-haired figure must have caused a sensation and creating the mystery he loved as he awaited his assistant Lopez under the hundred and seventh arch of the aqueduct of Segovia.

Epilogue

PRIOR to his five years in Spain George Borrow had survived largely on hackwork, writing for Sir Richard Phillips' *Monthly Magazine*, and employing his great facility with languages to translate from German, Danish, Swedish, Dutch and Spanish. In 1833 he obtained work with the British and Foreign Bible Society, first in St Petersburg to translate and oversee the printing of a Manchu version of the New Testament and then to distribute New Testaments in Portugal and Spain (1835-1840), undoubtedly the highpoint of his curious and often chaotic career.

Gypsies provided Borrow with the most enduring interest of his life, and on his return to England from Spain his first book, published by John Murray in 1841, was *The Zincali* about the gypsies of Spain. In 1843 he achieved his great success with *The Bible in Spain*. Later came *Lavengro* (1851) and *The Romany Rye* (1857), which are supposed accounts of his life prior to Spain. Both books are clearly a mixture of fact and fiction and met with mixed receptions because of the deliberate mystifications in which Borrow delighted. Nonetheless, they entered the canon of English literature.

On his return from Spain in 1840 Borrow married the widow Mary Clarke and spent the latter part of his life on her small estate in Suffolk. His last years were difficult and he frequently suffered fits of depression, which had begun in his boyhood. When he died in 1881 his reputation had long been in decline. His enduring works are four: *The Bible in Spain*, *Lavengro*, *The Romany Rye* and *Wild Wales*.

References

Introduction
1. Herbert Jenkins, *The Life of George Borrow*. John Murray, 1912, p.65
2. George Borrow, *The Bible in Spain*. John Murray, 1930. p.4
3. I am indebted to the Bible Society which gave me access to Borrow's correspondence which is now held in Cambridge University Library

1. Lisbon: "A Huge Ruinous City"
1. Borrow, *The Bible in Spain*, pp.4-5
2. *op cit*, pp.4-5
3. *op cit*, p.6
4. *op cit*, p.5

2. George Borrow, Eccentric
1. See chapters 85-100 in *Lavengro* and chapters 1-15 in *The Romany Rye* (George Borrow, *Lavengro*. John Murray, 1851 (1907 ed.) and George Borrow, *The Romany Rye*. John Murray, 1857 (1900 ed.)
2. Jenkins, *The Life of George Borrow*, p.65
3. See Jenkins, *op cit*, for references to the "veiled period"
4. See Jenkins, *op cit*, p.12, notes 1 and 2
5. Ivan A W Bunn, *George Borrow's Oulton*. St Michael's Church Oulton, 1981, p.11
6. Jenkins, *op cit*, p.88
7. Borrow, *The Bible in Spain*, p.67
8. Borrow, *op cit*, p.67
9. George Borrow Society, Bulletin No 2, Autumn 1991, pp.7-8
10. See Jenkins, *op cit*, p.88
11. See Jenkins, *op cit*, p.91
12. Quoted in Jenkins, *op cit*, p.112
13. Quoted in Jenkins, *op cit*, pp.100-103

14. See Jenkins, *op cit*, p.148
15. Borrow, *op cit*, p.12

3. To the Portuguese Paradise
1. Borrow, *The Bible in Spain*, pp.7-8
2. Borrow, letter to Rev. J Jowett, 30/11/1835

4. No Longer a Stranger
1. Borrow, *The Bible in Spain*, p.18
2. Guy Arnold, *Journey Round Turkey*. Cassell, 1989, pp.72-73
3. Borrow, *op cit*, p.76
4. Borrow, *op cit*, p.83
5. Borrow, *op cit*, p.85

5. The Province beyond the Tagus
1. Borrow, *The Bible in Spain*, p.33
2. Borrow, *op cit*, p.34
3. Borrow, *op cit*, p.35
4. Borrow, *op cit*, p.38
5. Bunn, *George Borrow's Oulton*, p.14
6. Borrow, *op cit*, p.88
7. Borrow, *op cit*, pp.88-89
8. Borrow, *op cit*, p.93
9. Borrow, *op cit*, pp.97-98

6. The Last of Portugal
1. Borrow, *The Bible in Spain*, p.103

7. A Little Spanish History: an Old Fascist
1 Borrow, *The Gypsies of Spain*. John Murray, 1901, p.223
2. David Urquhart in *The Pillars of Hercules* (published in 1850 by Richard Bentley) claims that Borrow's narrative is inaccurate and that the gypsies at the inn did not remember him as the English Gypsy. See Ann Ridler, "George Borrow in Seville, Granada and Cordoba", George Borrow Bulletin No 24, Autumn 2002, p.64. Ann Ridler makes the point that Urquhart "clearly detested

Borrow." Nonetheless, his "attack" on the veracity of Borrow's account raises questions about his veracity in relation to many other events he relates in *The Bible in Spain*.

3. Borrow, *op cit*, p.106
4. *The Gypsies in Spain*, Introduction, p.xi
5. Borrow, *The Bible in Spain*, p.109
6. Borrow, *op cit*, pp.109-110
7. Borrow, *op cit*, p.125
8. Borrow, *op cit*, p.130

9. The Conquistador of Jaraceijo

1. Borrow, *The Bible in Spain*, pp.136-37
2. Borrow, *op cit*, p.145
3. Borrow, *op cit*, p.145
4. In despatches to Major Barclay, 3 December 1909, quoted in Elizabeth Longford, *Wellington: The Years of the Sword*. Weidenfeld & Nicolson, 1969, p.197

10. Borrow in Toledo

1. Borrow, *The Bible in Spain*, p.512
2. Borrow, *op cit*, pp.508-09
3. Borrow, *op cit*, p.512n
4. Borrow, *op cit*, p.511

11. Madrid and the Spaniards

1. Borrow, *The Bible in Spain*, pp.172-73
2. Borrow, *op cit*, see pp.165-67
3. Borrow, *op cit*, p.531
4. Jenkins, *The Life of George Borrow*, p.184
5. Borrow, *op cit*, p.162
6. Borrow, *op cit*, p.529
7. Borrow, *op cit*, p.533
8. Borrow, *op cit*, pp.174-75

12. Cádiz and the south coast

1. Borrow, *The Bible in Spain*, p.213

2. Borrow, *op cit*, p.694

13. Gibraltar: Lion Chouchant
1. Borrow, *The Bible in Spain*, pp.709-10
2. Borrow, *op cit*, pp.711-12
3. Borrow, *op cit*, p.712

14. The Road to Seville
1. Borrow, *The Bible in Spain*, p.682
2 Borrow, *op cit*, p.683

15. Shimmering Seville
1. Borrow, *The Bible in Spain*, p.660
2. Borrow, *op cit*, p.215
3. Borrow, *op cit*, p.658
4. Jenkins, *The Life of George Borrow*, pp.299-301
5. Letter to Rev. Brandram, 29/9/1839, see Jenkins
6. Borrow, *op cit*, p.217
7. Stewart Perowne, *Hadrian*. Hodder & Stoughton, 1960, p.180

16. Pedro the Cruel
1. Quoted in Lewis Spence, *Spain*. Studio Editions, 1985, p.240
2. Borrow, *The Bible in Spain*, p.242

17. Córdoba within its Moorish Walls
1. Borrow, *The Bible in Spain*, p.238
2. Borrow, *op cit*, p.239
3. George Borrow Society, Bulletin No 4, Autumn 1992, p.14

18. Small Towns on the Road to Aranjuez
1. Borrow, *The Bible in Spain*, pp.253-54
2. Longford, *Wellington*, p.147
3. Borrow, *op cit*, p.254
4. Borrow, *op cit*, p.624
5. Borrow, *op cit*, pp.610-11
6. Borrow, *op cit*, p.611

19. Power and Perception
1. Borrow, *The Bible in Spain*, p.274
2. J A Froude, *History of England*. Longmans, 1870, Vol. 12, p.460

20. Inquisitor and Saint
1. J P de Oliveira Martins, *A History of Iberian Civilization* (1930). Trans F. G. Bell, Cooper Square Publishers, NY, 1969, p.252
2. Oliveira Martins, *op cit*, p.245

22. Alba de Tormes and the Dukes
1. Oliveira Martins, *A History of Iberian Civilization*, p.192
2. Oliveira Martins, *op cit*, p.173
3. Oliveira Martins, *op cit*, p.173

23. Salamanca: an Irish Dimension
1. Borrow, *The Bible in Spain*, p.275
2. Borrow, *op cit*, p.275
3. Borrow, *op cit*, pp.275-76
4. Borrow, *Lavengro*, pp.62-65
5. Borrow, *The Bible in Spain*, p.276
6. Eleanor Hull, *A History of Ireland*. George G Harrap & Co, 1926, Vol. 1, p.456
7. Hull, *op cit*, p.482
8. Hull, *op cit*, p.483
9. Borrow, *op cit*, p.276

24. Borrow's Religiosity
1. Borrow, *The Gypsies of Spain*, p.1
2. Jenkins, *The Life of George Borrow*, pp.346-47
3. Borrow, *The Bible in Spain*, p.237
4. Harriet Martineau, *Autobiography*. South, Elder & Co, 1877, Vol. 1, pp.300-301
5. Jenkins, *op cit*, p.105
6. Quoted in Jenkins, *op cit*, p.148
7. Jenkins, *op cit*, p.103
8. Jenkins, *op cit*, p.108

9. Quoted in Jenkins, *op cit*, pp.127 and 123
10. Quoted in Jenkins, *op cit*
11. Jenkins, *op cit*, pp.150-51

25. The Trojan Horse
1. Borrow, *The Bible in Spain*, p.291
2. Borrow, *op cit*, p.294

26. Palencia, León and Astorga
1. Oliveira Martins, *A History of Iberian Civilization*, p.100
2. Borrow, *The Bible in Spain*, p.315
3. Borrow, *op cit*, pp.321-25
4. Oliveira Martins, *op cit*, p.123n

27. The Pilgrim Way
1. Borrow, *The Bible in Spain*, p.327
2. Borrow, *op cit*, pp.330-31
3. Borrow, *op cit*, pp.331-32
4. Borrow, *op cit*, p331
5. Borrow, *op cit*, pp.333-34

28. Knights Templar
1. Borrow, *The Bible in Spain*, pp.343-44
2. Borrow, *op cit*, p.339

29. The Pass of Pedrafita: into Galicia
1. Borrow, *The Bible in Spain*, pp.344-45
2. Borrow, *op cit*, p.336

30. The Road to Lugo
1. Borrow, *The Bible in Spain*, p.350
2. Borrow, *op cit*, p.354
3. Borrow, *op cit*, p.359
4. Borrow, *op cit*, pp.359-60

31. A Foreign Strand

1. Borrow, *The Bible in Spain*, pp.374-75
2. Borrow, *op cit*, p.375
3. Borrow, *Wild Wales* (original John Murray, 1862). Century,1984, p.9
4. Louis Bertrand & Sir Charles Petrie, *The History of Spain*. Eyre & Spottiswoode, 1956, p.308
5. Arthur D Innes, *A History of England and the British Empire*. Rivingtons, 1915, Vol. IV, p.44

32. An Unlikely Saint

1. Borrow, *The Bible in Spain*, p.379
2. Borrow, *op cit*, p.381
3. Benedict Mol certainly existed although Borrow clearly embellished the doings of this strange man in order to enhance the drama of his own adventures in *The Bible in Spain*. See George Borrow Society, Bulletins 21, 22 and 23—Benedict Mol—"The Fabrication of a Treasure Hunt" by Peter Missler, Part 1 (Bulletin 21, Spring 2001), Part 2 (Bulletin 22, Autumn 2001), and Part 3 (Bulletin 23, Spring 2002), published by the George Borrow Society, Chairman and Editor Dr. Ann Ridler, St Mary's Cottage, 61 Thame Road, Warborough, Wallingford, Oxon OX10 7EA
4. Borrow, *op cit*, p.403
5. Borrow, *op cit*, p.406

33. To the End of the Earth

1. Borrow, *The Bible in Spain*, p.413
2. Borrow, *op cit*, p.429

34. At the End of the Earth

1. Borrow, *The Bible in Spain*, p.432
2. Borrow, *op cit*, p.433
3. Borrow, *op cit*, pp.433-34
4. Borrow, *op cit*, p.448

35. Germans, Statistics and Trees
1. Borrow, *The Bible in Spain*, pp.450-51
2. Borrow, *op cit*, p.452

36. The Dramatic Cantabrian Shore
1. Borrow, *The Bible in Spain*, p.454
2. Borrow, *op cit*, p.464
3. Borrow, *op cit*, p.470
4. Letter to the Bible Society, May 1837
5. Borrow, *The Bible in Spain*, pp.458-59
6. Borrow, *op cit*, p.470

37. Cracking the Bellotas
1. Borrow, *The Bible in Spain*, p.469
2. Borrow, *op cit*, p.471

38. Travellers' Fantasies
1. Borrow, *The Bible in Spain*, p.473
2. Borrow, *op cit*, pp.479-80
3. From Lt.-Col. E Napier, "Excursions along the Shores of the Mediterranean", quoted in Seaton Deardon, *The Gypsy Gentleman*. Arthur Baker Ltd, 1939, pp.239-40
4. George Borrow Society, Bulletin No 8, Autumn 1994, Book Reviews, Tom Bean, p.43

39. Rain and Cider, the Old Men of Colunga
1. Borrow, *The Bible in Spain*, p.491

41. The Lone Traveller
1. Borrow, *Lavengro*, p.210
2. Deardon, *The Gypsy Gentleman,* p.304
3. Deardon, *op cit*, pp.268-69

42. Over the Hills to San Vicente
1. Borrow, *The Bible in Spain*, pp.497-98

43. The Santillana of Gil Blas

1. Jenkins, *The Life of George Borrow*, p.349

45. Under the Hundred and Seventh Arch of the Aqueduct of Segovia

1. Borrow, *The Bible in Spain*, pp.602-03
2. Borrow, *op cit*, p.617
3. Borrow, *op cit*, p.617

Index